ECCLESIAL MAN

ECCLESIAL MAN

A SOCIAL PHENOMENOLOGY
OF FAITH AND REALITY

by

EDWARD FARLEY

FORTRESS PRESS   Philadelphia

Library of Congress Catalog Card Number 73-88359

ISBN 0-8006-0272-2

3781D73   Printed in U.S.A.   1-272

To three young people . . .
Mark
Wendy
Amy
          Farley

CONTENTS

PREFACE

"Where the path to new construction remains hidden, development can occur only in the sense of ever-mounting radicalization."[1] The following chapters fall more on the side of a construction than a mere radicalization. At the risk of even greater arrogance, I submit them more in the spirit of a discovery than a proposal, and an intuition rather than a theory, although, to be sure, they are not without their proposals and theories. The intuition is simply that the corporate historical existence which entered the world in and through Jesus of Nazareth involves reality-references and reality-apprehensions, and these are typically located in the pre-reflective, pre-institutional strata of this community. In order to gain access to these linguistic, social, and psychological depths, I have employed both the methods and gains of social phenomenology. I mean by social phenomenology that phase and aspect of phenomenological philosophy for which the life-world is central in the posing of the problems of knowledge and being.[2]

Because of my extensive use of phenomenological and especially Husserlian materials, I am using this work as an occasion for describing the relation between Husserlian phenomenology and theol-

1. Horst Stephan and Martin Schmidt, *Geschichte der deutschen evangelischen Theologie seit dem deutschen Idealismus,* 2d rev. ed. (Berlin: Topelmann, 1960), p. 12.
2. Social phenomenology originates in the social philosophy of Max Scheler and in Husserl's almost life-time reflections on the problem of intersubjectivity, formulated as early as the second volume of his *Ideen* (prior to 1913). It finds elaboration in Maurice Merleau-Ponty, Alfred Schutz, Maurice Natanson, and Otto Bollnow in their philosophies of body, social world, and lived-space.

ogy.[3] Because Husserl's philosophy is so often represented in theological literature only in its earlier forms (*Ideen* I and before) and in caricature, I include a rather technical but general chapter on Husserl. In addition, I have included an appendix on the history of phenomenology in twentieth-century Catholic and Protestant thought. So extensive is this literature that the Appendix contains little more than a typology and an annotated bibliography. Realizing that the careful historian will be frustrated by its brief expositions, I include it in order to provide some order in a largely unfamiliar group of materials and to defend the generalization that theology's typical use of phenomenology has been restricted to existentialist anthropology and its hermeneutical application. As this book will clarify, I am persuaded that pre- and post-existentialist phenomenological philosophy has made significant contributions to the philosophy of other minds, body, space, sociality, and consciousness. These contributions provide the theologian a potentially fruitful occasion to inspect the faith-world at the points where it concerns these themes. I hope, therefore, that this inquiry stimulates to some degree a reopening of that literature. On the other hand, the relation of theology and phenomenology is not the central concern of this monograph. The book is actually an exploration of religious knowledge by means of a morphology of its situation in a determinate community of faith. I invite readers with little interest in philosophy or phenomenology to avoid Chapter 2 and the Appendix. The remaining chapters form a continuous description and can be read without them.

To repeat, this inquiry describes a unique form of corporate historical existence and its role in mediating distinctive realities. "Corporate historical existence" means here an intersubjectively shaped redemptive consciousness, and this I am calling *ecclesia*. Ecclesia is not, therefore, a synonym for church with its sectarian and institutional connotations.

Several interests and fields of study converge in this work which would seem to have little relation to each other. One piece of the fabric is my earlier study of theological prolegomena in seventeenth-century reformed scholasticism. This brought into sharp focus the

3. See Chapters 2, 3, and 4.

legal models which pervade both Catholic and Protestant understandings of authority and the demolition of those models by historical-critical modes of thought. A second strand is Schleiermacher's ingenious synthesis of subjectivity (faith-consciousness) and history (the essence of Christianity). This synthesis did not find a completely consistent methodological expression in Schleiermacher. His stress on the determinate religious community and its historical "essence" played only a formal role in his critical assessments and his constructive moves. Or to put it differently, the presentation of reality in this historical faith did not find its way into a criteriology; hence, Schleiermacher's double commitment to history and subjectivity never found a consistent methodological expression.

The generation-long hegemony of Barthian and existentialist theologies continued this impasse created by the presence of both the historical and the subjective. In my opinion, Barth's repudiation of every sense of religious a priori and every sense of correlation resulted in a new heteronomy. Furthermore, buried in his method was an ambiguous irresolution concerning the effect of historical criticism on the authority of Scripture. On the other hand, Bultmann's individualism and its potentialities for translation into a new pietism made it an inadequate theological alternative. At the same time, the ecclesiological theologies of John Knox and the late Joseph Haroutunian, curiously reminiscent of the social approach to religious insight of Josiah Royce, suggested to me a new and valid way of understanding religious knowledge. For some years, I had been working in Husserlian phenomenology in the hope that its descriptive method might offer a way of salvaging both historical and existentialist components of faith. When these studies were extended from the descriptive method and its themes of the early Husserl (insight into essences, noetic-noematic correlation) to the phenomenology of world, life-world, and transcendental intersubjectivity, it created for me a social phenomenological method of inquiry by which I could explore the ecclesial dimensions emphasized by Schleiermacher, Knox, and Haroutunian. The present manuscript is the result. These remarks about the genesis of this work should not obscure my almost awesome gratitude and appreciation for the work of Barth and Bultmann or my dependence on many other theologians and philosophers as well.

Having briefly indicated the book's autobiographical and literary background, I should like to comment on its relation to the contemporary situation. First, I must rather regretfully admit that this *1* is yet another work in the general area of theological prolegomenon. Given the methodological paralysis bequeathed to us from the past, it is impossible for me to get on with theology's proper business and pretend that, if I do not look in their direction, maybe the problems will just go away. Most theologians would think they had died and gone to heaven if they awakened one morning with their methodological puzzles solved and their procedures ordered. This work is my struggle with the most paralyzing problem of all. Are there *2* any realities to which we can trace the normative language and the intellective acts of theology and the images resident in faith itself? If there are such realities, where and how are they apprehended? In this sense, this work is pre-methodological, being the attempt to lay the foundation for criteriological reflection in a second work of prolegomenon. On the other hand, because I locate the reality-references of faith in what was once called the "essence of Christianity," the inquiry involves descriptions which go far beyond "methodology."

Second, the heart of this investigation is a description of the more *2.* prominent strata of ecclesia, a portrait of ecclesial man. This should make it plain that the work has a positive relation to both Catholic and Protestant traditions. Since ecclesia and its consciousness-shaping power is propounded as the key to the problem of reality-reference, the book is a very Catholic one. It is also Catholic in its insistence on the priority of ecclesia over the Scripture principle. On the other hand, my formulation of the relativity of historical forms of institutionalization in relation to ecclesia is radically Protestant. Both communions, furthermore, pervade this work insofar as the problem of the loss of reality is a problem which both are now experiencing.

Third, I submit these explorations more in the spirit of a rap- *3* prochement between competing philosophical and theological options than a polemic against them. I realize that there may be no rapprochement between my own approach and narrowly linguistic or narrowly empirical commitments which insist that transcendental, depth sociological, and depth consciousness dimensions are reducible to observable behaviors, physical units, or linguistic expressions. But I see little in this work which is inconsistent with Whitehead's philosophy or with those kinds of linguistic philosophies which would permit religious faith to establish its own "game." Furthermore, although these inquiries are "theological" in the sense that they are conducted within the bounds of a determinate historical faith, they are pertinent beyond those bounds. If the basic intuition is correct concerning the corporate structure of religious knowledge, it suggests a datum to be taken seriously by philosophers and historians of religion who do not wish to carry on their work on the essence and truth of religion apart from specific religious faiths. Ecclesia names the particular form of corporate existence with which we are concerned, but all religious faiths are corporate in their own way and involve co-intentionalities and a distinctive intersubjectivity. If this is correct, then our study propounds a dimension of religious faith often bypassed in the history, phenomenology, and philosophy of religion.

Neither the research for nor the writing of this piece would have been possible apart from sabbatical leaves granted by Pittsburgh Theological Seminary and the Divinity School of Vanderbilt University, to which institutions I am grateful. Furthermore, like most authors, I had the effrontery to belabor friends with the manuscript. The result was that George Kehm of Pittsburgh Theological Seminary and Peter Hodgson of Vanderbilt University carefully combed the manuscript and gave me more criticisms and suggestions than I wanted to hear, forcing a grumbling author to better his manuscript. In addition, I wish to express thanks to James Duke and to Walter Lowe for helping out on some specific problems in the preparation of the manuscript.

PART I

THEOLOGY AND PHENOMENOLOGY

Chapter 1

THEOLOGY AND THE PROBLEM OF REALITY

Whatever a theologian feels to be true *must* be false: this is almost a criterion of truth. His most basic instinct of self-preservation forbids him to respect reality at any point or even to let it get a word in.[1]

Friedrich Nietzsche

A. THE PROBLEM BENEATH THE PROBLEM OF THEOLOGICAL METHOD

The story of theology's response to the sciences is one of abandoned claims and surrendered territories. So goes the commonplace interpretation. Not quite so commonplace but equally evident, theology's relation to its own content is also a story of reduction and diminution. The more this content is restricted, the larger looms the concern for "theological method" and its attendant themes of interpretation, language, sources, and norms. Never before has theology been more methodologically conscious and, we might add, methodologically dispersed. In recent theology, this gradual diminution of theology's subject matter has taken a new and difficult turn. With that turn theological method acquires a new problematic, the problem beneath the problem of theological method.

1. *The criteriological nature of traditional theological prolegomena*
In order to illuminate this new turn, we shall describe the domi-

1. Friedrich Nietzsche, "The Antichrist," in *The Portable Nietzsche*, trans. Walter Kaufmann (New York: Viking Press, 1954), p. 576.

nant methodological consensus which preceded it in an outrageously simplified overview. In patristic and medieval theologies, the controversies over the content of the Christian faith expanded rather than diminished that content. Although methodological consciousness did emerge in medieval theology in connection with the teaching of theology in the schools and with the theme of the relation between philosophy and theology, reason and revelation, such consciousness was still minimal in that theology was not yet a problem to itself. Hence, written theological prolegomena and treatises on material contents of theological method (tradition, Scripture) were rare. A general consensus prevailed concerning the realities to which faith, the liturgy, and the tradition referred. This consensus extended to the way in which these realities appeared and how one could appropriately settle controversies concerning their interpretation. Because of this consensus, patristic and medieval theological treatises usually begin with brief allusions to Scripture or to the teaching of the church without elaborate argument or polemic. When there was an argued thesis in the introduction to a treatise, it was usually apologetically oriented, attempting to give the work the status of rational and universal validity.

Two major shifts occurred in post-medieval Christendom to place theological method in the center of the stage. The first took place with the Protestant Reformation. Two issues dominated the Protestant-Catholic disputes of the sixteenth century: the nature of Christianity itself (law, freedom, justification, faith) and the autonomy of Scripture over tradition as a material source of knowledge and over the magisterium as an ever-present authority. With the second motif, methodological issues are drawn into the body of theology itself and theological prolegomenon is born. In post-tridentine Catholic thought, inclusive treatises in sacred doctrine were introduced by expositions of revelation as it is contained in the apostolic deposit of tradition and presided over by the magisterium. In Protestant theology, these treatises were introduced by exposition of revelation as it is deposited in Scripture.[2]

2. Both Catholic and Protestant theological prolegomena contain much more than these generalizations suggest, struggling as they do with the themes of natural theology, theology and philosophy, Christian certainty,

The second major shift in theological method occurred in response to the application of historical-critical method to Scripture, tradition, and subsequently to the phenomenon of Christian faith itself. Criticism de-supernaturalized and relativized the classical authorities. This rendered them ambiguous as authorities since neither Scripture nor tradition could be subject to historical origins and influences and at the same time carry supernatural qualities which guaranteed the facts, truths, and insights contained in them. Consequently, theological method becomes problematic in itself, and thus begins the search for some substitute for these truth-guaranteeing bearers of revelation. This search is in fact the one unifying characteristic of all post-historical-critical theology. The "Word of God," hermeneutic, the essence of Christianity, religious consciousness, and correlation are all moments in this search.[3]

Post-historical-critical theology de-supernaturalized not only the traditional authorities but the content of Christian faith as well. The spectrum ranges from the thoroughgoing de-supernaturalization of a Schleiermacher or Bultmann to a partial de-supernaturalization of Barth and Pannenberg. These theologies represent further stages in the paring of the content of Christian faith. In some instances, classical motifs are simply excised such as the resurrection of the

and true and false religion. But the central thrust remains Scripture in Protestantism and the deposit of apostolic truth in the church in Catholicism. The fullest study of traditional Lutheran prolegomena confirms this. See Robert D. Preus, *The Theology of Post-Reformation Lutheranism: A Study of Theological Prolegomena* (St. Louis: Concordia Publishing House, 1970).

3. Troeltsch saw more clearly than anyone the far-reaching implications of historical method for the nature of dogmatics. The result was an attempt to transform dogmatic method into historical method expressing the essence of Christianity within an evaluational framework. See his essay, "Uber historische und dogmatische Methode in der Theologie," *Ges. Schriften*, vol. II (Tübingen: J. C. B. Mohr, 1913), and "The Dogmatics of the 'Religionsgeschichtliche Schule,'" in *The American Journal of Theology*, XVII (January, 1913), pp. 1–21. Attempting to overcome the compromises which historical-critical considerations forced upon theology, Barth gave priority if not autonomy to a Christologically defined Word of God. Within the movement influenced by Bultmann, theology is rescued from traditional dogmatics and from historical relativism by becoming hermeneutics, the enterprise of translating the Word into contemporary language and meaning-frameworks. See, for example, James M. Robinson, "Theology as Translation," *Theology Today*, XX (January, 1964), pp. 518–27.

body, the determination of each individual's ultimate destiny prior to death and eternal punishment. In most cases, classical motifs were retained in an ambiguous rhetoric which still spoke of Jesus as the Word, God's mighty acts, the resurrection, and the trinity but in such revised senses that few could understand what was really retained.

Nevertheless, post-historical-critical theologies shared with classical Catholic and Protestant theologies the conviction that theological language and the cultic imagery beneath it did refer to realities. These realities were in some way the unique possession of the Christian faith. Their content included the transcendent creator, human beings and their salvation, and a historical past, including the historical event and person, Jesus Christ. Even the diminished content of the essence-of-Christianity theologies from Schleiermacher to Harnack still included these three realities. To summarize, the response of this historical faith to external and internal challenges from the patristic period to the present is marked by a diminution of "necessary" content. But the theologies of these periods are united in the conviction that this faith witnesses to distinctive transcendent, human, and historical realities. They also agree that theological method is concerned with the principles and procedures proper to the clarification of these realities. In short, theological method in its traditional meaning is criteriology.

2. *The problem of reality-reference in recent theology*

In recent years the theological community has entertained what might be called a nasty suspicion about itself. The rumor did not arise within that community but, once implanted, it had a certain self-fulfilling effect. Could it be that there are no realities at all behind the language of this historical faith? Could it be that the testimony, the storytelling, the liturgical expressions of this faith refer to entities that have only phenomenal status? Could it be that the mode of human existence which this historical religion calls faith involves no cognizing, no apprehendings, at all? Are Christian theologians like stockbrokers who distribute stock certificates on a nonexistent corporation? In this situation, the "reality" of the corporation, its size, type, power, and promise, turns out to be simply the broker himself.

Granting the dramatic impact of Feuerbach's challenge, this suspicion was still not implanted overnight. Many gardeners prepared the soil and planted the seeds. Historical criticism relativized the historical dimension of faith's references. The implications were clearly formulated by Lessing, Kierkegaard, and Troeltsch. Since the knowledge of a saving content cannot depend on the probabilities of empirical investigation, and since historical content is known only in the mode of probability, that content cannot be both historical and *necessary* to faith. If faith has a "cognitive" dimension, it cannot be directed to *historical* content. Traditional cosmological, ontological, and ethical frameworks of this historical faith are relative not only to the past but to the ongoing disciplines of natural and social sciences, as well as ethics and metaphysics. These frameworks are, therefore, dispensable to faith and are not part of whatever object faith apprehends by virtue of being faith. There is no nonfallacious deductive way from finitude to infinite being, certainly not one which is invulnerable to continuing relativizing counter arguments. The transcendent proves vulnerable to analysis by its incapacity to meet minimal conditions of meaning such as ostensive definition, falsifiability, and consistency. The transcendent, in the sense of the sacred, dies a socio-cultural death when something more powerful than the sacred comes on the scene, the secular. One stratum of content still remains to which the language of faith pertains, the individual and communal structures of the human being. But when these structures are specified, and when we listen to the ruthless questioning of the left-wing Bultmannians, we suspect that this historical faith is not the indispensable condition of the apprehension of these structures. The "knowledge" of this content is accessible universally. Faith being interchangeable with wisdom, common sense, and philosophical insight has no distinguishing content. It apprehends no distinguishing realities. Whatever distinguishes faith must, therefore, fall outside the spheres of cognition and reality. So goes the nasty suspicion.

The theological community is exceedingly sensitive to this final stage of reality diminution. The slogans of biannual theological responses to the suspicion as well as vocational, personal, and religious crises among theologians are symptoms. The flurry of responses to the unsynthesizable viewpoints which fell under the Nietzschean phrase, the death of God, expresses a momentary preoccupation. A more enduring symptom is the continuing response to the supposed metaphysically neutral questions raised by analytic philosophy. With this suspicion at work in the theological community comes a new problematic for theological method. Replacing the traditional disputes over criteriology is the prior problem of whether or not faith apprehends any distinctive realities at all. This prior problem is the problem beneath the problem of theological method. Nor is anyone surprised to find that this problem beneath the problem has paralyzed the theological community in its power to clarify the criteria appropriate to its work and in its power to interpret the realities themselves.

Contributing to this paralysis is the structural interrelationship between the methodological issues which have dominated different periods in the past. Instead of being "solved," the early problematics persist into the later ones. The problem of the proper function of tradition and Scripture endures into post-historical-critical theologies. The search for procedures which can incorporate historical-critical (relativizing) considerations into a method which serves faith and its object remains a genuine concern. At the same time, each new problematic transforms the previous one. Like any science historical-critical procedures undergo continuing correction and development, but a nucleus of evidence remains to prevent unhistorical interpretations of Scripture and tradition. More significant is the dependence of theological method in its total range of problems on the way in which the problem beneath the problem is settled. If the suspicion is confirmed that faith has no distinctive reality apprehensions, it would drastically alter theological method. If it is not confirmed and we discover that faith is directed toward distinctive realities, the manner of that solution will surely affect theological method. The reason is, the solution will have to somehow uncover the way in which realities appear in faith.

In sum we are arguing that the problem of reality pushes traditional theological method (criteriology) back to the pre-criteria situation in which realities are immediately grasped. The description of this situation has priority over criteriological clarificatons. Some may argue that, in theology, criteria (Scripture, tradition) replace all direct apprehensions. In our view, redemption itself involves direct apprehensions and falsifies this claim. Furthermore, the clues to the nature and function of the criteria lie in the pre-criteriological situation of faith. This is the only protection available against idolatrous and arbitrary manipulations of the authorities. In the light of the distinction between criteriological appeals and pre-criteriological descriptions of the situation in which realities appear, we can say that this present inquiry addresses the problem beneath the problem of theological method.

B. The Churchly Background of Reality-Loss in Theology

So far, we have confined our formulation of the problem of reality to the way that problem is sensed and expressed in the theological community. The academic community did not create the problem; neither is it the only community to possess the problem. Prior to the theological community and "funding" it cognitively is the religious community. In contrast to the customary assumption that a religious community lags behind its *avant garde* intellectual leadership, we shall stress the opposite. The loss or diminution of reality occurs first of all in the concrete historical community of faith which then gives it reflective formulation. If the community of faith experienced no diminution or loss of reality, it is difficult to imagine Messrs. Feuerbach, Ayer, and their successors being taken seriously by the reflective and self-critical component of that community. If a religious community does, in fact, undergo an existence-shaping redemption, proposals from the intellectual community about what is *really* going on have only a theoretical or hypothetical status. Conversely, proposals concerning the non-reality of religious representations fall on receptive ears because this is, in fact, what the religious community seems to be experiencing.

This pre-theological and churchly version of the problem presupposes the emphasis of our total argument on the social or corporate matrix of the "cognitive" component of faith. To say that the loss of reality is expressed in theology but generated first of all in the religious community presupposes the primacy of the community as the location of immediate apprehensions. For instance, this historical faith retains its own past not simply by means of a collective memory but through its corporately conditioned experience of redemption. If faith's reality-directedness does require these corporate conditions, the loss or even a strong modification of these conditions will affect its reality-orientation. The churchly formulation of the problem is simply that the social matrix of faith's apprehendings has undergone extensive modification.

Descriptions of the impact of the twentieth century on religious life and thought are commonplace. A massive and ever-growing literature from the social sciences ingeniously tracks the fate of religion in the modern world. Within this literature, we have a multiplicity of formulations of the changing sociality and social function of western Christendom. These descriptions illuminate the sense in which the traditional social matrix of faith has been altered. Most inclusive are the descriptions of the rise of a pervasive secularity. The residue is a thoroughly secularized religious institution which has traded religious for secular motifs masked in traditional language, rites, and polities. The so-called secular theology contains many descriptions of a new kind of human being who has emerged this side of the technopolis: man come of age, secular man, psychological man, therapeutic man, and technocratic man. Some interpreters qualify the thesis by acknowledging the presence of an embattled "cognitive minority" stubbornly clinging to beliefs which secular consciousness would ordinarily have swept aside. Nevertheless, the major emphasis of contemporary sociological studies of religion is that contemporary religious institutions function primarily to legitimate the goals and values of the society at large. Insofar as the suburban church is the model for this interpretation, the legitimation occurs through the antithesis of the religion-leisure (weekend) world and the urban-work world, and the resulting indifference to realities other than the familially centered suburb itself. In this interpretation, reality-denial is simply built into contemporary religious institutions.

A second observation about the changing social situation of the church focuses on the alteration of the specific congregation. Certain minimal corporate conditions are necessary if a congregation is to be the matrix of authentic testimony, experience, and worship. One of

10

those conditions is the existence of a social unit constituted by face-to-face relationships. In suburban Christendom, however, face-to-face congregations are giving way to large anonymous collectives. This transition alters every aspect of the congregation. The anonymous pseudo-congregation differs from the face-to-face congregation in the way the past is retained, the meaning and function of sacraments, the meaning of preaching, and the significance of such events as birth, puberty, marriage, divorce, injury, and death. In the pseudo-congregation, all of these events and activities are anonymously rather than personally experienced. A death in the face-to-face congregation, like a death in the family, alters the total entity, including the collective unconscious, and the ritual celebration of that death expresses this alteration. Since this is not the case in the pseudo-congregation, a certain unreality attends all of these events and functions.

In addition to a face-to-face social unit, the corporate matrix of faith requires what might be called a provincial social world. If the face-to-face unit prevents the relations and activities of the group from becoming anonymous, the provincial social world is the condition of continuity in the transmission of the faith from generation to generation. To make this clear, we must distinguish between a *provincial* and a *pluralistic* social world. A *provincial* social world is a bounded social unit like a tribe or nation which possesses a common, taken-for-granted stock of knowledge which permeates its valuational and institutional structures.[4] In addition, this social unit is stable enough and enclosed enough to transmit this stock of knowledge from one generation to the next before the recipients are introduced to the competing consensus of another social world. In other words, in the provincial social world one's access to competing systems of relevance comes only with adulthood and usually requires some initiating activity such as travel or investigation. A *pluralistic* social world is a cultural unit without such a consensus; hence, prior to maturation, a number of competing stocks of knowledge, including value systems, simultaneously shape the consciousness. It seems

4. For the notion, "stock of knowledge at hand," see Alfred Schutz, *Reflections on the Problem of Relevance* (New Haven: Yale University Press, 1970), pp. 66 ff.

evident that contemporary Western society is a pluralistic social world while small-town America in the nineteenth century was a provincial social world. It also seems evident that the traditional transmission of faith and its stock of knowledge occurred in and thrived on a provincial social world.

We have here a clue to the loss or diminution of reality in contemporary Christendom. In a pluralistic social world the consciousness is shaped in a pluralistic way simultaneously with the interiorization of the religious tradition. This relativizes the realities to which faith assigns cognitive status because it integrates them into the mass of competing systems before they can do their work, so to speak, in the redemptive modification of human life. Redemption is not interiorized in the mode of a reality which modifies human life but as one among many competing schemes. The reality status of redemption, its references and conditions, is compromised from the very beginning.

When we leave the rather dispassionate world of social science and look at reality loss from within faith itself, we find ourselves moving in a different region of interpretive categories. In the self-interpretation of the community of faith, the loss of God is God's own act. To paraphrase the New Testament writer, no one can "know" God and hate his brother. Since faith's apprehension of realities is bound up with a continuing redemptive alteration of existence which includes repentance, the faith community cannot reflect its own society's racism without those apprehensions being affected. If the historical community of faith is corrupt, no Feuerbach is needed to show that its theology is anthropology. God himself will make sure of that.

Both the loss of God and the alteration effected by cultural and social changes are mirrored in the subjective dimensions of religious life. There is a lack of correspondence between the intentions of faith, expressed in piety, life-styles, and valuations of religious people, and everyday social and psychological realities. The constant hue and cry about the irrelevance of the expressions of these intentions (images, liturgies, doctrines, and moral principles) is a symptom of this disproportion. Because of this lack of correspondence, reality-loss and reality-denial become a habitual and engrained quality of both Catholic and Protestant forms of the Christian faith.

In these alterations of the social matrix of religious cognition, we have the concrete, churchly background of the problem beneath the problem of method. A loss or diminution of reality is experienced in the community of faith itself which turns its language into slogans and clichés, depersonalizes its community, and desensitizes its conscience. Accordingly, the sensitivity of the theological community to the problem beneath the problem is not simply a response to a literary phenomenon, to the theoretical problems raised by theologians and philosophers. It also suggests that the cognitive springs which flow from its social matrix are drying up.

C. PHENOMENA AND REALITIES: A SYSTEMATIC FORMULATION

Theology has a new problematic owing to a diminution, if not loss, of reality, and this diminution is grounded in the reality-loss in the cultus itself. So goes the historical and social description. We shall now attempt a systematic account of that problematic itself.

1. The "phenomenal" subject matter of theology

Does theology have a "subject matter," a content to which its inquiries, controversies, and clarifications can be traced? In a phenomenal sense, the answer is clear. There are "phenomena" about which theology constantly talks. These phenomena have empirical dimensions which measure up to the narrowest kind of empirical concern, space-time entities apprehendable in sense perception. There is "before our eyes" the historical phenomenon of the Christian religion which extends into the past and is partially reconstructable by historical method, and which embraces a continuing living cultus. Like other religions, the Christian religion contains within itself an origin and development, various epochs, signal events, significant individuals, visible institutions, and, perhaps, a persisting though developing distinctive "essence." If we attend to the present cultus, we find observable activities amenable to description in ordinary language: attending church, saying prayers, baptizing and other sacraments and ordinances, seasonal celebrations, a visible leadership, and a corporate structure. With a slight switch in perspective, we find also before our eyes a linguistic stratum which ranges from the elusive imagery of the liturgy to the highly conceptual refinements of theology itself. Through this linguistic tradition occur the behaviors, as well as the "mental acts," of the cultus; worshiping, believing-in, believing-that, celebrating, remembering, anticipating in hope, confessing, and the like. When historical faith critically assesses these behaviors and acts under the demands of its own essence and of new cultural and linguistic situations, it creates a reflective enterprise which has its own literary history. This, too, is part of the phenomenal content of this faith, the phenomenon of theology itself.

Theology may have a subject matter in any or all of these senses. It may see its content as "Christianity" and its essence.[5] It may insist that its only content are the behaviors and activities of the religious "form of life" and cultus which come to expression in a distinctive logic and in specific functions and games of language. It may focus on the linguisticality of that mode of human existence called faith and develop a hermeneutic appropriate to the correspondence between language and self-understanding. A serious ambiguity pervades these proposals. Are the realities to which faith is directed reducible to this empirically describable content (cultic behaviors, language games, self-understanding, historical essence), or is that content simply the mode in which the realities appear? A

5. Ever since Schleiermacher's inclusion of *das Wesen des Christentums* in "philosophical theology," which in his view is intrinsic to theological encyclopedia, this motif has been a feature of liberal theology's programmatic. In post-Schleiermacher Protestant dogmatics, the essence of Christianity, along with the essence of religion, was usually a moment within, but not identical with, dogmatics. For instance, note the dogmatics of Kaftan, Haering, and Wobbermin. After a flurry of reaction to Harnack's famous monograph at the turn of the century, the motif passed out of favor in the period of dialectical theology. Now it is undergoing a slight renascence. Ebeling, Nygren, and Cobb have written works on it. Unfortunately, the importance and the persistence of this theme in continental theology has been obscured by imprecise translation of the phrase into English. Haering's section in *das Wesen des Christentums* is rendered "the nature of Christianity." Harnack's work of the same title becomes in English, "What Is Christianity?" Ebeling's *Das Wesen des christlichen Glaubens* is translated, *The Nature of Faith* (Philadelphia: Fortress Press, 1961). This present work on ecclesial man falls within this tradition of essence-of-Christianity theologies.

flying-saucer sect has a distinctive essence, involves characteristic behaviors and activities, and possesses a linguistic tradition marked by symbols and their conceptual translation. This sect could easily fund a theology in the modest sense of an empirical, historical, linguistic, or psychological enterprise. The presence, therefore, of distinctive historical, cultic, linguistic, and literary phenomena is not coincident with the realities laid claim to or experienced in a historical faith. Social structures and individual behaviors and attitudes are at best vehicles for whatever realities faith apprehends but are not the realities themselves. Believing in God simply does not mean believing in believing in God. If theology settles for this "vehicular" subject matter as its defining content, we have a symptom of the loss or diminution of reality and, also, of a refusal to take up the problem beneath the problem of method. If theology accedes to the total translation of its subject matter into these phenomena, it ceases to be theology. It successfully metamorphosizes itself into the history or psychology or phenomenology of religion.

2. *The logical peculiarity of reality-reference in traditional theology*

We are now ready to pose the question which pushes behind behavioral or attitudinal matters. Are there any realities at all which faith apprehends through linguistic and historical phenomena, or are the "realities" of faith simply these phenomena themselves? A cursory review of the Christian religion makes clear its own claim in this matter. Historical study of the origin, development, events, personages, and "essence" of Christianity reveals a prevailing consensus that faith is directed to realities which are unreducible to the images, experience, or behaviors of this historical religion. Even if we grant the "doxological" dimension in the language about God in this historical faith, the praise of God is not praise of praise.[6] It is not intended as praise of a communally engendered symbol or image. When an early church father or reformer criticized an opponent's Christology, a state of affairs was intended which pertained to Jesus himself, not simply the literary, psychological, or sociological features

6. On the issue of doxological language, see Edmund Schlink, *The Coming Christ and the Coming Church* (Philadelphia: Fortress Press, 1968), pp. 16–84, and Wolfhart Pannenberg, *Basic Questions in Theology,* vol. I (Philadelphia: Fortress Press, 1970), pp. 211–38.

of the opponent or of the tradition. There is no question that this historical faith in its very "essence" testifies to realities which transcend its own determinacy, representations, and theology.

There is, however, something very peculiar about the status of these testimonies as cognitive claims. In order to clarify that peculiarity, we must call attention to a universal feature of cognitive claims, the axiom of object-evidence correspondence. The axiom is simply that the evidence for a given type of fact or reality must occur within the "region" of that reality. We cannot apprehend certain facts about an ancient civilization simply by examining our own stream of consciousness. We cannot grasp the present contents of our own consciousness in an act of sense perception. Analytic judgments cannot serve as evidence for synthetic judgments. The reality claims of historical faith are peculiar because they appear to suspend this axiom. Historical states of affairs such as events in the life of Jesus are *meant* as historical but they are not grasped by gathering historical evidence. The reality of God is affirmed but not through evidence of a type appropriate to God's being. Structures and features of the human being are insisted upon in doctrines of sin and redemption but not on the basis of psychological, sociological, or philosophical investigations.

This leaves us with this problem: Present-day theology appears to be trapped within two impossible alternatives. First, acknowledging that the faith in which it is grounded does, in fact, suspend the axiom of object-evidence correspondence, it can charge this faith with being grounded on a several-thousand-year-long logical fallacy. Theology itself is, therefore, scientifically purified. Its cognitive grounding is no longer suspect, for it now does what all genuine disciplines do; it describes and explains on the basis of genuine evidence. Therefore, theology's historiography is genuine historiography. Its ontology is genuine ontology. The difficulty with this rather simple and "honest" alternative is that it reduces historical faith to something other than itself, and, therefore, puts theology out of business. Second, theology can make a heroic attempt to do justice to the "realities" on which this faith insists and to which it testifies. In this case, it must live with the impossible situation of admitting that these realities are arbitrarily asserted. Present-day theology is trapped by what appears to be a paralyzing feature of faith itself, a deadly seriousness about and a sublime indifference to reality.[7]

We anticipate at this point the following rejoinder. Is this not a simplistic account of the way in which things obtain cognitive status even in the everyday world? We, ourselves, verify directly only a small portion of the facts which we take for granted in everyday life. The majority of these facts come to us through socialization and formal education and are never directly confirmed by us. We trust instead in the investigations of others and take for granted that the distribution of the results is accurate and honest. And we find a consistency between this panorama of unconfirmed facts and our own immediate apprehensions. In the case of this historical faith, so it has been argued, there is good reason to trust in the authorities which mediate the realities that elude the circle of object-evidence correspondence.

This rejoinder calls for several comments. First, because the authorities have become ambiguous under historical-critical probing, they are a tenuous substitute for the axiom of object-evidence correspondence. Second, the grasping of the realities of faith through mediating authorities falsifies the actual situation of faith. According to this formulation, the only realities faith directly apprehends are the authorities themselves. If that is correct, and if the authorities are eroded, faith is left without any reality-orientation at all. We are ready then to formulate precisely our problem. Are there in faith's situation apprehensions of realities which are not simply apprehensions of authorities, and which are sufficient bases for judgments about realities not directly apprehended? Do representations such as God, Jesus Christ, creation, end-time, or salvation touch ground, so to speak, in direct apprehensions? Systematically formulated, this is the problem beneath the problem of theological method. Does faith involve apprehensions of realities which transcend a mere phenomenal status?

7. Our use of the term *reality* may be somewhat perplexing. For a fuller treatment, the reader may consult the section on "realities" in Chapter 3. In the present section, we mean little more than simply "the way things are," "what is the case." This suggests that a reality has at least the minimal feature of being correlated with evidence of some sort and of, therefore, offering a certain resistance to the will. We cannot "wish" a reality to be anything we want it to be.

D. PHENOMENOLOGICAL THEOLOGY AS THE FOUNDATION OF THEOLOGICAL PROLEGOMENON

Although the problems of the loss of reality and the logical peculiarity of reality claims can be given precise and straightforward expression, the procedure for exploring these questions is complex and elusive. Do we really expect to clear up this matter? Are we to assume that reflective procedures and discursive inquiries can be successfully applied in this case? The issue divides into two questions: First, can the question of faith's reality reference be pursued *1* within theology itself? Second, if the loss or diminution of reality *2* is occurring in the cultus itself, what then can a reflective procedure do other than simply describe and possibly lament that loss?

1. *Is the problem of reality-reference a theological problem?*

We have argued that the problem of reality-reference does not fall within theological method proper, that is, in criteriology. Does this mean that it is a non-theological matter? There are those, no doubt, who would see this formulation of the problem as at best an impertinence and at worst a surrender. There appear to be, furthermore, logical grounds for excluding the problem from theology. If a discipline casts into question its own "realities," nothing remains by which to settle or even work with the question. This judgment is correct and it forces us to a further refinement of the problem. We must distinguish between an absolute denial of reality, a confident exclusion of reality, and the problem of reality. Although faith has always had a reality-apprehending aspect, this has been largely obscured by faith's traditional, authority-oriented self-interpretation. As long as an authority functions unambiguously as the source and criterion of faith's assents, the apprehensions of faith which do, in fact, precede that authority tend to remain hidden. Prior to the rise of such authorities as the New Testament canon or the crystallization of a doctrinal tradition, believers apprehended Jesus Christ, the power of evil, and the eschatological community in the redemptive shaping effected by participation in the community of faith. With the emergence of canon and tradition came a mode of engaging in disputation and interpretation which obscured the apprehensions concomitant with faith itself.

The problem of reality does not arise, therefore, because there are no realities. It occurs because the modes in which the realities present themselves are obscured. The result is confusion about the sorts of realities to which faith is intrinsically directed. When this confusion combines with a diminution of reality in the cultus itself (the "loss of God"), it creates the widespread suspicion that faith is concerned not with realities but only with phenomenal or vehicular representations. If faith has no realities, theology can make no headway since it would lack data to be clarified. On the other hand, the *problem* of reality can be taken up only if there are realities present to faith. The procedure called for is a procedure of turning back to the obscured or diminished realities and reflecting on them. This procedure involves a number of categories and moves which will be specified in later chapters. Negatively, it excludes formulations of the problem which make the appearance of reality depend upon one element alone such as language, experience, or revelation. On the constructive side, the procedure ties to uncover the strata beneath the surface of faith in which faith appears to itself as something wholly individual, wholly conscious, and occurring in theoretical or assertive expressions.

This pentration attempts to obtain to the communal matrix, the pre-theoretical imagery, and the pre-conscious structures of faith, at which levels most of faith's reality apprehensions take place. Because the procedure concentrates on what is already present in faith, what is shaped in the communal matrix of faith, it occurs within theology but prior to theological method as criteriology. Since our purpose is to gain access to pre-conscious and pre-individualistic dimensions of faith by means of the Husserlian method of "questioning back," we call the first moment of prolegomenon "phenomenological theology." Phenomenological theology is that inquiry within theological prolegomenon which attempts to expose the situation in which realities are apprehended by faith. It occurs prior to theological method proper and its results materially affect the interpretation of sources and norms, that is, criteriology. In short, we are pursuing in theological prolegomenon what Scheler calls "the epistemological question *par excellence*."[8]

8. In this passage, Max Scheler attempts to clarify the question of the

2. "Establishing the possibility of . . ."

The second issue is what phenomenological theology can and cannot accomplish in the face of the concrete loss or diminution of reality in the cultus itself. If reality-loss extends to the actual matrix of faith and of faith's cognitive funding, the problem beneath the problem of method appears to be intractable to a reflective inquiry. We must clarify further both the meaning of reality-loss in the cultus and the meaning of the retrogressive analyses of phenomenological theology.

First, we reject on both empirical and theological grounds the *1* possibility of an absolute or unqualified statement about reality-loss in the community of faith. It is empirically untenable because we can never know on empirical grounds that an actual historical faith has been *absolutely* emptied of all reality and apprehensions of reality. It is theologically untenable because of the *hubris* involved in any unqualified statement about God's presence or absence. In our interpretation of reality-loss in contemporary Western Christendom, we attempted to describe the experience of a lack of correspondence between the language, actions, and piety of the cultus and the realities to which they refer. The statement describes an experienced diminution and the confusion which accompanies it rather than the absolute removal of all reality. Yet, even within this experienced diminution, and even by means of it, persist some kinds of realities.

Second, what then can theological reflection accomplish and what *2* are its limitations? Since it is reflection, a second-order enterprise, theology itself will not restore reality to the cultus. Phenomenological theology cannot solve the problem of reality in the concrete sense of making that reality available. What can it do? We recall that there is "before our eyes" a living historical faith which in its fullness (its history, institutions, beliefs, telos, and essence) is not reducible to any one specific period of its history, including the pres-

origin of the knowledge of other minds. To do so he distinguishes between the questions of criteria and justification of knowledge, the logical critique of knowledge, and the "epistemological question *par excellence.*" By this latter, Scheler means the transcendental conditions of knowledge which can be investigated independently from particular objects of knowledge and from actual phases of the empirical development of an individual. *The Nature of Sympathy,* trans. Peter Heath (London: Routledge and Kegan Paul, 1954), pp. 218–19.

ent period. This implies a distinction between the empirical content and situation of this faith in any specific time and its persisting structures which lie below the surface. It also implies the possibility of penetrating beneath the surface layers of what is specific, visible, and contemporary to what is constitutive and persistent. We may not settle the question whether a particular reality is in fact apprehended in a specific place and time. We can describe the conditions of reality-apprehending distinctive to this historical faith. In Husserlian language phenomenology itself does not actualize cognitive potentialities but attempts to understand how specific actualized cognitions were possible.

In his early lectures on time-consciousness Husserl does not pretend that phenomenological analysis establishes time-consciousness. Rather, he inquires into the conditions by which time-consciousness is a possibility.[9] Time-consciousness itself is a given datum. The phenomenological exploration attempts to uncover the structures, capacities, and transcendental conditions which time-consciousness requires. Husserl never suggests that if the investigation failed, we would have no basis for affirming that datum itself. Phenomenological theology, that initial moment of theological prolegomenon, makes a similar attempt. Its analyses do not establish the realities of faith's apprehensions. They are efforts to understand the conditions of those apprehensions whereby such reality-apprehensions are possibilities. However, the conditions of faith's apprehensions differ from the conditions of knowledge as such in several important respects. For one thing, these conditions reach all the way into the mystery of being itself, the mystery of God himself, and, therefore, they are not accessible in the same way as transcendental consciousness. Furthermore, the "conditions" of faith's apprehensions are not simply transcendental and, therefore, the exploration of these conditions is not merely consciousness analysis. The conditions of faith's apprehensions are created in a very special situation which involves both redemption and a specific form of human corporate existence (ecclesia). Establishing the possibility of faith's cognitivity means setting forth this special situation.

9. Edmund Husserl, *The Phenomenology of Internal Time-Consciousness* (Bloomington: Indiana University Press, 1964), sec. 2.

3. New eyes and new ears

We have insisted that phenomenological theology cannot itself restore faith's present-day reality-loss. We mean by this that no reflective enterprise funds itself. Reflection is never simply about itself, but is always turned toward something given to it. Yet, we would avoid giving the impression that phenomenological theology is a second-order or theoretical discipline in the sense of being so totally severed from our present situation that it is merely a technical instrument available for use but helpless to offer any assistance whatever. We are convinced that the problem of reality-loss is largely an *intellectual* problem. Faith's realities have not simply flown away; they have been obscured by the emergence of a certain kind of human being, civilization, historical consciousness, all of which are attended by an insistence on playing the games of intellectual inquiry by some very narrow rules. The result, as William James expressed it, is "a certain blindness in human beings." That sort of situation requires not simply a new instrument but a reshaping of the consciousness in which we are given new eyes and new ears. In our view, this is precisely what the phenomenological reduction in its fullest sense effects, the effecting of a special perceptivity.[10] Yet we do not wish to qualify in any way our statement that phenomenological theology is unable to establish the realities of faith. Rather its consciousness-reshaping role serves to uncover those realities and to this extent it may play a positive role as a theological therapeutic.

Phenomenological theology, therefore, can perform analyses and obtain insights which may not be present even to those who participate in the concrete reality-apprehending situation. There is nothing mysterious or arrogant in such a claim. For while the reality may, in fact, be present to given individuals or even to a

---

10. Paul Ricoeur persuasively argues for this "existential" interpretation of the phenomenological reduction. See his *Husserl: An Analysis of His Phenomenology* (Evanston: Northwestern University Press, 1967), pp. 8–9, 11–12, 146–47. Husserl saw phenomenological procedures as actually effecting and replacing a specific *attitude,* the "naturalistic attitude" (not to be identified with the "natural attitude" of the *Ideas*). See Edmund Husserl, *The Crisis of European Sciences and Transcendental Phenomenology; an Introduction to Phenomenological Philosophy,* trans. David Carr (Evanston: Northwestern University Press, 1970), p. 315. Hereafter referred to as *Crisis.*

corporate group, the mode of existence and essential structure may be quite hidden. We should expect this since the majority of apprehensions occur as components of practical activities. Hence, a couple may fall in love, marry, have children, face crises, and retain mutual affection, and, through it all, their pre-conscious apprehension of marriage may lack a focus on the essential structure or mode of existence of this reality. Accordingly, a religious community may apprehend the realities of the sacred and of the alienated-reconciled human being in and through the activities of worship or reciprocal forgiveness with little or no awareness of the essential structures and mode(s) of existence of such realities. What phenomenological theology can do is to render explicit the contours, the essence, the modes of existence which lie present but hidden in these apprehensions. This, in fact, is the aim of this present work. We would investigate the kinds of apprehensions and the kinds of realities which occur in this determinate community of faith and their locations and conditions. What phenomenological theology cannot do is to so duplicate the apprehensions themselves that they are actually and concretely mediated to a reader. In other words, the actual reality-apprehendings of a determinate community do not occur in the "uncovering" analyses of phenomenology but in participation in the community itself.

Chapter 2

THEOLOGY AND HUSSERLIAN PHENOMENOLOGY: SOME GENERAL CONSIDERATIONS

> Even though for practical purposes the author had to tone down
> the ideal of his philosophical ambitions to those of a mere begin-
> ner, he has, at least for his own person in his old age, reached
> the perfect certainty that he can call himself a *true* beginner. He
> could almost dare to hope that, if he were granted the age of a
> Methuselah, he might still become a philosopher.[1]
>
> Edmund Husserl

A. THE AMBIGUITY OF "PHENOMENOLOGY": PHENOMENO-
    LOGICAL PHILOSOPHY, METHOD, AND ATTITUDE

"Phenomenological theology" is that founding moment in theological prolegomenon which attends to faith's reality-directed apprehensions and their conditions, on which depends the second moment,
theological method or criteriology. Even in the beginning of the
phenomenological movement, the term *phenomenology* was obscure,
and in these faddish times it is even more so. In the following
chapters of Part I, we shall attempt to clarify the sense in which
phenomenological theology is "phenomenological." Almost insuper-
able difficulties attend any program which purports to be phenomenological. "Phenomenology" is now a faddish term and it carries
with it a faddish jargon which can more easily obscure than illu-

---

1. Edmund Husserl, "Author's Preface to the English Edition," *Ideas:
General Introduction to Pure Phenomenology* (London: Allen & Unwin,
1931), p. 28.

minate. Part of the reason for this is that the term never acquired a standard and conventional meaning.[2]

If "phenomenology" itself is a *philosophical* movement whose founder is Edmund Husserl, phenomenological method is a philosophical method serving a philosophical program. Even this restriction is not unambiguous because of the difficulty of deciding what falls within this philosophical movement. In the narrowest sense, the phenomenological movement embraces those philosophers who made some attempts to perpetuate the program of Edmund Husserl. This statement, however, clarifies little, partly because of continuing controversies over the nature of Husserl's program and partly because almost no one was a loyal or literal follower of the founder. A broader sense of the phenomenological movement includes philosophers who utilize Husserlian operative concepts (although not always the Husserlian vocabulary) for philosophical purposes which depart from Husserl in fundamental ways. In this sense Heidegger, Sartre, Marcel, and others within existentialist philosophy are within the movement.[3] Broader still, phenomenology can mean a method employed by any philosophy which attends to phenomena, essences, meanings, or simply to human subjectivity. In the widest sense of all, phenomenology suggests a method exportable from philosophy into other disciplines (history, social science, psychiatry, religion) by which they study phenomena, essences, meanings, or subjectivity.[4] An additional reason for the ambiguity of "phenomenology" is the long history of disagreement over Husserl's philosophy due to polemical caricature, the unavailability of materials, and the susceptibility

2. On the problem of defining phenomenology and identifying the phenomenological movement, see Herbert Spiegelberg, *The Phenomenological Movement,* vol. I (The Hague: Nijhoff, 1965), pp. 1–20; Quentin Lauer, *Phenomenology: Its Genesis and Prospect* (New York: Harper & Row, 1965), chap. 1; and Paul Ricoeur, *Husserl: An Analysis of His Phenomenology* (Evanston: Northwestern University Press, 1967), pp. 202 ff.
3. Klaus Schwärzwaller's *Theologie oder Phänomenologie; Erwägungen zur Methodik theologischen Verstehens* (Munich: Chr. Kaiser, 1966) exemplifies this broader meaning. He simply identifies phenomenology with Heidegger and the Heideggerian hermeneutic.
4. For a survey of the exportation of phenomenology into non-philosophical areas, see Anna-Teresa Tymieniecka, *Phenomenology and Science in Contemporary European Thought* (New York: Farrar, Straus and Giroux, 1962), parts II and III.

of his content and style to varying interpretations. The result of all this is that "phenomenology" means "Cartesianism," "neo-Kantianism," introspection, Platonic essentialism, and indifference to reality. Although we do not expect to resolve these alternative interpretations, we shall make an effort at least to introduce some order into the terminology and to correct some of the more glaring caricatures, thereby, clarifying the sense in which this project appropriates phenomenological philosophy. We begin this ordering of terms by distinguishing between phenomenological philosophy, phenomenological method(s), and the phenomenological attitude. Like any philosophy, phenomenology is easier to identify in its beginning than in its development. In the case of phenomenology, Husserl influenced a whole generation of continental philosophers, but none of them perpetuated his "transcendental" program in a manner which would have obtained his approval. Yet, a continuity marks this post-Husserlian philosophical family. Like Husserl, these philosophers begin philosophical reflection not simply with being, language, visible behaviors, or even perceived events and qualities of nature, but with the human being in his pre-reflective intentionality. Even if the Husserlian vocabulary (consciousness, intention, essence, noesis-noema) is not used, the starting point of a noetic-noematic correlation is present in Heidegger, Sartre, Marcel, Merleau-Ponty, and Ricoeur. To the degree that philosophy attempts to find the key to being, nature, or reality by attending to the very structure of pre-reflective directedness, it is phenomenological philosophy. In this sense, the philosophers just mentioned are members of the Husserlian family.[5]

There seems to be no such thing as phenomenological method in the singular. It is not even possible to locate in Husserl himself one procedure which he always follows. This is partly due to the programmatic changes which occurred between the *Logical Investiga-*

5. In our view the issue of an egological or non-egological view of consciousness which is the occasion of criticisms by Heidegger, Sartre, and Gurwitsch does not disqualify these figures as phenomenologists. Nor is the so-called priority of existence an issue which transports the philosopher outside of phenomenology. Both existentialist and non-egological methods retain, if not the vocabulary, the moves of reduction, noetic-noematic structures and the primacy of the *cogito* over objectivized and everyday world realities.

tions (1900, 1901) and "transcendental phenomenology."[6] Husserl's own account of this development distinguishes between the "phenomenological psychological method" of the *Investigations* which uses the "phenomenological psychological reduction" and focuses eidetically upon essential structures of specific types of subjective processes *(Erlebnisse)* and transcendental phenomenology, the science of transcendental subjectivity and intersubjectivity.[7] These two reductions prevent "phenomenological method" from being a unitary thing.' At the same time, this distinction between two methods is responsible for the early exportations of the method outside of philosophy. Although Husserl's lifelong program is clearly "transcendental phenomenology," he did acknowledge the possibility of an "eidetic science" based on an "eidetic reduction" which could focus on essences of any given consciousness-act or its intentional object. And in spite of the fact that Husserl's distinction concerned a "pure" psychology, eidetic analysis by its very nature can be applied to any act of consciousness and its object. This is the basis in phenomenology itself for the exportation of its method into non-philosophical disciplines. In such an exportation, the formal characteristic of the Husserlian structure persists, namely, the attending to the object or reality under consideration in its status as intended by the act of consciousness which is directed toward it. The methods of both Scheler and Van der Leeuw reflect this structure since they approach the religious object (the Holy, the Power) as an object of a certain

6. The *Logische Untersuchungen* (Halle: M. Niemeyer, 1900, 1901) underwent substantial revision in the period of Husserl's earliest programmatic publications of his philosophy, and the second edition (1913) reflected these alterations. The English version, *Logical Investigations,* 2 vols., trans. J. N. Findlay (London: Routledge and Kegan Paul, 1970), is based on the 1913 or revised edition. Hereafter we shall refer to this work as *Investigations.*
7. This distinction is sharply posed in the successive versions of the German text behind the Encyclopedia Britannica article on phenomenology prepared by Husserl and his assistant, Martin Heidegger. See *Phänomenologishe Psychologie,* ed. Walter Biemel (The Hague: Nijhoff, 1968), pp. 237–99. Husserl summarizes his own deepening of the problematic of the *Investigations* in his lectures on phenomenological psychology. Ibid, pp. 31–42. For his distinction between "descriptive" and "transcendental" phenomenology, see the "Author's Preface to the English Edition," in *Ideas.* The German text of this essay, containing some additions and alterations, is "Nachwort," in *Ideen III: Die Phänomenologie und die Fundamente der Wissenschaften,* ed. W. Biemel (The Hague: Nijhoff, 1952).

specific intending in the religious subject.

When phenomenological procedures are exported from philosophy into another discipline, they adapt themselves to the objects and regions of that discipline and, thereby, become something different in each case. This adaptability rises out of the central feature of phenomenological method itself, intentional analysis. The treatment of a consciousness-act and its intended object *must* follow the kind of act-object under consideration. For example "willing" presents itself to the inquirer in a very different way than "religion," which appears in conjunction with historical and social data. "Phenomenological method," therefore, looks very different in the hands of Ricœur or Pfänder (phenomenologies of the will) than in Van der Leeuw or Scheler. To speak about the *one* phenomenological method suggests that Van der Leeuw and those like him proceed in history of religions exactly as Husserl does in his transcendental enterprise. More accurately, methods employed outside of philosophy are "phenomenological" insofar as they use intentional analysis to isolate and describe essences. "Phenomenological method" in this sense resembles the "eidetic analysis" of Husserl's distinction, but even that undergoes alteration when it migrates outside of philosophy.

There are some whose work seems to reflect the "spirit of phenomenology" without even the minimum feature of eidetic and intentional analysis. Working with the phenomenological *attitude,* they not only attempt to deal with a subject matter as it shows itself; they also permit it to generate the terms, categories, and methods appropriate to itself.[8] The phenomenological attitude tries not to determine the object in advance by imposing arbitrary or foreign interpretive categories and methods. The antithesis of the phenomenological attitude is the reductionist or dogmatic attitude. Since the phenomenological attitude is a way of being predisposed toward an object, it is susceptible to degrees of realization. "Scientific method" in the sense of empirical or experimental method can operate within either the dogmatic or phenomenological attitude but is not intrinsically related to either one. To illustrate this distinction between phenomenological

8. We are using "phenomenological attitude" to designate a specific relation to phenomenology within our threefold typology, not in its Husserlian sense of the "phänomenologische Einstellung" of *Ideen* I, sec. 50.

method(s) and phenomenological attitude, Paul Ricoeur, Ludwig Binswanger, Alfred Schutz, and Gerardus Van der Leeuw utilize phenomenological method, while Karl Barth, Dietrich Bonhoeffer, and perhaps Erik Erikson reflect the phenomenological attitude.

B. PHENOMENOLOGY AND REALITY: PARALLELS BETWEEN THE CRISIS OF PHILOSOPHY AND THE CRISIS OF THEOLOGY

Guiding our reflections on the meanings of "phenomenology" is this general question: In what sense is phenomenological theology, the founding moment of theological prolegomenon, "phenomenological"? Although the question is best answered in the specific investigations of this work, we are attempting now some preliminary clarifications. In the face of the ambiguities of the term *phenomenology,* we have propounded a brief typology of phenomenological philosophy, method, and attitude. In the framework of that typology, phenomenological theology does not merely reflect the phenomenological attitude nor does it appropriate the Husserlian transcendental program. It exports from the phenomenological movement a procedure which it adapts to its own object-act content.

Any proposal to use phenomenological method for theological purposes, especially for the sort of problem outlined in Chapter 1, faces two serious objections. First, how can an investigation whose problem is the *reality* reference of the religious community obtain any help from a philosophy whose trademark is the bracketing of "reality"? Second, will even the minimal features of phenomenological method (essence analysis and intentionality) restrict theology to the domains of immanence and universality, thereby undermining in the very beginning the determinate content of historical faith? Does not phenomenological theology inevitably transform transcendence into immanence, the determinate into the universal, and theology into anthropology? The second question requires a clarification of the sense in which theology not only appropriates phenomenological method but alters it in the appropriation. We shall attempt clarification in Chapter 3 where we set forth the operative principles of the investigation. Because of its assumption that phenomenology brackets "reality," the first question is primarily a question about phenomenology itself. I shall address this question by first indicating in an autobiographical way why Husserlian phenomenology appeared to bear on the problem of theology and reality. Then I shall try to show (Section C) why Husserl's program is not a suspension of reality.

I was initially attracted to Husserlian phenomenology because of some general parallels between the philosophical situation to which phenomenology was a response and the theological situation with its problem of reality. According to Husserl, philosophy was in the doldrums because it had lost its subject matter, and it lost its subject matter because of its attempt to imitate discrete logical or scientific enterprises. This imitation is doomed to failure because natural and cultural sciences including logic and mathematics rest on unclarified and even uninvestigated presuppositions. Knowledge is an "accomplishment" of human beings not simply because it involves physical experiments and the like but because it rests on structures and performances of human consciousness which synthesize disparate impressions into meanings and meant objects so that these objects can be retained as unified objects over a period of time. His complaint was that the philosophy of his day had lost sight of the one problematic whose investigation distinguishes philosophy from all discrete sciences. It lost this subject matter because it appropriated from the natural sciences models pertinent to their investigations but absurd when applied to consciousness. Philosophy, therefore, became committed to psychologistic or historicist explanations of the foundations of logic and mathematics. The result was that philosophy became a science of itself, a dog chasing its own tail, a "writing of books about books in philosophy."[9] To assist in its own self-immolation, philosophy foisted onto human consciousness laws and terms which describe relations between objects in space.

Traditional accounts of Husserl's philosophy are often limited to description of his philosophy as a neo-Kantian revivification of the problem of knowledge and the problem of transcendental founding. Yet, behind Husserl's preoccupation with *Wissenschaftslehre* was the

9. This remark of Husserl's is quoted by Helmuth Plessner and cited by Hermann Lübbe in "Die geschichtliche Bedeutung der Subjectivitätstheorie Edmund Husserls," *Neue Zeitschrift für systematische Theologie,* Band 2 (1960), p. 305.

broader issue of the crisis of Western man.[10] The unclarified foundations of knowledge and the sciences and the crisis of Western man have the same root, which Husserl in his early works called "the naturalization of consciousness" and in his later works "the mathematization of nature and of the life-world." The result is the dualism which now paralyzes the history, institutions, consciousness, and life-world of Western man. The dualities are "reality," which means what is researched, experimented with, and known in the sciences, and non-reality about which we guess, emote, opine, and have superstitions. The reality of the human being means what is researched, experimented with, and known according to the procedures of natural science. The human being is acknowledged as a reality only in the sense of a naturalized, mathematized object. The consequence is that Western man has no way of interpreting himself. His entire life and life-world, the world of concrete decisions, values, aesthetic objects, history, evil, hopes, and dreams all fall outside of "reality." So goes Husserl's version of the Spenglerian vision.

This two-sided crisis involving both formal knowledge and historical existence requires a two-sided remedy. To the philosophers who have abandoned their subject matter for books in philosophy or for imitations of the sciences, Husserl addresses the slogan, "to the realities themselves."[11] So inclusive is the slogan that its interpretation refers us to Husserl's total program. We should say provisionally that it means an appeal to go not only behind the arguments, interpretations, and terms of the philosophers, but even behind the phenomenal levels of *Weltanschauungen* and *Vorstellungen,* which pertain more to historical and psychological than to philosoph-

10. Husserl's early writings, *Philosophie der Arithmetik* (Halle: C.E.M. Pfeffer, 1891) and the *Investigations* (1900–1901), including his articles through 1906, struggle almost exclusively with the foundation of logic and mathematics. However, his first published programmatic essay, "Philosophy as a Rigorous Science" (1910–11), opens up the theme of the *"geistliche* need of our time," a theme which became dominant in the last work of Husserl, the *Crisis.*

11. Although the term, *Sachen,* in the German phrase suggests "things," "objects," even "facts," that to which Husserl has reference is so inclusive that "realities" is the best English term. Husserl's application of this slogan suggests Whitehead's concern for processes and things rather than concepts as the subject matter of philosophical analysis. See Victor Lowe, *Understanding Whitehead* (Baltimore: Johns Hopkins Press, 1962), pp. 367–68.

ical investigations. Because the mathematization of reality spills over to man's reality and is an element in the crisis of Western man, the *Sachen* or realities of the slogan connote, in a special way, human realities. One of the nuances of the slogan, therefore, can be translated, "to the human subject himself," and this does not mean subjectivity in the sense of the flow of experience but in the deeper sense of transcendental structure.

In Husserl's usage "phenomenology" was both an inclusive term for this philosophical enterprise and also the name for a method designed to get at the foundation of human knowledge in transcendental structures and accomplishments. Influenced as he was by Locke and Hume, as well as Brentano, Husserl did not see consciousness as a noumenal thing in itself grasped only by speculation or analogy, but as something which presents itself to immediate insight. One need not speculate about consciousness: he need only to turn to it and view it.

We are not attempting here to describe Husserl's total program; only certain features of it, especially in its inception, which are addressed to a philosophical situation which parallels the present situation in theology. We find these parallels in the two motifs of the Husserlian problematic, the crisis of knowledge and the crisis of man. Theology like philosophy seems to have lost its subject matter in the sense of "realities themselves." The symptoms of this loss which philosophy manifested appear now in theology: the writing of books about books in theology, the displacement of theological inquiry by theological journalism and by "phenomenal" descriptions of the religion, doctrines, or language of the Christian faith. "To the realities themselves" seems to be a ready-made slogan for theology as well as philosophy. Furthermore, the situation of philosophy and theology is a parallel one because both participate in the "crisis of Western man," the separation of the political, cultural, aesthetic, and moral life of human beings from the cognizings and facts of science and technology. Given this dualism, religious man has no "reality" before him and no way of interpreting himself. The "crisis of Western man" has not only shaken the foundations of philosophy but of religious man and his reflective life in theoology.[12]

12. Theobald Süss makes a similar point in "Phänomenologische Theologie"

The instrument constructed by Husserl to focus the attention back upon human consciousness is important to theology to the degree that the problem of reality is a problem of the distinctive consciousness-acts or even pre-consciousness structures (the imagination) of religious faith. Phenomenological method in the sense of eidetic and intentional analysis is a potentially useful instrument in theology for several reasons. Since this procedure involves viewings of what is immediately given, it is not a system, metaphysical or naturalistic, into which faith's content must be fitted. The procedure can be employed without metaphysical commitments in the sense of one reality scheme serving as the criterion for judgments about another reality scheme.[13] Although it does focus on the human subject, intentional analysis is not "subjectivism," partly because it is not an introspective description of contingent mental processes or feelings and partly because the intentional object directs the analysis beyond the subject to what appears to the subject.

These remarks are not intended to clarify how phenomenology enters into the present investigation. The question to which they are addressed is how phenomenology with its bracketing of "reality" can ever be pertinent to theology with its problem of reality. We are simply pointing out the crisis and problematic that generated the Husserlian program and why the method devised to meet the crisis might attract another discipline whose problematic is similar and whose crisis is a common one.

C. PHENOMENOLOGY AND REALITY: THE HUSSERLIAN PROGRAM

We now take up that part of the question which concerns the nature of Husserlian phenomenology itself and the issue of its supposed disinterest in reality. We shall attempt, perhaps foolishly, an

---

in *Neue Zeitschrift für systematische Theologie,* Bände 5–6 (1963–4), p. 39.
13. Süss argues that Husserl can be more easily appropriated for theological purposes than Heidegger because Husserl does not foster particular conditions and demands which in content could destroy Christianity. "The only demand which Husserl makes is, as he occasionally expresses it, that Christianity possesses characteristic, genuine themes, that it therefore has its law in itself, in its own unique structures and essential forms. Theology obtains from this the task of clarifying these themes, structures, and essential forms and formulating Christian doctrine with regard to them." Ibid., pp. 38–39.

exposition which could easily require several volumes. We shall have to omit most of the pertinent technicalities and refer the reader to sources in Husserl's works and to secondary studies. The question before us is whether or not the Husserlian program eschews reality. In this form the question is imprecise. "Reality" connotes that which *is* rather than that which simply appears to be, that which is transcendent to human cognition rather than that which is simply a meaning or an essence. Although we find serious limitations in these ways of distinguishing reality from unreality, we shall work with the question in this form. Does Husserlian phenomenology turn away *Q* from existing, transcendent, and objective references in favor of meant, immanent, and subjective appearances?

The question brings us face to face with the standard caricatures of Husserlian phenomenology. At this point, we must be quick to acknowledge that these caricatures were almost unavoidable. For one thing, the full range of Husserl's work was largely inaccessible until the 1950's and almost totally inaccessible outside the German language.[14] Because of the lack of available materials, *Ideen* I (1913) has functioned as the standard source for interpreting Hus-

14. For the first forty years of Husserl's publishing life (1889 to 1929), he published only three works; *Philosophie der Arithmetik,* the *Investigations,* and *Ideen* I. In this period Husserl wrote significant monographs which he would not release for publication (*Ideen* II and III), and he gave lectures which figure significantly in his development such as those on time-consciousness in 1904–5, on "first philosophy" in 1923–24, and on phenomenological psychology in 1925. Throughout this period only Husserl's students and assistants had access to the developing program. Husserl himself complained bitterly over the caricatured reception of the *Investigations.* Reactions to the few works which saw publication described his program as either a "realism" or a subjective idealism. Neo-Kantians such as Zocher complained about Husserl's methodological empiricism, his orientation toward sense experience, and accused him of accounting for beings *(Seienden)* by means of other beings. Those in the naturalist or realist tradition accused Husserl of an idealism which was not significantly different from the critical philosophy.

From 1929 to his death in 1938, only one significant work of Husserl's was published in Germany, *Formal and Transcendental Logic,* trans. D. Cairns (The Hague: Nijhoff, 1969). The *Cartesian Meditations* (trans. D. Cairns [The Hague: Nijhoff, 1960]) had been published in a French translation, but Husserl held back its German edition. The *Crisis* was written but not completed and only Parts I and II saw publication, and not in Germany but in Belgrade. The writings, therefore, which are indispensable for a picture of Husserl's development and program were not publically available. These included many materials written in the 1930's on the theme of *Lebenswelt.* The early caricatures, the inaccessibility of his late philosophy, and the growing dominance of the˙ *Existenzphilosophie* com-

serl's thought. In addition, Husserl's own terminology and modes of expression, especially as found in the *Ideas,* lend themselves to a caricature of phenomenology as subjective idealism and as a philosophy uninterested in reality. The term *phenomenon* suggests an appearance in contrast to reality. The phenomenological *reduction* seems to be a reduction to the phenomenon and, therefore, a turning away from reality. Phenomenology puts in brackets the *natural attitude* which naïvely takes existents for granted; hence, existents and existing things are suspended. Husserl's demand for *apodictic* evidence, his goal of presuppositionlessness, suggests that phenomenology has to do with a priori matters rather than matters of fact, existence, or reality. *Intentionality* is directed structurally to meanings and meaning-aspects, hence, dispenses with fact or existence aspects. Putting this together, the Husserlian program seems to be an attempt to deal with human subjectivity, the realm of immanence, the flow of experience.[15] Programmatically speaking, Husserlian philosophy would seem to be a philosophical psychology with no interest in or means to deal with metaphysics.

bined to obscure Husserlian phenomenology before it found full expression. Therefore, to most philosophers and theologians of the 1930's and 1940's, "Husserlian phenomenology" meant the methodological preoccupations of *Ideen* I. In this period Husserl's former assistants, Eugen Fink and Ludwig Landgrebe plus a scattering of philosophers, including Paul Ricoeur and Maurice Merleau-Ponty, made thoroughgoing studies of Husserl's late writings, available after 1938 only in the Husserl Archives of the University of Louvain It was not until the 1950's that these materials began to find their way to the public in the volumes of *Husserliana.* Archive materials on the *Lebenswelt* are yet to appear.

For the English-speaking world the problem of accessibility has been far more serious. Until the late 1950's the only work of Husserl's available in English was the Gibson translation (1931) of *Ideen* I, and it was more obscure than the German text. In conclusion, the works of Husserl which provide an overall picture of his program have not been available until fairly recently except to a small circle of Husserl specialists.

15. Both Lonergan and Gilkey read Husserl this way. "But the whole enterprise is under the shadow of the principle of immanence, and it fails to transcend the crippling influence of the extroversion that provides the model for the pure ego." Bernard Lonergan, *Insight: A Study of Human Understanding* (New York: Philosophical Library, Inc., 1957), p. 415. "If it is to be methodologically certain, phenomenology can apparently only study immanent objects *in* experience; clear, particular, definite essence which result from particular experiences and are the objects of definite, unique, and clear intuitions." "Phenomenology was thus a careful, methodological study of immediate, direct experience; its characteristics and structures..." Langdon Gilkey, *Naming the Whirlwind: The Renewal of God-Language* (Indianapolis: Bobbs-Merrill, 1969), p. 244, p. 242.

1. Husserl's philosophical development

We enter now into that stream of disagreements about Husserl's philosophy and its development which have continued since the early neo-Kantian criticisms.[16] We should differentiate among these controversies between interpretations which depend exclusively upon the first phase of Husserl's thought because of lack of access to or interest in other phases and those which reconstruct his program out of every period using material from the Husserl Archives. Examples of the former would be the neo-Kantians, Zocher and Kreis; Marvin Farber, who locates genuine phenomenology in the *Investigations* and sees Husserl's subsequent development as an idealist corruption, and theologians.[17] For those who utilize the whole Husserlian corpus of writings, the key issue is the sense in which the last phase of

16. We suggest the following sources and procedures in interpreting Husserl's philosophical development. In addition to the key works from various periods, the investigator should give particular attention to the few places where Husserl assesses his own earlier works and interprets his own development. Unfortunately, most of these comments are limited to the shift from the eidetic disciplines of the *Investigations* to transcendental phenomenology. For the fullest account, see *Phänomenologische Psychologie*, sec. 3, pp. 20–46 and p. 347. Cf. *Erste Philosophie*, ed. Rudolf Boehm (The Hague: Nijhoff, 1959), 2d part, Beilage XX. Husserl also formulated the issue of the eidetic and transcendental reductions as the issue of phenomenology. See *Phänomenologische Psychologie*, p. 25, n. 1.

A general but moving account of his philosophical pilgrimage is the extract from his diary from 1906–8, "Persönliche Aufzeichnungen," *Philosophy and Phenomenological Research*, XVI (March 1956), pp. 293–302. The most important survey of Husserl's work through the *Meditations* with which Husserl himself is associated is the article written by his assistant, Eugen Fink, entitled, "Edmund Husserl" in W. Ziegenfüss and G. Jung, *Philosophen-Lexikon*, vol. I, pp. 569–75. For a brief but important passage on the difference between the "Cartesian" reduction of *Ideen* I and his *life-world* path to the reduction of the *Crisis*, see *Crisis*, sec. 43.

Among secondary sources the most detailed study of Husserl's development is Theodorus de Boer's *De Ontwikelingsgang in het Denken van Husserls* (Assen: Vangorcum, 1966), which contains in an appendix a useful German summary of the results. A brief but helpful account is Walter Biemel's "The Decisive Phases in the Development of Husserl's Philosophy" in R. O. Elveton, ed., *The Phenomenology of Husserl: Selected Critical Readings* (Chicago: Quadrangle Books, 1970). Pertinent also is Oscar Becker's article in the same volume. See also Ricoeur's insightful essay, "Introduction: Husserl (1859–1938)" in *Husserl*. The Introductions to the various volumes of *Husserliana*, written by Walter Biemel, Rudolf Boehm, and Stephen Strasser provide many details of Husserl's development available nowhere else.

17. See Appendix for an account of the use and interpretation of Husserl in Catholic and Protestant theology.

Husserl's thought develops, contradicts, or throws light on his program as a whole. More precisely, is Husserl's final phase a departure from his early "Cartesianism" (Landgrebe) or a development of what is throughout a philosophy of transcendental foundations? The disagreements among careful students of Husserl like Ricoeur, Fink, and Merleau-Ponty are more matters of emphasis. They all agree that Husserl's thought retains a continuity marked by identifiable stages of development.

A fairly standard analysis yields four stages. In the first, Husserl investigates in a quasi-psychologistic manner the foundations of arithmetic and other a priori sciences. Although in this period of the *Philosophie der Arithmetik,* Husserl is already influenced by Brentano and the intentional structure of consciousness, his formulation is sufficiently affected by current psychological terminology to attract Frege's accusation of psychologism. In the second phase, that of the *Investigations,* Husserl is still at work on the foundation of logic and mathematics, but he begins with a critique of psychologism and develops a descriptive or eidetic phenomenology in Volume II.[18] In the third phase, Husserl's program of trancendental phenomenology is born, and phenomenology becomes, to use his metaphor, a pilgrimage toward the promised (transcendental) land. Instrumental in the shift from the eidetic descriptions of the *Investigations* to the transcendental explorations of *Ideen* I (1913) is Husserl's discovery of the synthesizing and self-constituting accomplishments of the consciousness.[19] The earliest programmatic expressions of phenomenology were his Göttingen lectures of 1907–8, *Die Idee der Phänomenologie,* and an essay written for *Logos,* I (1910), "Philosophie als strenge Wissenschaft."[20] These were only anticipations of the *Ideas* which was one of three systematic attempts

18. See especially *Investigations* V, "On Intentional Experiences and Their Contents," and VI, "Elements of a Phenomenological Elucidation of Knowledge."

19. Contributing to this discovery are insights into the temporality of consciousness on which Husserl lectured in 1904–5. These lectures were edited by Martin Heidegger and published in 1928 under the title, *Vorlesungen zur Phänomenologie des inneren Zeitbewusstseins."* They are available in vol. X of *Husserliana* and in the English translation already cited.

20. See *The Idea of Phenomenology,* trans. William Alston and George Nakhnikian (The Hague: Nijhoff, 1964), and *Phenomenology and the*

Husserl made in his lifetime to formulate and publish an introduction to transcendental phenomenology.[21] The fourth phase finds its fullest expression in the unfinished work, the *Crisis,* and centers around the theme of transcendental intersubjectivity and the life-world. Life-world is present *in nuce* in Husserl's early notions of "natural attitude," body (*Leib*), and apperception, and in his attempts to formulate the constitution of the other in his philosophy of perception. The fourth phase is anticipated in his lectures of 1923–24 published in the second part of *Erste Philosophie.* The themes of the last phase are also developed in Archive materials written in the 1930's and in the fifth Cartesian Meditation.

2. *The exploratory nature of Husserl's program: reduction as a continuing attempt at "questioning back"*

Whatever the shifts in Husserl's developing thought, there is no abandonment of the program of transcendental phenomenology. The only stages which Husserl himself acknowledges in the sense of different formulations of his program are the early descriptive phenomenology of the *Investigations* and transcendental phenomenology. Husserl characterizes his development after the *Ideas* as a deepening and extending of the attempt to reach the transcendental region, and these deepenings involve new proposals concerning the "point of departure" or the "path" to the transcendental region.

As a transcendental philosophy, Husserl's life-time program is an attempt to obtain access to and disclosure of the pre-reflective structures and accomplishments (*Leistungen*) by which the taken-for-granted objects in the everyday world are perceived, meant, associated, distinguished, and thereby known. For instance, it is at the pre-reflective (and even pre-psychic in the sense of the concrete flow of experience) level where consciousness performs a synthesis of an amalgam of colors and shapes into an enduring and "meant" object such as a tree, man, or table. In his initial formulations of the

Crisis of Philosophy, trans. Quentin Lauer (New York: Harper Torchbooks, 1965) .

21. The other two are the *Cartesian Meditations* and *The Crisis of European Sciences and Transcendental Phenomenology,* trans. David Carr (Evanston: Northwestern University Press, 1970).

problem, Husserl argued that philosophy could only recover its own scientific integrity and rigor by attending to its proper task, the investigation of the transcendental foundation of knowledge as such. Although he never abandoned the notion of the "crisis of European sciences," the title of one of his late essays indicates a broadening understanding of the task of transcendental philosophy to include the crisis of Western (we would say, technological) man.[22] This extended problematic can best be understood in Husserl's scheme of various "worlds" or regions of being and the consciousness-acts associated with them.

In the *Ideas* we find the following three regions of entities with their corresponding attitudes and enterprises of investigation: the surrounding-world *(Umwelt)* in which men live their everyday lives in the natural attitude; the sciences with the scientific world and the scientific attitude; phenomenology, the transcendental world and the phenomenological attitude. Husserl never questioned the actual results of the sciences but argued that the validity of these results rested not only on a priori sciences of logic and mathematics but on yet unclarified transcendental accomplishments. The surrounding-world and its common-sense attitude cannot be the ultimate foundation of the sciences since man lives in this world naïvely and practically, taking for granted its validities and existing objects. To get at the founding transcendental region, Husserl's proposal was to suspend both the sciences and the natural attitude and, in one leap, gain access to the transcendental realm.

In Husserl's late philosophy the program is the same but the scheme of "worlds" is greatly extended and the natural attitude and its "world" play a different role.[23] Husserl sharply distinguishes the

22. "The Crisis of European Man," in *Phenomenology and the Crisis of Philosophy.*

23. By Husserl's "late philosophy" we mean the fourth or final stage of his thought, which finds definitive, although incomplete, expression in the *Crisis* and in the unpublished works on the theme of the life-world written in the 1930's. Among the many studies of Husserl's late philosophy, we recommend the following as especially helpful: Paul Ricoeur, *Husserl,* chaps. 6 and 8; David Carr, "Translator's Introduction" to the English translation of Husserl's *Crisis;* Alfred Schutz, "Type and Eidos in Husserl's Late Philosophy," in *Collected Papers,* 3 vols (The Hague: Nijhoff, 1966), vol. III; H. G. Gadamer, "Die phänomenologische Bewegung," in *Philoso-*

sciences, "scientific world," and scientific knowledge from the life-world in which occur the everyday acts of practical life and the kinds of knowledge which they require. For if the ordinary acts of sense perception and ordinary relations between human beings are invalid, the simplest acts of scientific research and verification are called into question. Hence, the validities of science itself depend upon the validities of the life-world. As in the *Ideas,* the life-world presupposes and rests on the transcendental region, but the problem has now become much more complicated. First, since the life-world / itself founds science, transcendental philosophy faces the problem of the validity of the life-world and its acts and attitudes. In the *Ideas,* the natural attitude presented itself as naïve but not as involving *valid* cognitive acts. Second, Husserl discovers among the structures 2 and accomplishments of the transcendental region itself a pre-reflective constituting not only of the ego in its temporality but of other egos, and also of the life-world. The following levels or regions are thus to be distinguished:

A. *Scientific world* which transforms life-world material by mathematizing it into laws, structures, and the like.
B. *Life-world,* an open realm of actual acts, processes, thoughts, relations, etc.
C. *Transcendental consciousness* which includes the foundational level of the self-constituting transcendental ego, the sphere of "one's own" (*Eigenheitssphäre*) in which one's own body is constituted, the level of the other or transcendental intersubjectivity, and finally the life-world in the a priori sense of the universal structures of what is intuitable in principle.

When one attempts to place the life-world in brackets in order to gain the transcendental (cf. *Ideas*), he finds present in the transcendental consciousness after the bracketing a constituted pre-given world. Placing science as the formal, technical, and explicit product of human knowledge at one end and the almost contentless

phische Rundschau, 11 (May 1963); Ludwig Landgrebe, "Husserl's Departure from Cartesianism," in Elveton, *Husserl;* Aron Gurwitsch, "The Last Work of Edmund Husserl," in *Studies in Phenomenology and Psychology* (Evanston: Northwestern University Press, 1966); H. Hohl, *Lebenswelt und Geschichte: Grundzüge der spätphilosophie E. Husserls* (Freiburg: Karl Alber, 1962).

transcendental ego at the other end, it would not be too simple to say that Husserl's efforts from the *Ideas* to the end of his life were devoted to the exploration and discovery of layers of reality, both actual and transcendental, between the two.

With these discoveries comes a change in the operation of the transcendental reduction. In an important passage in the *Crisis,* Husserl distinguishes between his early "Cartesian" way of carrying out the transcendental reduction and his later procedure. The "Cartesian" procedure attempted in one application of radical *epochē* to arrive at the pure and presuppositionless realm of the transcendental ego. In this move, the natural attitude and its taken-for-granted everyday world are simply suspended. In the later philosophy, Husserl sees the realm of the transcendental as itself comprised of many layers of constituted entities which include a pre-given world and its structures. The problem is to work through these strata on the way to the deepest layer of all. This is the situation described in Husserl's metaphor of a "path" or "way" to transcendental phenomenology. Transcendental method becomes then a process and an attempt at a *Rückfragen* or *Rückgang,* questioning-back or uncovering.[24] Throughout his later writings he differentiates various *Stufen* (grades) and *Schichte* (strata) to which he would penetrate. Husserl's overall program then is a series of *attempts* to obtain to and describe the transcendental region, on which he can build formal and regional ontologies. For this reason, Husserlian method is best seen as a process and attempt rather than as a static, once-for-all successful reduction.[25]

24. See *Erfahrung und Urteil; Untersuchungen zur Geneologie der Logik* (Hamburg: Claasen Verlag, 1964), secs. 5 and 10. Note also the titles of the following Archive manuscripts: "Rückfrage von der Wissenschaft auf der Welt als Welt der Erfahrung," B, I, 32 III; "Rückfrage zur Hyle," C, 3, VI; "Rückfrage, Methode des Abbaues," B, III, 3 (1931).

25. Husserl always saw his own life-time program as a pilgrimage, a march to a hoped-for promised land ("Nachwort" in *Ideen* II, p. 161). In a moving passage from his diary of 1906 he is so overwhelmed by the enormity and challenge of the task that he invokes heavenly aid, and looks to great spirits such as Carlyle for inspiration ("Persönliche Aufzeichnungen"). In the "Nachwort" essay of 1930 (published as the "Author's Preface to the English Edition" in the Gibson translation of *Ideas*), he says that he is satisfied that now at 71 years of age, he is a "true beginner" and if he could obtain the age of Methuselah, he might even be a philosopher (p. 28). In the *Crisis* he wants simply to speak "as one who has lived

This picture of phenomenological procedure as a continuing inquiry adds subtle changes to the usual meanings of the transcendental reduction. Instead of being merely a momentary shift of standpoint, a predominantly intellectual act, the reduction becomes an enduring and even existential structuring of a person's consciousness in which he receives new eyes and new ears. This is clearer in Husserl's later and more historical way of seeing the problem of philosophy in the framework of the crisis of Western man. In the later version the "natural attitude" of contemporary man is more than simply the naïveté which accompanies practical, everyday tasks. It is also the attitude of a historically shaped consciousness which reflects the mathematization of all reality. Insofar as this "natural scientific attitude" dominates the natural attitude, the problem of man is a problem requiring a transformed existence.[26] Furthermore, the shift to dynamic inquiry also alters many of the operative concepts of phenomenology from the status of accomplishments to the status of goals. "Presuppositionlessness" becomes that which characterizes the transcendental foundation *when* it is reached and *insofar* as it is purely described rather than a feature of any and all phenomenological statements and inquiries. It is more a goal, criterion, or ideality than an intellectual or psychological capacity of the investigator or a feature of his method.[27]

3. Husserl's "discovery": "worldly" transcendental subjectivity

So far we have confined ourselves to some general characterizations of the direction of Husserl's life-time program, stressing his renewed attempts to discover strata of the world already pre-given in the transcendental region. We now pose the issue central to the problem of reality-orientation of phenomenology, the issue of the relation between the transcendental realm and the world. We have

through a philosophical existence in all its seriousness." See also the self-interpretation of his philosophical life expressed in an autobiographical piece written in the summer of 1935 (see *Crisis,* appendix IX).

26. Cf. Ricoeur, *Husserl,* p. 12.

27. "The method now requires that the ego, *beginning with its concrete world-phenomenon,* systematically inquire back, and thereby become acquainted with itself, the transcendental ego, in its concreteness, in the system of its constitutive levels and its incredibly intricate (patterns of) validity founding." *Crisis,* p. 187, italics mine.

acknowledged that Husserl is a transcendental philosopher, and this means that he locates the conditions of human knowledge in the structures and in the passive, synthesizing "accomplishments" of human consciousness. In addition, this realm of the transcendental has its own laws and features which are not reducible to empirical laws, or to the relations between transcendent objects. Neither can these laws be accounted for by appeal to everyday world objects. There is in other words a certain "independence" about transcendental subjectivity; hence, Husserl describes it as "irreal." We would submit that Husserl's categories of apodictic certainty, presuppositionlessness, and the apprehension of essences (*Wesenschau*) express his attempt to describe the methodological requirements appropriate to the transcendental realm.

More specifically, the knowledge of an object presented to consciousness presupposes on the part of consciousness the capacity to apprehend that object in its unity. This unity is at the same time a *meaning* since its unifying features endure through specific instances of perception and can be referred to even if the object itself is destroyed. If this "capacity" to unify and to "mean" depends itself on such contingencies as psychic events, sense perceptions, or external facts, the foundation of knowledge is removed by a circularity of contingencies. For it would mean that the consciousness-acts and structures on which knowledge depends rest on the very empirical "facts" whose validity themselves require these structures. In such a case, cognitive activity is traced to perceptions and verifications which involve pre-reflective capacities and performances which are either arbitrary or unknown. Instead of being a matrix of cognitive accomplishment, transcendental consciousness becomes simply an abyss. We should clarify at this point that the "independence" of the transcendental region refers to the sense in which human consciousness has the structure and capacity to synthesize and "mean" entities, and that actual knowledge depends upon this structure. It does not mean that objects themselves exist by virtue of "productions" of that consciousness. Nor does this primarily formal understanding of the independent status of the transcendental region involve the ontological doctrine that the transcendental consciousness is factually conceivable apart from the world. Husserl

43

was always adamant in his rejection of subjective idealism.

Although these remarks do locate Husserl's program within the critical philosophy, they do not indicate that which makes Husserl's transcendental philosophy distinctive, comprising a step beyond the critical philosophy. The simplest way of expressing the central thesis of phenomenology, Husserl's "discovery" so to speak, is that the region of the transcendental necessarily "mirrors" the structures of — the world. This thesis is neither realistic nor idealistic in the ordinary meanings of these terms. Reality is neither the things, facts and relations "out there" which become written on a merely receptive and passive consciousness "in here," nor is it simply consciousness or subjectivity writ large. What prevents these one-sided judgments is the character of subjectivity as intersubjectivity, the nature of the transcendental region as worldly. This discovery is latently present in Husserl's early notion of the intentional character of consciousness in which every consciousness-act as well as consciousness as such has a necessary noematic correlate to which it is directed. Husserl's primary model and example of a consciousness-act is perception, and the object of an act of perceiving has in a necessary or a priori way features such as spatial extension and the differentiation between the directly grasped facade and appresented back-sides and background.[28] The important point is that the "accomplishments" (constitutions) of transcendental consciousness are such that they are structured by the nature of the object in question. This is why the transcendental accomplishments by which knowledge is possible do not impose "subjective" acts onto the world so that the "world" is simply a product of those accomplishments. That which the transcendental region "contributes" to knowledge are unifying syntheses by which an object can be "meant" as that object and can be grasped in its own mode of being according to the noematic features which comprise it.

In his later version of this discovery, Husserl sees that the very structure of the life-world, including its intersubjective aspect, is pregiven in the transcendental realm. Transcendental consciousness is intersubjective consciousness and this precedes and is the condition

28. *Ideen* II, p. 79.

for all objective knowledge and knowledge of reality. To go beyond the mere phenomenal level of saying, "X is there for me," to the truth claim, "X is there in reality," implies that it is there for anyone to apprehend. The degree of its reality status is the degree of its accessibility to a plurality of apprehensions. The cognizing "I" is, therefore, always an intersubjective "I."

We must acknowledge at this point that these analyses are *transcendental* analyses. They represent deepenings and extendings of the transcendental region. With the exception of occasional hints and side remarks, Husserl does not follow inquiries into the ontological question of the conditions of this "worldly" transcendental subjectivity. He speaks of a science or ontology of the life-world.[29] He speaks of and even pursues in a brief way "regional ontologies" of human spirit, personal body *(Leib),* and the material thing.[30] Some of his more specific explorations concern what he calls "formal ontology," the ontology of the objects and regions of logic.[31] Except for formal ontology, these investigations are, for the most part, of a preliminary nature, making a beginning at setting forth the essences and essential structures of these regions. Husserl distinguishes ontology and phenomenology by assigning to the former the task of describing the essences and contour of a determinate region of being, and to the latter the task of probing in the transcendental sphere that by which those same essences are constituted. The presupposition of this way of relating them is the "worldly" structure of transcendental consciousness.[32] Briefly put, Husserl's alternative to the

29. *Crisis,* sec. 51.
30. See *Ideen* III, secs. 1–4 and also sec. 15, and *Ideen* II for Husserl's attempt to expose the constitution of material nature, animal nature, personal body, and the realm of psychic processes.
31. For instance, *Erfahrung und Urteil* and *Formal and Transcendental Logic.*
32. One of the most explicit passages in Husserl's work which expresses the revision of his early bracketing of the world by reintroducing the world into transcendental subjectivity is the following: "First, it would be better to avoid the expressions *phenomenological residue* and *the bracketing of the world.* They too easily can mean that the world is now excluded from phenomenological themes, leaving only "subjective" acts, modes of appearance, etc., which refer to the world. Rightly understood this is correct. But if universal subjectivity is validly dealt with in its full universality and as truly transcendental, then the world itself lies in it in the correlative-aspect as lawfully existing, according to everything which it in fact is. Thus,

solipsistic formulation of transcendental idealism, his solution to problems inherent in Cartesian dualism, is his portrait of the transcendental subject as intrinsically having a world, and along with that, having the other ego as well as the sphere of "one's own." While Husserl never paints the whole picture, his total scheme seems ⋄ to be a monadic one, with the structure of the world at large repeated in the microcosm of human consciousness. This is why Husserl's most careful interpreters do not see his phenomenology as a mere antithesis to metaphysics or even to the existential philosophy of Heidegger.[33]

To summarize, then, Husserl's language sharply differentiates transcendental subjectivity from all other regions including that of

a universal, transcendental investigation also embraces as its theme the world itself, according to its total, true being. Therefore, phenomenological investigation includes all sciences of the world; and indeed, as an eidetic, transcendental science, it embraces all a priori ontologies of the world; and as "empirical" transcendental science, it includes all fact-sciences of the factual world." *Erste Philosophie Zweiter Teil,* p. 432.

33. Ludwig Landgrebe, one of Husserl's early assistants, argues that the analyses in his last period of the loss of the foundation of all contemporary life and his proposal that phenomenological philosophy can be an instrument for the renewal of life involves a potential metaphysics. He also thinks that Husserl's deepening of the Kantian problematic to the level of intersubjectivity means that the ego discovers its own immanence as open-being, and open-ness to a transcendence in the sense of absolute being, not just ordinary worldly being. "Phänomenologische Bewusstseinsanalyse und Metaphysik," in *Der Weg der Phänomenologie* (Gütersloh: Gerd Mohn, 1963). Merleau-Ponty argues that Husserl linked philosophy and the sciences of man (psychology, linguistics, history) in a closer way than Heidegger. Although Husserl made the distinction between philosophy and the sciences as the starting point of phenomenology, he later saw this as a problem and saw a hidden connection between the two kinds of research. *The Primacy of Perception* (Evanston: Northwestern University Press, 1964), p. 94. Pierre Thévenaz argues that Husserl's reduction involves a rejection of both reality-in-itself and isolated consciousness, bringing into contact the "essential intentional contact between consciousness and the world." *What Is Phenomenology and Other Essays,* ed. James M. Edie, trans. Charles Courtney, et al. (Evanston: Northwestern University Press, 1962), p. 47. Alwin Diemer's summary of Husserl's threefold scheme of sciences (phenomenology, formal and regional ontologies, and empirical sciences) exemplifies the reach of Husserl's concern toward various dimensions of reality and shows that his "philosophy" embraces more than simply the philosophy of the transcendental foundations of knowledge. *Edmund Husserl: Versuch einer systematischen Darstellung seiner Phänomenologie* (Meisenheim: Anton Hain, 1956), pp. 358–59. In addition see Rudolf Boehm's essay, "Husserl's Concept of the Absolute," in Elveton, p. 199, and also Ricoeur, *Husserl,* p. 12.

the specific "flow of subjective experience" because the synthetic and meaning accomplishments of transcendental consciousness precede and condition every cognitive act. This is why the transcendental cannot be confused with the empirical or psychological. On the other hand, the transcendental reflects in the first place the very structure of the world in which objects appear.[34] In its inmost structure, it is world-oriented, intersubjective, and even corporeal in the sense of personal body. There is a correspondence, therefore, between the world and transcendental subjectivity so that in their very being they are ordered toward each other. We repeat that Husserl does little in setting forth the ontological grounds of this correspondence. The program of his published writings was to expose the pre-reflective accomplishments of transcendental subjectivity and to show how they found the taken-for-granted life-world which in turn "founds" the worlds of the sciences. We might say that Husserl was "on his way" toward the ontological, which is the meaning of his remark that now, at the end of his life, he is ready to be a true philosopher.[35]

In the light of Husserl's doctrine of the worldly and intersubjective strata of transcendental subjectivity, we must reappraise the reality-bracketing language associated with phenomenology. We have already indicated how reduction, apodicticity, and presuppositionlessness undergo alteration in his later philosophy. Does Husserl focus on "phenomena" as "appearances," thereby turning away from reality? The phenomena yielded by the eidetic reduction are essences and essential structures of what shows itself. These can be consciousness-acts like dreaming or suffering pain, or regions of reality like nature or man. These essences are neither the reality in all of its concrete fullness nor are they mere "appearances" in contrast

34. To express this summary in terms of Husserl's development, the formal delineation of transcendental subjectivity with the accompanying methodological requirements is Husserl's primary concern from *Ideen* I through the 1920's. The "filling in" of that region with strata that mirror the world, plus occasional efforts at formal ontology, is the guiding concern of the late philosophy.

35. The famous Husserl-approved article written by his assistant, Eugen Fink, in 1933 clarifies to the neo-Kantian critics that the "basic question phenomenology is in the process of raising" is simply "the origin of the world." Elveton, pp. 97 ff. Cf. Elveton's "Introduction," pp. 10–11.

to the thing itself. They are features which order and unify the entity or region without which the entity can neither be thought nor be meant. The phenomena yielded in the transcendental reduction are the structures and accomplishments of transcendental intersubjectivity and, as such, they are neither external facts nor mere appearances, but are features of a distinctive region.

Is Husserl exclusively concerned with mere "meanings" at the expense of existents, subjectivity or immanence at the expense of transcendence? This complex question calls for several comments. One, the purpose of the whole program is to *justify* the cognitive activities of the natural attitude which takes existents for granted, and to do this by uncovering the transcendental accomplishments which are presupposed but never examined in the natural attitude itself.[36] Two, the subjectivity which Husserl uncovers is not the flow of actual consciousness but a complex of strata involving other persons and worldly structures. Three, Husserl lays out a program of regional ontologies going beyond transcendental subjectivity to regions of being. Finally, Husserl's "discovery" resulted in an unveiling of human consciousness as something uniquely individual, temporal, and as a perpetual open-ness with an ever-changing horizon of possibilities. We have here the undeveloped seeds of a philosophical anthropology and fundamental ontology anticipating the *Daseinsanalyse* of Heidegger.[37]

One gets the strongest impression of Husserl's concern for reality

36. "How is the naive obviousness of the certainty of the world, the certainty in which we live — and, what is more, the certainty of the *everyday* world as well as that of the sophisticated theoretical constructions built upon this world — to be made comprehensible?" *Crisis*, p. 96.

37. One of the most insightful descriptions of the way in which Heidegger's *Being and Time* continues Husserl's program is Gadamer's "Die phänomenologische Bewegung," *Philosophische Rundschau* (May 1963). The occasion of these remarks is the appearance of a number of works on Husserl including Spiegelberg's *The Phenomenological Movement*. The differences between Husserl and Heidegger have been overdrawn for a number of reasons: the usual caricatures of Husserl as a "formalist" and epistemologist, indifferent to reality and being, the inaccessibility of materials which would correct this picture, the growing tension between Husserl and Heidegger toward the end of Husserl's life, causing Husserl himself to disassociate his work from *Being and Time* and Heidegger to work outside of the Husserlian vocabulary. Thus, Heidegger eschews even the term *consciousness*, as well as constitution and reduction. *Intendieren* occurs in Heidegger but rarely.

by recalling that against which Husserl addressed himself, the opponent so to speak. In his attack on psychologism in the *Investigations,* on "naturalistic" misinterpretations in the *Ideas,* and against the mathematizing of nature in the *Crisis,* Husserl is addressing the same adversary. It is not science itself but the philosophical attempt plus its cultural counterpart to impose the model of empirical and mathematical knowledge upon all reality. Husserl's complaint against this naturalizing and mathematizing of man, consciousness, and life-world is simply that we have here a mislocation of reality, a misidentification of knowledge.[38] The result is not only a loss of the transcendental region and its role, but the loss of its worldly correlate; hence, the true nature of being and its regions is obscured.

4. *The "discovery" and other disciplines*

We began with the question of how phenomenology with its so-called bracketing of reality could have any significance for a theological enterprise concerned with the problem of reality. We have argued that Husserlian phenomenology not only does not contradict a concern for reality, but offers analyses which open up at least certain strata of reality, thus, laying the groundwork for other enterprises. The traditional way religious disciplines have used phenomenology has been to appropriate eidetic reduction (in contrast to the transcendental reduction) in order to describe the essential structures of religious "phenomena." We would go beyond this and propose that Husserl's later attempts to "fill in" the worldly and intersubjective strata of the transcendental region offers important materials and procedures for non-phenomenological disciplines. We recall that Husserl's program is a transcendental one; therefore, it is conducted at the level of universality and is concerned with universal structures of world as such, personal body as such, etc. The life-world, however, is always concretely experienced as a determinate world, involving, as Schutz says, "finite provinces of meaning." In such determinate worlds as Western man, urban America, or black religion, these universally present "accomplishments" of transcendental consciousness become the conditions for the particulate pre-reflective accomplishments required by that world. Personal body, social

38. Cf. Whitehead's description of the fallacy of misplaced concreteness.

49

world, the role of the other, all become determinately transformed in, for instance, black religion. A reality-oriented investigation of such matters possesses in Husserl's program a powerful instrument for grasping the subject-world correspondence of a determinate region of reality. Husserl's own program, concerned as it is with the problem of world and knowledge as such, occurs at the level of universality. In other words, it is a philosophical program. But once the structures of body, consciousness, intersubjectivity, and world are exposed to view, they can hardly be ignored by those disciplines studying determinate realities, for in determinateness is disclosed what happens to these universalities. The Husserlian program should, therefore, be useful for any and all disciplines (history, psychology, aesthetics, social sciences, and religion) concerned with the individual and social realities of the human being.

Chapter 3

PHENOMENOLOGICAL THEOLOGY AND
ITS OPERATIVE PRINCIPLES

Now what makes it difficult for us to take the line of investigation
is the craving for generality.

The idea of a general concept being a common property of its
particular instances connects up with other primitive, too simple,
ideas of the structure of language. It is comparable to the idea
that *properties* are *ingredients* of the things which have properties;
e.g., that beauty is an ingredient of all beautiful things as alcohol
is of beer and wine, and that we, therefore, could have pure
beauty, unadulterated by anything that is beautiful.

Ludwig Wittgenstein[1]

A. The Nature and Function of Operative Principles

Phenomenological theology, the attempt to penetrate and describe
the pre-reflective matrix of faith's acts and structures, requires certain
operative principles. While these principles are not mere idiosyn-
cracies, they do not exhaust the ways in which phenomenology can
be appropriated in theology, nor do they exemplify the one and only
relation between theology and phenomenology. Phenomenology in
some sense of the term appears to be at work in valid but variant
ways in the thought of Karl Barth (the phenomenological attitude),
Paul Tillich, Karl Rahner, and Gerhard Ebeling.

1. Ludwig Wittgestein, *The Blue and Brown Books* (New York: Harper
Torchbooks, 1965), p. 17.

1. Phenomenological theology as anti-formalist correction

The corrective aspect of these operative principles functions to expose the formalism which has always plagued Christian theology. This must surely sound paradoxical and strange to those who think of phenomenology as a structuralism. Some clarifications are, therefore, in order. If theology from Schleiermacher to the present is marked by any consensus at all, it is in the perpetual attempt of theology to overcome its own formalism. Pietism's reaction against Protestant scholastic theology expresses this correction from within the Protestant religious community. Kant's criticism of speculative or "physicotheology" continues this correction within the framework of philosophical idealism. Schleiermacher's attempt, caricatured as romanticism and subjective theology, to reassign the locus of religious acts from the cognitive and moral dimensions of consciousness to *das Gefühl* or immediate self-consciousness is the most inclusive and profound theological anti-formalism to date, beginning a tradition which ranges from investigations of a religious a priori to Christian existence, and which includes such diverse groups as the Ritschlian school, the new hermeneutic, and Wittgensteinian fideism.[2] Almost

2. "Wittgensteinian fideism," a phrase coined by Kai Nielsen, may be the best way to describe this position. Nielsen used the phrase to call attention to a common Wittgensteinian interpretation of religion in such people as Peter Winch, Norman Malcolm, G. E. Hughes, and Robert Coburn. That interpretation is "that religion is a unique and very ancient form of life with its own distinctive criteria." See Kai Nielsen, "Wittgensteinian Fideism," *Philosophy*, 42 (July 1967). Nielsen accuses the fideists of so formulating the distinctiveness of religious reality, rationality, and coherence that it has no carry-over at all into more universal usages of these terms. This article called forth a response by W. D. Hudson, "On Two Points against Wittgensteinian Fideism," *Philosophy*, 43 (July 1968), and is continued in a counter-response by Nielsen, "Wittgensteinian Fideism: A Reply to Hudson," *Philosophy*, 44 (January 1969). If there is a school of Wittgenstein fideists, it seems to be divided already into two groupings: those mentioned in Nielsen's original article and Kierkegaardian Wittgensteinian fideists. For the latter, see David Burrell, "Religious Life and Understanding," *The Review of Metaphysics*, 22 (June 1969); Paul Holmer, "Wittgenstein and Theology," in Dallas High, ed., *New Essays in Religious Language* (New York: Oxford University Press, 1969); and D. Z. Phillips, *The Concept of Prayer* (New York: Schocken Books, 1966), *Death and Immortality* (New York: St. Martin's Press, 1970), and *Faith and Philosophical Inquiry* (New York: Schocken Books, 1970). One of David Burrell's statements illustrates why we characterize this position as "phenomenal." "What religion offers to understanding, then, is not primarily data, but rather a new light on oneself as responsive." Burrell, "Religious Life," p. 698.

the whole of modern theology resists accounts of religious knowledge which objectify the relation between faith and its "object." Both the apologetic grounding of theology by means of a natural theology and the view that revelation resides in a rationally established authority and in a propositional mode exemplify this objectification. Consequently, theologies which attempt to order themselves "systematically" out of Scripture or tradition are very much out of vogue. Dialectical theology fought this battle through its attack on propositional revelation, its stress on encounter and subject-to-subject relation, and on dialectical method. Wittgensteinian fideism enters the fray not only in its suspicion of metaphysics and rational theology but its focus on the ordinary utterances of the man of faith in the concrete situation of faith. Existential theology drove a sharp wedge between *existence* where faith resides and reflective and speech acts "about" God.

So vigorous is anti-formalism in modern theology that some theologians are reticent to do technical work since it is unavoidably "propositional," esoteric, and "irrelevant" to the concerns of the ordinary man of faith. Although this anti-formalist consensus in modern theology represents a certain gain and a genuine insight, it is not without its confusions. A certain formalism is inevitable in every second-order enterprise simply because of the inescapable and unbridgeable difference between concrete occurrences, consciousness-acts, processes, decisions, and transcendental structures on the one hand, and the linguistic and reflective moves which attend to such for the purpose of explication and understanding on the other. In this sense, Kierkegaard's writings are as "formalist" as those of Thomas Aquinas. Insofar as the anti-formalist literature gives the impression that it can transcend formalism even in this sense, it obscures the issue of *ways* of formalizing the object and improper formalizations of the subject.[3]

3. Alfred Schutz offers the following suggestive example. Noting that a city-dweller and a cartographer experience a city in very different ways, he accuses social scientists of being mere "cartographers" insofar as they are indifferent to the elements of the everyday life-world, the "meaning" the city has for the city-dweller himself. *Collected Papers* (The Hague: Nijhoff, 1966), II, 66-67. What Schutz is objecting to is the error of improper formalizing in which the concrete life-world dimension is lost in a plethora of statistics, demographic charts, and population studies.

At this point it seems that each anti-formalist theology exemplifies not only formalism but even an improper formalization of faith. Existential theology's contribution to anti-formalism is of inestimable value. But its attempt to appropriate the categories of *Dasein*-analysis (anxiety, despair, nothingness, inauthenticity) as correlates of the symbols of Christian tradition, liturgy, and doctrine turns out to be in the end an individualism which largely ignores both process and sociality. An individualist structure is imposed upon the situation of the believer, closing out corporate and intersubjective elements in that situation and thereby ending up with a scheme imposed on and not extracted from the situation. Wittgensteinian fideism certainly renders a service in its attempt to locate religious speaking in its everyday situation. However, the everyday situation (attending church, taking communion, praying) is part of but does not exhaust the situation of the believer. The everyday situation occurs within a social form involving institutional and pre-institutional corporate structures as well as a believing consciousness shaped in this matrix. If these dimensions are dismissed as unempirical, meaningless, or inaccessible, then even Wittgensteinian fideism is imposing upon the situation a model of the human being which suggests behavioristic restrictions. Here, too, a scheme formalizes the situation by excluding most of its strata.

Let me repeat that phenomenological theology stands in the line of these anti-formalist corrections. Like them, it may be susceptible to improper formalization. However, its overarching purpose, which the operative principles are designed to serve, is to locate and set forth the founding apprehensions of religious faith in the setting distinctive of that faith and with attention to the various strata of that setting. For this reason, phenomenological theology cannot be simply fundamental theology, existence theology, or linguistic theology. Faith does not occur simply in some individual consciousness but, as in human beings in general, occupies its own "world." Uncovering this world and its strata is the undertaking to which the operative principles are guidelines.

2. *The priority of the theological given*

The present project is a theological one. We do not propose to carry it out at the expense of theology, diluting theological content by synthesizing it with another content, or working at a natural theology as a way into theology. For this project the theological object and content is there from the beginning. Hence, the operative principles are not foundations on which we build theological content or theses from which it is deduced. They are instruments for the uncovering that content or categories and insights which the procedure of uncovering presupposes.

The theological given is simply that which is present constitutively making this historical faith what it is. The theological given precedes doctrines and even confessions since these are attempts to bring to expression in a specific time and place the theological given. The *doctrine* of salvation is not the theological given but salvation is. The doctrine of Jesus Christ is not constitutive of the theological given but Jesus Christ is.[4] Phenomenological theology is, therefore, not a contrast term to "Christological" theology if this means that the former "begins" with phenomenology while the latter "begins" with Jesus Christ. "Jesus Christ," "Word of God," or "Church" are as points of departures not so much problematic as ambiguous. Do we mean by these terms the doctrines about such in the church tradition? Do we mean by Jesus Christ the one testified to in Scripture or in the church tradition? Scripture and church tradition are themselves not unambiguous since they involve particular historical and possibly arbitrary ways of understanding what Scripture is and how it functions as the witness to Jesus Christ. If this is the case, what appears to be a "Christological" point of departure becomes a doctrinal one. The presence of Jesus Christ is identified with a certain tradition's provisional and possibly erroneous interpretation of Scripture and its mediations. The alternative to such a procedure is an attempt (which may, of course, be unsuccessful) to attend to Jesus Christ in his actual mode of givenness. This is why, as we argued in Chapter 1, phenomenological theology must precede theological criteriology. This is not because "phenomenology" precedes such, but because the question of the mode of givenness of

4. Because this investigation addresses the situation of a specific historical faith, its given must involve the one whose presence founds and unifies that faith. However, the principle of the priority of the theological given and the method which reflects it are not limited to the Christian religion but find expression in other historical faiths such as Islam and Buddism.

the object is that which should found decisions about authorities and norms, not vice versa.

To say that the theological given has priority means first of all that the mode of givenness in the situation of givenness is prior to *i* second-order interpretations which come and go in the course of the history of the community of faith. Secondly, it means that theology's *2* object precedes and controls theology's method of clarifying its own given. And with this arises the central problem involved in a proposal that theology make use of phenomenological resources. In the light of the priority of the theological given, we must derive theological method from its object. If this is our procedure, will not "phenomenological" method always be a foreign intruder threatening to disrupt or distort the object? So must the problem be formulated by theology insofar as it would preserve the priority of its own given.

But the problem can also be formulated from the phenomenological side. Husserlian phenomenology or transcendental analysis is directed to that which is universally accessible and universally valid. How can such a program be applied to the object or region of a historical faith which (1) involves a specific shaping of consciousness, (2) is a primarily corporate mode of existence, (3) has a verification which is not a universal possibility but is conditioned on participation in this corporate mode of existence, and (4) has a content which has in its very core mystery and transcendence? These features are simply there in theology's pre-given object. They cannot be ignored or transformed, and the phenomenological attitude would distort its own goals if it did so. We are left then with this problem. How can the methods and instruments of the Husserlian program, *Q* oriented as they are toward universality, be applied to a historical, determinate subject matter? It is this problem to which the following operative principles pertain.

What do we mean by operative principles? The expression comes from Eugen Fink who distinguishes between concepts which express the explicit and extensive investigations of a philosopher *(concepts thématiques)*—such as *ousia* in Aristotle, the absolute idea in Hegel, or transcendental subjectivity in Husserl—and functional or instrumental concepts *(concepts opératoires)* which serve to mediate understanding and give expression to the elusive situation of human life and finitude. Examples might be participation in Plato, positivity in Schleiermacher, and reduction and constitution in Husserl.[5] Operative concepts tend to resist explicit and unambiguous analysis although they help uncover other themes and entities. They are not discrete entities easily susceptible to definition. They appear to be both obvious and at the same time elusive, and their clarity is in proportion to the success with which one uses them to enlighten something else. They are not arbitrarily or pragmatically fabricated; hence, they are not mere tools. Our present project makes use of three kinds of operative principles. The first, the principle of positivity, is ontological in import. The second, apprehensions, realities, and meant-objects are inclusive terms whose meaning and clarity is revealed in a particular "apprehension" of "reality" rather than in second order discussions of these terms as such. The third, "theological reflection," stands for the procedure in which these terms and principles operate.

B. THE PRINCIPLE OF POSITIVITY

The first operative principle is the very cornerstone of this project because it guarantees the integrity of both the determinate (the theological given) and phenomenological method and at the same time brings them together. This principle, however, does not itself originate in phenomenological philosophy. Pascal anticipates it in his distinction between the God of the philosophers and the God of Abraham, Isaac, and Jacob, a distinction which is not between the false and the true but between a universal, speculatively apprehended entity and the God of a determinate religious faith. While Schleiermacher does not explicate it thematically, it forms the very structure of his work.[6] Several contemporary philosophers of religion who work within the phenomenological movement have asserted this principle. Theobald Süss argues that Husserl himself

---

5. Eugen Fink, "Les concepts opératoires dans la phénoménologie de Husserl," in *Husserl: Cahiers de Rayaumont III,* ed. M. A. Bera (Paris: Les Editions de Minuit, 1959), pp. 214–30.
6. See especially "The Religions," the fifth address of *On Religion: Addresses in Response to Its Cultured Critics,* trans. Terrence Tice (Richmond: John Knox Press, 1969). We also have in mind Schleiermacher's lifetime propensity to permit the universal structures of religiousness to undergo transformation under the conditions of a particular faith whose *Wesen* or essence is not translatable without alteration into such general structures.

observed it in his treatments of Christianity.[7] Henri Duméry, the Roman Catholic philosopher-theologian, calls attention explicitly to the principle. He names Hegel the "first philosopher of Christian positivity" in the sense of religious institution, and he finds in recent phenomenological philosophy an attempt to "determine the possibility, the validity of the conditions of the religious act" without reducing the act to these conditions or dissolving it into its theoretical exposition.[8]

The presence or absence of this principle affects all theological work even though the principle itself rarely comes to even indirect expression. Although positivity is an ontological principle, awareness of it usually occurs in connection with the problem of interpretation or hermeneutic. We shall try to bring this awareness to light by focusing on two hermeneutic procedures which ignore the principle. A *provincial* hermeneutic attempts to understand a his- *1* torical faith from the standpoint of one of its specific historical forms; for instance, the specific piety of a denomination in a decade of American history. In provincial hermeneutics the essential features and "truth" of the historical faith are identified with one of its specific historical expressions. They are not related, except by way of opposition, to other historical forms of that faith, or to other religious faiths, or to universal features of man and his world. At the other extreme *generic* hermeneutics attends to universal structures such as *2* the fundamental ontology of the human being or a general metaphysical scheme, and sees a specific historical faith as the exemplification of these generic (genus-related) structures and as translatable into them. Even when the focus is on a "religion" the procedure is the same if it translates the historically determinate (Jesus Christ, ecclesia, justification) into the general or analogous counterparts in all religions (founding figure, the dying-rising god, religious cultus, salva-

7. The only demand which Husserl makes is, as he occasionally expresses it, that Christianity possesses for him distinctive, genuine themes, that it therefore would have its law in itself, and in its own structures and essential forms. This yields for theology the task of making clear these motifs, structures, and essential forms and of formulating Christian doctrine with regard to them." Phänomenologische Theologie," in *Neue Zeitschrift für systematische Theologie,* Bände 5–6 (1963–64), pp. 38–39.
8. Henri Duméry, *Phénoménologie et Religion. structures de l'institution chrétienne* (Paris: P.U.F., 1962), p. 97.

tion). Generic hermeneutics "understands" a determinate historical faith in the light of phenomena, categories, and terms which are induced from an assortment of faiths, philosophical anthropology, or metaphysics. Provincial hermeneutics "understands" by simply excluding, or attempting to, phenomena which are more universal than the specific cultus in question, thereby, severing it from the human being, society, world, and being. Provincial hermeneutics violates the essence of a historical faith by narrowing it to the contingencies of one of its historical periods and expressions. Generic hermeneutics violates that essence by expanding it to the universal. Generic hermeneutics may be rooted in what Wittgenstein called the "craving for generality."[9]

We have to do in these examples with an ontological principle because the issue is that of the relation between universal and determinate strata of being and the effect of these strata on essences or essential structures. We are not at this point talking about "essential structures" as merely the products of analysis as if these were mere abstracted ideas correlative to intellection alone and reality were the concrete entity or process. Rather, these essential structures are structures of regions of being. They are in other words features of the human being, of history, and nature. Reality, however, is neither simply the concrete existent nor the structures of various regions. Or to put it differently, one has not described a human being in his "reality" if he limits himself to the actual existing process and entity in a moment of time or to the generic features of humanity. Reality cannot dispense with the actual nor is it reducible to such.

Our problem, however, is the problem of the relation between universal or regional structures and actuality. To express it differently, what happens to universal structures under the conditions of existence and actuality? They do not disappear. A human being cannot "be" without the constituents of body, consciousness, sociality, and the like. Instead these structures undergo transformation. This has a temporal dimension in that they are constantly changing. But it is also true hierarchically and structurally. A situation viewed

9. Wittgenstein, *Blue and Brown Books*, p. 17. I am grateful to Phillip Hallie who cited this passage in Wittgenstein in a paper read on the philosophy of evil.

statically involves multiple levels of determinacy or positivity. Western man is more determinate than simply human being. American is more determinate than Western man. Black American is more determinate yet. At more restricted levels, we have urban black youth in a specific city, and finally the individual himself. The individual is, of course, an unrepeatable and unique being, but his uniqueness occurs finally in the way these levels of determinacy are taken up and filtered through his decision-making, plus of course countless other organic, historical, and psychological factors not mentioned here. All of these strata are themselves in process, which feature we need not elaborate at this point. What becomes evident from these changes which determinacy effects is that *each general stratum undergoes transformation when it is incorporated into the strata more determinate than itself.* This, in brief, is the principle of positivity. To illustrate, being an American is transformed in the determinacy of being a black American. Being a black American undergoes transformation in the determinate situation of urban black youth. What we have before us is a hierarchy of forms which range from the most general (those which characterize being as such) to the most restricted. The more general forms are transformed by the more restricted forms.

In some philosophies of forms, the impression is given that reality is a concrete entity which retains a number of forms in the sense of enduring meanings abstractable from the entity and which offer themselves so to speak to other concrete entities. In this view an entity can simultaneously "participate" in a variety of types of forms, but the forms themselves are unaffected by the participation. Forms then are simply self-identical and are unaffected by determinacy. For instance, in the *Sophist* Plato sets forth angling as an acquisitive art *(technē)* of a coercive nature which engages in the hunting of a certain kind of water animal by a certain method. The analysis roots the specific activity in ever more general classes. According to the principle of positivity the coerciveness is itself of a different nature because it is hunting than it would be if it were (to use Plato's alternative) fighting. Certain features of coercion are carried from the one to the other, but they are altered by the determinate situation. Coercion itself means something different in war and in hunting, and therefore it is not a self-identical form which then gets attached to an existent. This principle finds contemporary illustration in the treatment of existence in Kierkegaard or Marcel, temporality in Heidegger, and spatiality in Merleau-Ponty. Hence, human beings are not "spatial," "temporal," or "existing" in identical ways with other levels of being. It is characteristic of more narrow types of empiricism to ignore this, thereby sharing with idealism the repudiation of the principle of positivity.

This ontological principle pervades every stratum or region of actuality. Historical faiths exemplify it as well as cultures, governments, institutions of leisure, and all the rest. It is apparent that both provincial and generic hermeneutics violate the principle: provincial hermeneutics because it does not see itself as reflecting or participating in structures more universal than its own actuality; generic hermeneutics because it presupposes that more universal strata simply reappear unchanged in more determinate levels. To illustrate, the resurrection of Jesus is another case of a "rising god." Christian freedom is simply this religion's pictorial or symbolic expression for authentic existence.[10] According to the principle of positivity, the specific images and realities of the historical faith are not unrelated to the universal human structures which Whiteheadian metaphysics or Heideggerian hermeneutics might disclose, but these universal structures actually undergo modification in the determinate situation of a historical faith. This is why the "correlation" of the symbols of a religious faith to general ontological structures is not an unambiguous procedure. If the correlation is carried out by suspending the principle of positivity, it means the attempt to disclose the general ontological structures hiding unchanged in the symbol. This appears to be what is happening in the naïve correlativism

---

10. Although most contemporary theologies are united in attempting to correct formalism by recourse to what is concrete, contemporary, or existential, their commitment to the principle of positivity is an ambivalent one. Existential theology is tempted to see *existence* reappearing as "Christian existence" relatively unaltered. Existence, derived generally and ontologically, becomes simply the "meaning" of determinate images of sin and salvation. Religious language reappears simply as language generically described and according to models of language as such; hence the situation of faith and faith-community does not really modify the language, but simply "uses" it as its own ceremonial or prescriptive game, or as a Word unveiling being.

of relevance theologies. Within the principle of positivity, correlation ?
means locating the way in which a universal ontological structure ?
has in fact undergone modification in the situation of the historical
faith and the imagery which expresses it.

1. *Phenomenology and the principle of positivity*

Granting that the principle of positivity is not an original contribution of phenomenological philosophy, what is the relation between Husserlian phenomenology and this principle? We should
first observe that any philosophy, phenomenology included, can be
used in such a way that the principle is violated. For instance,
phenomenological method can be employed for the purpose of philosophical anthropology which then is correlated with the symbols of
a historical faith in the framework of generic hermeneutics. Yet
Husserlian phenomenology seems to provide new ways of exploration within the principle of positivity. Although Husserl's own program is directed toward the universal (the transcendental foundations
of truth and knowledge as such), one of his key categories in his
investigations of transcendental intersubjectivity is personal body
(Leib) distinguished from objective body *(Körper)*. Body thus reappears in the determinate region of human being in a transformed
and distinctive way. This line of thought permits more specific
determinations of body such as male and female body, body in a
bachelor-oriented or Playboy culture, or body in Protestant sect-
groups. The principle of positivity is not a Husserlian discovery,
but intentional analysis does offer a new way of being sensitive to
the transformation of general structures in determinate situations.

Husserl in fact anticipates such a step in his occasional hints concerning the possibility of investigations of the determinate. In one
passage he acknowledges that the *residuum* of a phenomenological
reduction carried out toward a particular object, a specific house for
instance, is the noema not of house in general but of this particular
house.[11] In other words particularities themselves can be subject to
phenomenological investigation. In many passages Husserl speaks
of "regional eidetics" and regional ontologies which investigate the

---

11. *The Idea of Phenomenology,* trans. William Alston and George
Nakhnikian (The Hague: Nijhoff, 1964), p. 57.

essences and structure of a determinate region of objects.[12]   The most important "hint" is found in Husserl's category of a particular human surrounding-world *(Umwelt)* which, because of its determinacy, is not universally accessible.[13]   In other words, the home-world is a determinate world and offers itself as an object to be known in a different mode from an alien-world.

2. *Theology and the principle of positivity*

Since faith has a determinate object and a determinate matrix, the principle of positivity is indispensable to theology.   However, human reflection, driven as it is by the fears and malice which characterize historical existence, constantly fluctuates between provincial and generic interpretations.   These interpretations are rooted in the human drive to self-securing because both are ways of dehistoricizing human being.   Accordingly, the principle of positivity is not an automatic possession of theology but must be continually regained.   To this extent, it is as much a goal as a feature of theological reflection.

Prior to our actual investigation, we cannot display the results procured by a reflection operating with this principle.   We can point out certain features of the theological given to which phenomenological theology must adapt if it retains the principle.   A merely external and superficial adaptation would give Christian truths or doctrines an unapproachable status.   To so locate "Christian truths" involves also grasping their mode of presence and the meaning of their "truth," and this presupposes the very things phenomenological theology would investigate.   If we begin with Jesus Christ but refuse

12. Cf. *Ideas,* sec. 9, sec. 59, plus much of the inquiry in *Ideen* II and III.
13. *Meditations,* sec. 58, p. 133.   In this passage Husserl argues that phenomena such as personal body are universally accessible, but then observes that, in the cultural world, a specific surrounding-world is relative to the undstandings of the participants.   Its distinctive reality is not present to general experience or distributed universally.   "Each man understands first of all, in respect of a core and as having its unrevealed horizon, *his* concrete surrounding-world or *his* culture; and he does so precisely as a man who belongs to the community fashioning it historically.   A deeper understanding, one that opens up the horizon of the past (which is co-determinate for an understanding of the present itself), is essentially possible to all members of that community, with a certain originality possible to them alone/and barred to anyone from another community who enters into relation with theirs."

to acknowledge his distinctive mode of presence, we are not actually beginning with Jesus Christ, that is, with the theological given in its givenness. Ultimately, the distinctive mode of givenness is founded in the nature of the object itself. The "object" present and given to the community of faith is not a single entity such as "God" or man. It is a multidimensional object presented in and through a variety of human acts which reflect corporate, liturgical, existential, and even transcendental structures and which find expression in a constellation of images which bear on various kinds of realities. Because this multidimensional object is what it is, pertaining to the sacred and to man alienated from himself, its mode of presence involves mystery, human existence, and human self-alienation. The theological given presents us with something through which our very being has already been modified, and this modification permeates and guides all of our attempts to apprehend, reflect on, or investigate that given. Because our historical existence is marked by a kind of rift, a structural flaw, we apprehend the sacred and ourselves in and through this rift. Because the theological given concerns a built-in directedness to transcend this rift, as well as salvific events and processes pertaining to this transcending, its mode of presence to us finds expression in relations, testimonies, and imageries which occur at the pre-reflective level of existence. Because the sacred touches and unifies all the imagery of the theological given, a dimension of mystery is present which is constitutive and unremovable.

We do not want our emphasis on the pre-reflective nature of the mode of presence of the theological given to be taken as an obscurantism or an esoteric fideism which eschews all analysis and reflection as a pseudo-intellectual alteration of the faith of the "ordinary man of faith." We have seen enough of this pietism masked in the sophistications of contemporary existential and linguistic theologies. The point is that the principle of positivity requires an adaptation of phenomenological method to the specific modes of givenness of the historical faith with which we are concerned. Furthermore, these interrelated features of mystery, alienation, and existence are themselves not identical with some general version of the phenomena but pertain to the concrete reality of this historical faith.

2 C. "Apprehensions" and "Realities"

The two operative concepts, apprehensions and realities, play an important role in the way the problem and proposal of this essay are formulated. Chapter 1 posed the following problem: In the network of symbols, acts, social structures, and experiences of this historical faith, are there *any* apprehensions of *any* realities? But what are apprehensions and realities? As operative concepts they resist thematic clarification and explicit definition. These terms or concepts are as old as philosophy itself and occur frequently in metaphysical schemes from Plato to Whitehead. A complex vocabulary of apprehension and reality is employed by Husserl in his program of transcendental exploration.[14] For this reason our usage of the terms will depart somewhat from that of Husserl.

1. *Apprehensions*

In the term *apprehension* we are searching for an inclusive and ontologically neutral expression which avoids association with a particular kind of object or entity and therefore avoids being reduced to a specific type of apprehending such as sense perception or imagination. Its very flexibility and adaptability make it constitutively elusive. Described in a general way, an apprehension is an act which grasps realities directly or immediately. We could, therefore, speak of apprehensions as intuitions except for the unfortunate connotations the term *intuition* has in English. To many intuition means a kind of whim, a spontaneous feeling which dispenses with evidence

---

14. Husserl expresses the concept of "immediate apprehension" in the following verbs and substantives: *schauen, anschauen, erschauen, erfassen, auffassen, originär gebender Anschauungen,* originär *Evidenz, unmittelbare Sehen, Intuition, Wesenschau.* He contrasts these immediate apprehensions with the second-order acts of *Darstellung, Gegenwärtigung,* and *Reflektion.* The usual function of this vocabulary is to display the act which grasps transcendental subjectivity. However, Husserl does not limit the vocabulary to the transcendental region, but also uses it to describe the grasping of any entity, mathematical or otherwise, which is present in such a way that one must base judgments about it simply on "seeing" it. A few of Husserl's most important passages on immediate apprehensions are the following: *Ideas,* sec. 19 and secs. 136–45; *Meditations,* sec. 24; *Formal and Transcendental Logic,* chap. 4; *Crisis,* sec. 34; *Erfahrung und Urteil,* pp. 17–18. See also Maurice Natanson's essay, "Phenomenology: A Viewing," in his *Literature, Philosophy, and the Social Sciences* (The Hague: Nijhoff, 1962).

and which is at the mercy of one's own subjectivity. Apprehension, as used here, means an act in which evidence occurs in its most individual and basal form. This is the most distinctive trait of apprehensions. Because the object is given immediately, an apprehension cannot be corrected by searching for the way the object is *really* given. Apprehensions do not of course provide the total object, and in this sense investigations can continue concerning the nature, essence, relationality, and development of the object in question.

We must clarify that there is a certain ideality about apprehensions which differentiates them from the actual apprehendings of everyday life which only approximate genuine apprehensions. For instance, I may apprehend a certain object which I see at a distance as an existing house. The object may turn out to be an existing thing but not a house, or it may be a mirage-type house without existence. Or again, I may remember that I received a certain grade on a fifth-grade history test, when in fact I have synthesized this incident with a subsequent one and have mislocated the test. The mark of a genuine apprehension is its unsusceptibility to continuing confirmations or disconfirmations. The house seen at a distance calls for more confirmation. On the other hand, if I visit the house, explore it, purchase it, and reside in it, there comes a time in this continued exposure to the object that future exposures add nothing as far as evidence for houseness or existing house is concerned. A genuine apprehension is present to the degree that attempts at confirming the judgments in which the apprehension is expressed only repeat but add nothing to former confirmations. In the case of spatial entities the confirmations occur in relation to the complexity and accessibility of the entity. But with a priori entities such as essences or consciousness-acts, the confirmation is simultaneous with the apprehension. For instance, once one "sees" that his own consciousness is so structured that former acts, experiences, emotions, and the like persist into the present and are co-present in perception, he does not continue to confirm this in a series of investigations. Furthermore, in "seeing" this, we are not apprehending an "apparent" entity behind which, if we properly conduct our investigation, we may obtain to the "real" entity. A genuine apprehension is not confirmed because it itself is that consciousness-act in which confirming evidence is grasped as evidence.

Having set forth the fundamental feature of apprehensions, we shall now attempt a closer delineation. First, since apprehensions are immediate, they are to be distinguished from various cognitive activities which are not; arguing, calculating, inferring, concluding, re-presenting, reflecting, etc. This is a rather commonplace distinction between the direct apprehending of entities and the sophisticated apparatus of explanation which is constructed on it.[15] The relation between the immediate apprehension and scientific or reflective knowledge is that the latter requires the former for validity. Without immediate apprehensions second-order empirical, historical, or philosophical investigations would have no subject matter. Furthermore, genuine apprehensions ground the "knowing" of the practical life and guide its activities. These everyday world apprehensions are neither hypotheses nor wagers. When the housewife cooks a meal, she is neither hypothesizing nor wagering about the existence of her stove or the heat of the fire.

Second, since apprehensions are apprehensions of various contents or entities, they vary in type as the entities and contents vary. Different sorts of consciousness-acts are involved in the apprehensions of physical entities, relationships between such, logical relationships, the moods and predispositions of another person, one's own bias, and the nuances and tones of language.

Third, because an apprehension is an apprehension of, an act directed toward some entity or content, it involves a singling out of that entity (or process, object, relationship). This differentiating

---

15. C. I. Lewis distinguishes between "apprehension of the familiar" and philosophical conceptualization of such apprehensions. *Mind and the World Order* (New York: Dover Publications, Inc., 1956), pp. 1–7. Paul Ricoeur's distinction between understanding and explanation (*Freedom and Nature: The Voluntary and the Involuntary* [Evanston: Northwestern University Press, 1966], pp. 222 ff.) resembles a similar distinction Max Weber makes between direct observational understanding (*aktuelles Verstehen*) and explanatory understanding (*erklärendes Verstehen*). *The Theory of Social and Economic Organization* (New York: Free Press of Glencoe, 1964), pp. 94 ff. Whitehead's wider definition of perception, "non-sensuous perception," resembles what we are calling apprehension distinguished from explanation. See *Adventures of Ideas* (London: Cambridge University Press, 1935), p. 231.

or focusing need not be highly deliberate. Most apprehensions, serving as they do the more deliberate purposes of everyday life, are in fact unconscious or, better, pre-conscious focusings.[16] The housewife does not "make a decision to apprehend" the water boiling on the stove. On the other hand, reflection and deliberation can also lead to new apprehensions. For instance, when a married couple deliberately attempts to arrest something which is disrupting their relationship, they may come to "see" certain patterns of their lifestyle of which they hitherto had not been aware.

2. *Realities*

Apprehensions resist definition because they come to life at the concrete level of the specific entity grasped. Realities resist definition for the same reason. Like apprehensions the term *reality* is general and unfocused and comes to life at the level of the specific. Since realities are correlates of apprehensions, they are subject to similar formal characteristics. Realities occur in the mode of differ- | entiation; they stand out and exhibit themselves in the mode appropriate to their kind.

But what counts as a reality? Are phenomena, appearances, and consciousness-acts realities? They are in some sense apprehended. This poses the difficult problem of the relation between the *noema,* the meant or intended meaning and content of an entity which is present in the apprehension, and the reality status of that entity. We distinguished previously between psychological apprehensions which may or may not be reality-directed and genuine apprehensions which are so directed. Both kinds of apprehensions have at least an intentional content. Even a mirage house has the *noema,* the meant-object, house. However, unless we simply define reality as whatever a consciousness-act intends, the *noema* must be distinguished from reality. The problem is further complicated by the fact that the essence or essential structure of an entity may not be grasped in a given psychological apprehension, and therefore we must distinguish the *noema,* the meant content, from the essence or essential structure. Here an example is called for. My own consciousness, or at least a portion of it, is in some sense present to me in an apprehension.

16. See p. 94, n. 11, on the term *pre-conscious.*

Insofar as this is the case, I necessarily intend a certain noema or meant-content when I grasp or make judgments about my own consciousness. I intend the consciousness of the sphere of "my own," not the other's consciousness. I intend something in which my own past perdures as memory and is a present factor in my responses. All this can be the case and is the case in self-awareness without my apprehending the distinguishing trait of consciousness itself. If intentionality is the essence of consciousness, it is quite possible to be aware of consciousness and, with that, a certain noematic content without that particular insight into essence. In other words, essence-apprehension (*Wesenschau*) is not a necessary concomitant of noematic intending.

These distinctions offer us a provisional and quite formal way of filling in the term *reality*. A reality is an entity which has a certain (noematic) content, a certain unification and differentiation (essence), and which occurs in a certain mode of existence. We say mode of existence rather than existence to call attention to the many and varied forms of existence reality can take. We are not suggesting that realities are necessarily space-time entities or transcendent entities or even independent entities. According to this usage of the term, the following would all qualify as realities: the human body; acts, emotions, structures and processes of consciousness; regions such as nature or animal life; corporate entities such as nations and tribes; and the structures of dependence between individuals and collectivities. Naturally, these entities have conditions for their existence in complex matrices more inclusive than themselves; hence, apprehending them involves focusing, an abstracting process which seems to lift them out of their matrix. But they do have noematic content, essential structure, and a differentiated mode of existence. It makes little sense to say that the above sorts of things have no existence at all, although the greatly impoverished reality-sense of a technological civilization is constantly tempted so to judge them.

When we say that human beings apprehend realities, what do we mean? We mean that an entity which has a noematic content, essential structure, and exists in a certain mode of existence is immediately present to consciousness. A genuine apprehension of a house qua reality grasps the noematic content (including its function as a dwelling) plus the mode of existence proper to a house. What cannot be done is to transfer that particular mode of existence to other types of reality such as consciousness or social structures as the criterion of their reality: an act so arbitrary as to resemble superstition.[17]

D. THE REFLECTIVE METHOD OF PHENOMENOLOGICAL THEOLOGY

Finally, we take up operative concepts which guide the reflective procedures which we shall be following. As operative concepts they too are difficult to explore thematically, and the nature of these procedures will only be clarified in their employment. We shall characterize these procedures with the aid of two of Husserl's methodological concepts, one *(epochē)* which occurs throughout his writings and the second (questioning-back) which occurs mostly in the late philosophy. Husserl refined these procedures for his own transcendental investigations, but in appropriating them for phenomenological theology we shall alter them somewhat for our own purposes. So far we have said in this chapter that the principle of positivity requires the investigation of the theological given to adapt itself to that given, and that the theological given appears to be rooted in apprehensions of realities which occur in the community of faith. We now ask about the procedure by which phenomenological theology explores this determinacy or positivity of this historical faith.

1. *The theological epochē*

The method of phenomenological theology is primarily reflective. This reflection is not so much a "thinking about" an explicitly given totality as it is an attempt to penetrate and open up matters which are present but hidden. Theological reflection is a continuing and at best partially successful enterprise, a reflection in process. The reflection is not without its challenges and obstacles. Since its goal

17. It should be clear that this discussion of realities does not involve the classic metaphysical problem of what is ultimately real, what is the *res vera*. Monads, atoms, material particles, and actual entities have all been candidate answers to that problem. Realities in my usage refer not to the ultimate constituents of the cosmos, but to anything and everything which has the status of being over against us, and has the capacity to evoke from us an acknowledgment of that status.

is the situation of faith, the components and structures which make possible the reality-apprehensions of faith, it will be easily turned aside if it simply appeals to the authorities of the church tradition. The meaning and function of the authorities themselves are rooted in this reality-apprehending situation. Instead of the authorities being the key to the situation of reality-apprehension, it is the other way around. Because theological reflection can be disrupted in its initial efforts, the procedure calls for a negative moment resembling what Husserl called the *epochē*. We call it negative not in the sense of denial or repudiation but in the sense of suspending, putting into brackets, or temporarily not taking into consideration.

We must suspend two sorts of commitments or belief-systems in this initial moment of theological reflection. The first is the belief-ful or theological commitment to the church tradition, especially as it presupposes its own authorities such as Scripture or confessions. Two questions may help clarify this epochē. Does it contradict the principle of positivity? Is it a psychological impossibility? In regard to the first, we recall that the goal of the inquiry is to expose the structure of the situation of faith's apprehensions as the structure pertains to the concrete or determinate religious community. This structure, however, will not come into view if we substitute the appeals (Scripture citations, etc.) which occur in the everyday activities of that community for an inquiry into the matrix of such appeals and activities. In regard to the second question, we clarify that the epochē does not entail the concrete erasing of one's tradition from memory. It simply means an investigation which "makes no use of" the methodological commitments of the faith community.

What remains after the theological epochē? We are calling the post-epochē residue the *matrix* of the reality-apprehensions of the community of faith. This suggests that the theological epochē is not a radical one in the Cartesian sense.[18] Cartesian radicalism is the use of radical doubt to expose the apodictic or undoubtable region of the cogito. Such doubt is not a possibility in .theology, even phenomenological theology, partly because its exploration is not ad-

18. See Pierre Thévenaz, "The Radical Point of Departure in Descartes and Husserl," in *What Is Phenomenology and Other Essays* (Evanston: Northwestern University Press, 1962).

dressed to the foundation of rationality as such, and partly because the mysterious and existential nature of that which is theologically given limits and relativizes absolute doubt. Methodological doubt in phenomenological theology does not expose the foundation of rationality as such but opens the way to the "determinate" foundation and structure of the community of faith. The theological epochē is, therefore, not a radical one but occurs in the service of the principle of positivity.

Accordingly, the theological epochē is not performed for the purposes of a fundamental theology in the sense of exploring *transcendental* foundations of the possibility of faith. We are not setting everything out of action except the religious a priori. We do not repudiate fundamental theology, nor do we reject a religious a priori in the sense of that structure constitutive of the human being by which revelation accords with and does not distort or neutralize humanness. Although fundamental ontology may be an appropriate first step in philosophical schemes (cf. Heidegger), it can occur at the beginning of theology only in conjunction with other elements in the matrix of faith. In philosophy the various cognitive and human acts which the transcendental region "founds" are universally available and are already grasped by the philosopher. In the case of faith and a faith community in which the content itself has become problematic, that which the so-called religious a priori founds is not initially clear. If the determinate is elusive, attempts to isolate the ground of its possibility will, lacking guidelines, be unfocused. And if the determinate, the content of the faith-community itself, is problematic, a program of fundamental theology will not render it less so. In short, the guiding clues for fundamental theology need to be taken from the determinate imagery, social structure, and reality-apprehensions of the faith community. This is why fundamental theology needs to succeed or accompany rather than precede phenomenological theology.

The second set of commitments or belief-systems which would be set out of action in the theological epochē are "metaphysical" schemes which determine beforehand the criteria, scope, and nature of faith's reality-apprehensions. I do not wish to aid and abet the standard easy dismissal of metaphysics found in the empiricist, pietistic, and American temper. Neither would I wish to declare as insignificant those programs of philosophical theologies (Thomist, Whiteheadian) which explore relationships between the reality claims of a religious faith and a particular ontology. I do want to postpone (put out of action) this sort of thing in phenomenological theology because the ways in which realities are apprehended in the particular historical faith will remain hidden if they are allowed to be realities only to the degree that they are translatable into the scheme in question. This is, of course, simply another way of expressing the principle of positivity. It presupposes a certain distinctiveness in such historical entities as religious faiths which reflect but also particularize (and sometimes explode) the ontological structures discovered by philosophers.

Yet a far more serious reason lies behind this appeal to suspend philosophical criteria for reality and knowledge. Philosophy, even analytic philosophy, is never simply a neutral instrument unrelated to the culture in which it occurs or the human being who works with it. No human being escapes the emphases, valuations, and predispositions of the life-world in which he is shaped. And no human being escapes that rift of self-alienation which has characterized human history and its collectivities and individuals as far back as we know them. More specifically, no human being in America escapes the West and all it means. Our life-world and our interiority are actualizations of Spengler's prophecies. None of us escapes science, Western education, the technocracy and the militarizing and computerizing of human life into patterns of anonymity, emptiness, and fanatical searchings. With these effects come subtle models of reality and knowledge. And although many rebel against the accumulating and debilitating consequences of a civilization's decline, these models are implanted in us. So successful and prestigious have been the natural sciences in the precounter-culture epoch that other intellectual pursuits could survive only to the degree that they imitated their procedures and categories of explanation. In these imitations the human being simply disappears. Lost or distorted are human consciousness, human body, human time, human spatiality, human sex, human decision-making, and human reciprocity. Dismissed as speculative, intuitive, and prejudicial are the issues of freedom, hope, bondage, and evil, and in their place come various physiological, social, and psychological mechanisms. We are not saying that industrialists and generals are responsible for these substitutions while academia is a prophetic opposition. Technocratic models of reality and knowledge permeate academia as much or more than any other cultural region. They probably originated there. In such a civilization "philosophical criteria" have a very specific meaning. The philosopher like the theologian and other academics is technocracy's child, and he imbibes its models of reality. These models function in subtle and hidden ways. They are rarely explicated but they determine what are valid and invalid issues, what regions can and cannot be investigated, how issues are formulated, what is allowed to count as evidence, and what words, images, and expressions are acceptable or taboo.

Because of the effect of our civilization upon our modes of thought and our patterns of inquiry, the theological epoché is more than an easily performed intellectual act. It involves a shift in deeply habitual ways of looking at reality, a kind of alteration of consciousness which attemps to be self-aware of the hidden models of reality that restrict and impoverish our apprehension of most of our life-world. The issue is far deeper and more serious than the professional conflicts of competing frameworks: "phenomenology" or analysis, being or language, science or religion. We are faced here with the way we use our powers and skills to perpetuate or oppose the darkness now descending upon the West. The theological epoché in other words is partly an *existential* act involving not just a temporary change of stance but a permanent attempt, perhaps always only an attempt, to put out of action the reality models which have shaped our consciousness, so that the specific realities of a determinate faith can appear. In this sense the epoché is a turning around, a transformation, or as religious people would say, a kind of repentance.[19]

19. This passage summarizes a main thesis from Husserl's *Crisis,* pp. 71–73. In this work he describes contemporary philosophers as receiving predispositions from the intellectual heritage of the West, and he invites a reflection which would open up the historical situation of the philosopher himself.

2. Theological reflection as "uncovering"

In addition to the negative bracketing of the epochē, theological reflection includes a constructive aspect which we shall call *uncovering*. Terminologically, we are following Husserl who spoke of his own reflective method as a "way back" (*Rückgang*) and a questioning-back (*Rückfragen*) to the life-world. Since reflection always follows its object and adjusts itself to it, theological reflection cannot be a mere instance of Husserlian reflection, directed as it was at the transcendental region. But even a provisional description of theological reflection forces us to anticipate future development of our argument. Alfred Schutz's lifetime project was a delineation of the life-world in the sense of the world of everyday life, the social world. Schutz's social world is neither the particular or concrete environment of a specific time and place nor Husserl's transcendental intersubjective world. The components of Schutz's social world are successors, predecessors, consociates, and contemporaries which at some time or other have empirical existence but which are not understandable apart from subjective or intending acts of human beings. Schutz's concern is with the essential structures of social world as such, which find empirical exemplification in particular social worlds.

We are not concerned with the social world in this sense. The theological thrust of this investigation with its principle of positivity drives us to realities more determinate than the transcendental region and the general structure of the social world. On the other hand, the object of our inquiry, the matrix of the reality-apprehensions of faith, resembles a social world in that the apprehensions of faith like all apprehensions occur in a determinate and pre-formed corporate reality (faith-world). Like the social world this corporate reality exists in the form of concrete social units in space and time (church, churches, sects, parishes, denominations) and has a distinctive structure which persists through these empirical exemplifications. The matrix of the acts, language, and apprehensions of faith is neither merely subjective, a matter of the interiority of the individual consciousness, nor objective, a matter of contents presented to a rather empty and receptive subject. The intentional relation between consciousness-acts and their objects constitutes this matrix as well as the social world as such. The problem of theological reflection then is to obtain access to this determinate region or structure which is neither empirical in the sense of the actual day-to-day contents of a specific sect nor subjective in the sense of the actual flow of experience of an individual.[20]

The faith-world like objects of perception presents itself in the mode of a facade, or, to change metaphors, a surface. This is inevitable and proper since life in the faith-world formally resembles life in the world of everyday life in that it is primarily practical and unreflective. Religious people attend church, take communion, pray, seek forgiveness, organize projects for justice, and console those in pain and misery. They do these things in whatever attitude is proper to them. And although these very activities may be guided by a consciousness already shaped by participation in the community and by interiorized images, this shaping and the shaping matrix remain hidden in the background. The activities themselves occupy the foreground. All this, as we said, is proper and inevitable, unless we wish to find out in what sense reality-apprehensions occur in such a setting. At this point we are tempted to permit the everyday acts of the cultus (praying, communing, and the like) to answer the question. If someone asks whether and in what sense Jesus Christ is present in all this, whether faith is in "God," or how one knows that salvation is a human and not a demonic power in human life, one possibility is simply to point to people praying, working for justice, etc. Such an answer is no answer for the participants themselves if their own religious acts become problematic, if they themselves ask these questions. It tends to capitulate to the Feuerbachian suggestion that religious acts are finally simply self-directed. Most seriously, if there are structures beneath these

20. One of the most lucid expositions available of the multi-strata nature of consciousness is Richard M. Zaner's *The Way of Phenomenology* (New York: Pegasus, 1970), chap. 3, "The Theory of Consciousness." On one point I must depart from Zaner's interpretation. Zaner indicates that the *founding* strata of consciousness-acts must be investigated at the beginning. While this does justice to Husserl's method in *Ideas* I, it should be said that in the *Crisis* Husserl's method was more of a working back from founded to founding strata, from life-world back to transcendental structures which it presupposed. Further, this present work attempts to open up founding strata by attending to what is founded.

everyday acts in which the realities appear that impel religious people toward these acts, and if there is some access to such, then the occasionalistic solution is not only arbitrary but reality-denying.

Our proposal is that the everyday activities of the religious cultus are founded in a "world" that contains many strata; institutional, pre-institutional, intersubjective, subjective and experiential, and transcendental. For instance, the inclination of a community of faith compassionately to relieve human misery may rest in part on the way the people in that community intend each other as human beings, an intention that is interiorized, that is guided by Christological images, and that produces a structure of reciprocity, which the participants take for granted but not in a conscious way. If this structure has no existence, reflection remains imprisoned in the foreground. If it does exist, but there is total preoccupation in the everyday activities themselves, the background remains unexplored but offers itself as explorable. If the background structure is present only in the pathological sense of a psychological block, it may be simply inaccessible. Yet the structures of the social world as such are available to those who would turn back to them. Our proposal is that the faith-world, the matrix and background of religious acts, has a discernible content and structure. What enables this discernment is a reflection which is a conscious second-order act that turns back, questions back to the accessible strata beneath the everyday acts of the cultus. We assign what is uncovered neither to the conscious nor to the unconscious, but to a pre-conscious stratum of which there is dim but indirect awareness.[21] We are not proposing that this reflection can give a total or exhaustive account of itself. The dimension of the sacred, the mystery of the human being, and the obscuring effects of alienation will limit and sometimes defeat the attempt to penetrate the background. Nevertheless, some pene-

---

21. The following passage from Merleau-Ponty is exemplary of this shadowy realm between the conscious and unconscious. "What we have just said about the dream applies equally to that ever slumbering part of ourselves which we feel to be anterior to our representations, to that individual haze through which we perceive the world. There are here blurred outlines, distinctive relationships which are in no way 'unconscious' and which, we are well aware, are ambiguous, having reference to sexuality without specifically calling it to mind." *The Phenomenology of Perception* (London: Routledge and Kegan Paul, 1962), p. 168.

tration of the matrix of faith seems possible, and this is the object of theological reflection, at least as it serves the purposes of phenomenological theology.

At this point several clarifications are in order. First, the reflec- *1* tion we are talking about is reflection in service of this first stage of theological prolegomenon, phenomenological theology. But other sorts of reflection can and do occur in the faith community, for instance, an "existential" reflection which brings together the elements of one's present situation (temptation, grief, political struggle, a familial problem) with the imagery and commitment of faith. Second, theological reflection is descriptive rather than speculative. *2* Its procedure is not so much an argument or a series of inferences as it is sifting the empirical and subjective materials which are before our eyes in search of essential structures. Third, if phenomenological *3* theology probes for a region which is not so specific as a particular church in space and time, does it then lose itself in a universality which has no bearing on Catholic, Protestant, or black churches and pieties? We would defer this question since it drives us in the direction of criteriological issues. We can say that theological reflection is an instrument adaptable to a community of faith in many of its forms, both universal and particular. Since a particular religious tradition such as the Roman Catholic church participates in but is not synonymous with the general structures of this faith shared also by other communions, theological reflection will attend to these universal features and to the way they are altered in this particular communion. The criteriological issue is present here in the question of how universally Christian structures function as measures of the faith of particular communions.

In summary, the problem of the essay as a whole, the problem of reality, required us to pursue the matter of apprehensions and realities. Husserlian phenomenology offers us some insights concerning the kind of reflective inquiry needed to gain access to the faith-world and its strata. The principle of positivity makes the object of our work determinate, and requires constant adaption of phenomenological materials. All this should make it clear that we are not attempting to exhaust the possible uses of phenomenological philosophy in theology. In later stages Husserlian methods and categories may assist in fundamental theology, the ontological conditions of faith constitutive of human consciousness.[22] Theological anthropology can be deepened and extended by phenomenological studies of personal body, lived-space, time-consciousness, and phenomenologies of the will, the imagination, and language. Most of these we leave aside, even as we make little use of other potentially helpful sources in process, linguistic, and existentialist philosophies.

3. Theological eidetics

Phenomenological method in its earliest Husserlian moment was an *eidetic* method. This means that it was a descriptive method based on a special kind of intuition into the *eidos* or essence of something.[23] When Husserl's philosophy developed into a transcendental program, he then distinguished the eidetic from the transcendental reduction.[24] Both reductions presuppose the intentional (noetic-noematic) structure of consciousness. The essence or eidos in eidetic intuition and analysis is not merely an event in the stream of consciousness but a *noema,* a meant unity which structures an object or individual. It is a *meaning* in that it is the objective correlate of an act of meaning. On the other hand, it is that in or about an object without which the object cannot be grasped as a unity, as a differentiated entity. Therefore, the content of the noema or essence does not depend simply on what the subject wishes to make it. Its fate is not merely turned over to the subject's will. If anything the subject's act is elicited by or ordered toward the

22. Ricoeur's *Fallible Man,* trans. Charles Kelbley (Chicago: Regnery, 1965), although without theological emphasis, may be the most explicit example of the use of phenomenology in portraying the transcendental conditions of one aspect of faith's situation, the possibility of human evil rooted in man's fragility. *Ray Hart's Unfinished Man and the Imagination* (New York: Herder and Herder, 1968), is the most inclusive and profound attempt at a Protestant fundamental theology.

23. For Husserl's philosophy of essence and the place of eidetic analysis in phenomenology, see the following: J. J. Kockelmans, ed., *Phenomenology: The Philosophy of Edmund Husserl and Its Interpretation* (Garden City, N.Y.: Doubleday and Co., 1967), part IV; Herbert Spiegelberg, *Phenomenological Movement,* vol. II, chap. XIV, C.; Ricoeur, *Freedom and Nature: The Voluntary and the Involuntary,* trans. Erazim Kohák (Evanston: Northwestern University Press, 1966).

24. See pp. 26-27, 33-37 above; also M. Natanson's "Introduction," to *Essays in Phenomenology* (The Hague: Nijhoff, 1966).

noema, the meant essence. *Eidetics,* a term used by French phenomenologists, refers simply to the method of essence inquiry. Hence, Ricoeur's eidetics of the will is a description of that about the will without which one cannot "mean" the will, on which all consciousness-acts which have the will in view depend, and which all modifications of the will (such as the fault) presuppose.[25]

The method of phenomenological theology is in some way an eidetic method. A glance at the chapters which follow will indicate the descriptive and morphological character of this inquiry. We are attempting no less than an eidetics of religious cognition (the apprehending of realities) under the determinate conditions of a historical faith. In connection with this we have attempted an eidetics of redemptive existence (Chapter 6) and of the communal matrix of that existence (Chapter 7). This should make it clear that our incorporation of eidetic method into theological prolegomenon rejects one of the alternatives before us, namely, an eidetics of the religious act or faith. Although most of the phenomenological philosophies of religion from Scheler to the present involve an eidetics of the religious act, the principle of positivity makes this impossible for our own project. At this point the principle of positivity intervenes to create the complexity and the distinctiveness of theological eidetics. The theological character of our inquiry requires that our work be done in the determinacy of a historical faith. Under the principle of positivity, the noemata with which we are concerned are not the universal essences of religious man but the more specific essences of a concrete and corporate historical existence. But how is such a concrete, historical faith available to us? Two modes of availability tend to be acknowledged in contemporary theological thought: an internal availability by way of an "inner history," in which the historical faith is perpetuated and disclosed to its constituents; and a historical availability in which the community's past, past epochs, language, polity, and liturgy are available to historical consciousness and by means of historical reconstruction.[26] Because of these

25. See p. 95 for a brief example of eidetics, applied in this case to the phenomenon of marriage.
26. In both Wittgensteinian and hermeneutic theologies, it is fashionable to emphasize language as *the* way in which this historical faith is available.

"inner" and "outer" historical modes of presence, theological eidetics involves historical consciousness and historical method. In other words theological eidetics, the attempt to set forth the determinate noemata in the situation of reality-apprehension of this historical faith, includes what Ricoeur calls symbolics. It cannot avoid the stories, imagery, and doctrines of this faith in its attempt at an eidetics of ecclesia or redemption.[27]

Theological eidetics may be a contemporary and phenomenological version of the nineteenth-century attempt to obtain the "essence of Christianity." Theological eidetics differs from that program because, in its attempt to obtain the eidos or essence, it focuses on the noema, the meant correlate of the consciousness-act which "means" such entities from within. When the method is applied to the situation of religious knowledge we find before us the specific matrix of that knowledge, therefore a historical phenomenon. And we find ourselves working with historical data. Because our method is eidetic, we are attempting to sift this data to distinguish the features necessary to, and distinctive of, this phenomenon. To this degree we remain within the program of the essence of Christianity. However, the method of distinguishing these features is to locate the *noemata,* the objects or contents which are correlative to acts of consciousness which are characteristics of the participants in this historical existence. Accordingly, we would miss the (essential) character of ecclesia if we failed to take into account how its partici-

While agreeing that language has a certain priority as a bearer of that availability, we would argue that this formulation is subject to an unfortunate abstractness. First, the focus on only one dimension of language (language behavior, statements, speech-acts) involves an abstraction insofar as the language of faith is itself multidimensional, involving strata of imagery which occur beneath the level of utterance or speech, the actual linguistic interchanges in the cultus. Second, this historical faith has vehicles of availability other than its own language, namely, its cultic acts, institutional structures, and the like, which in any given present are available both to intuition and to the historian.

27. For this reason theological eidetics is quite different from a philosophical eidetics as we find it in Ricoeur's philosophy of the will. In the philosophical program an eidetics of human will and a symbolics of man's situation in which the "fault" is taken into account can be sharply differentiated. Because theological eidetics faces the determinate from the very start, symbolics must play some role in its eidetic procedures, making available the data with which it works.

pants "mean" it, and this is bound up with ways in which they typify and co-intend each other. It was this sort of questioning which uncovered one of the features of ecclesia, its intrinsic universality (Chapter 7).

PART II

THE CORPORATE MATRIX OF FAITH'S APPREHENSIONS

CHAPTER 4

LIFE-WORLD AND FAITH-WORLD

The constitution of the world of culture, similar to the constitution of any "world," including the world of one's own stream of experience, has the lawful structure of a constitution, oriented with respect to a null-point, i.e., to a personality. Here am I and my culture; it is accessible to me and to my cultural companions as a kind of experience of Others.[1]

Alfred Schutz

The problem beneath the problem of theological method is whether and in what sense faith with its cognates of revelation and redemption is directed toward realities. This investigation cannot pretend to restore reality to the faith-community, partly because every second-order enterprise depends on apprehensions which occur in a concrete situation, and partly because the reality-loss in the present Christian community is rooted in contemporary events which make that community both a victim (of the technocratic invasion) and a perpetrator (of racism, escapism, and other crimes). We must be content to set forth the essential components in the situation of faith, and try to work back to those largely hidden dimensions of faith's situation where realities may still be making their appearance. What follows is an eidetics of faith's situation. The effort is not so much an argument as an attempt simply to uncover or discover what is already there in the way of elements, interrelations, levels of community, and intentions of consciousness.

1. Alfred Schutz, *Collected Papers* (The Hague: Nijhoff, 1966), I: 127.

85

The central thesis of this exploration is that most of faith's founding apprehensions are pre-reflective, and that they are mediated through the distinctive sociality of the community of faith. This is not to be taken in the sense of a sociological determinism which simply has people acting and believing in ways in which tradition and social heritage predispose them, nor is it a refinement of the same point in the framework of the sociology of knowledge. We are not talking about the social conditions or sociological "explanations" of belief but the role of a social matrix in *apprehensions of realities*. We will, however, make little progress in this investigation if we restrict sociality to visible and measurable social units. The apprehensions which occur through the matrix of sociality occur in depth strata which resemble the depth dimensions of the human psyche dealt with in psychoanalysis. The first two chapters of Part II attempt to explore these strata and their presence as essential conditions of genuine cognitive acts. Since the key terms, life-world, social world, and intersubjectivity, are cognates of "world" as it appears in phenomenological thought, we shall begin with the operative concept, world, in Husserl's philosophy.

A. LIFE-WORLD AND ITS COGNATES

1. *"World" in Husserl's thought*

The motif *world* is central to Husserl's philosophical development. According to the "official" exposition of Husserl's thought in Fink's article, the origin of the world was the unifying problem of Husserl's program.[2] If the "founding" role of the transcendental ego was the center of Husserl's thematic investigations, that which was founded was the world whose existence and structures we take for granted

2. Of the many passages in Husserl's writings on world and life-world, the following are the most indicative: *Ideas,* secs. 27-29, sec. 47; *Meditations,* sec. 28; *Crisis,* sec. 9, H and part III, A, especially sec. 34 (see also appendices V, VI, and VII to the English edition of the *Crisis*); *Erfahrung und Urteil,* secs. 6–10. Although Husserl's assistant, Ludwig Landgrebe, actually wrote this part of *Erfahrung,* he based the writing on a manuscript of Husserl's and the final formulation was approved by Husserl. It is one of the most explicit passages in Husserl's writings on the theme of life-world. There are also a number of unpublished studies of world and life-world in Husserl's papers, most of them falling in the 1930's. See especially Series A, V–VII and B, I and E, III of the Archive materials. A volume of *Husserliana* collecting the more important manuscripts on world is to appear in the future.

in all acts of knowing and specific scientific inquiries. Husserl's distinctive approach to world as a *noema* occurs as early as the *Ideas*. Present here are the main ingredients of what later came to be called life-world. However, we shall not trace the development of this theme in Husserl's thought but rather shall discuss it systematically.

Needless to say, certain of Husserl's key concepts are central to his portrayal of world. The basic one is intentionality which operates passively in every act of consciousness by which that consciousness-act is structured toward an object. Husserl carried this insight into his analysis of perception, and the result was the discovery that every perception carried with it an intentionality which went far beyond the perceived face of the object. The perceiver fills in or completes by way of intention what is not directly perceived (other aspects of the object, its background, its past), and this intentional completing is what Husserl calls appresentation. And while perception always involves drawing an object into the foreground, the background (which shades off into infinity) is present intentionally. Hence, each perceived object has a background, part of which is present to us along with the object but which shades off into the unperceived. For this reason background is always present in the form of a horizon. This analysis of perception with its elements of intention, horizon, and appresentation was the occasion of Husserl's philosophy of world. For the human being intends not merely *one* object as having a background to which he could then turn to investigate, to which he is related in the mode of "I can." Every object has such a background and horizon. This intention of a background and horizon is present prior to any actual perception. The result is that world is "passively pre-given."

Furthermore, there is an essential correlation of world in this pre-given sense and any particular perception or consciousness-act. For all perceptions occur in a situation in which it is possible to substitute the perceived object for something in the background. A perceived object always has an *explorable* background. And although thing-consciousness directed toward other *things* (and their background) is the founding structure of world, this structure (with its intentions, horizons, and appresentations) extends to every kind of consciousness-act and every kind of object and region of objects:

mathematical, cultural, aesthetic, and the like. Persisting through this tremendously varied set of acts and objects is always the pre-given intention toward a landscape, only part of which is ever actually viewed or explored, but whose presence makes future explorations possible. Because world is what it is, an ever-present horizon of possible future explorations; it can never be thematized in itself in the way some worldly region or object can be the object of thematic inquiry. One suspects, therefore, that world functions in Husserl's philosophy much like *being* in Heidegger's philosophy.

World, the totality of backgrounds and of possible future acts and intentions, is the world in the sense of the common-sense world, the world of everyday life. As early as 1924 Husserl labels it the life-world. In our everyday practical activities, we take for granted an underlying landscape or structure which enables us to maneuver in such a way that we can correct mistakes. Any one perception or conclusion may be incorrect in the everyday world, but if it is *correctable,* it requires some foundation of validity which is not identified with any particular thing or percept.

On the basis of this formulation of world and life-world, Husserl elaborates insights about world which became commonplace in the phenomenological and existential philosophies after him. First, even though Husserl's basic model of self-world relation is that of perception, with things and thing-consciousness having a certain primacy, the world's furnishings are not simply things. The furnishings of the world are present to me in the various modes of my passive as well as conscious intentions toward them. Hence, my world is comprised not just of things but of facts, and not just of facts but entities which exist for me in graduations of importance. The chair in my living room is not simply a thing with a certain shape and color. In my life-world it is present as expensive, as early American, as having been inherited from a revered ancestor, as being too frail to be used. Not only intentionally graded "things" make up the life-world, but all intentional objects of whatever kind: symbols, nations, sentiments, laws, taboos, sanctions, sports, the other person in various relations, structures of power.

Second, because the life-world is the field of my possible acts, experiences, and maneuverings, whose objects correlate with my evaluating, acting, thinking, I am the center of my world. And the "I" at the center of the world is not a disembodied spirit but a bodily "I," an embodied self which acts on the world, makes plans, and carries out tasks. This embodied self has a temporality all its own and a spatiality all its own, in the sense of various times and spaces which have significance to the self. Furthermore, in the life-world I do not perform those sophisticated and solipsistic philosophical acts which question the existence of the other person. I apprehend my own embodied "I" to which my personal name applies as the object of experience of other body-selves. The only self I know in the life-world is a self in reciprocal interaction with other selves. In short the life-world is at the same time an intersubjective world. And this intersubjectivity is not a general phenomenon but involves the actual intersubjectivity of a world in my reach. Thus the home-world as over against the alien-world is the social expression of the fundamental structure of the life-world as centered around myself.

3   Third, it is in the life-world where occur the actual perceptions, apperceptions, and insights which found all cognition, including the knowledge obtained by science. For life-world connotes that concrete level of experience where objects immediately appear to us, and includes things, objects of nature, other persons, and cultural entities. Hence, without life-world there would be no science at all for two reasons. One, there would be no subject matter to explore, and no way to trace a theory or explanation back to an immediate apprehension. Two, there would be no room to maneuver so that an erroneous judgment could be corrected, since the background or life-world is what contains the evidence making possible continued inquiry. This is why any transcendental attempt to ground knowledge and science has as its problematic the critique of the life-world. All three of these Husserlian insights appear in some form in the philosophies of the so-called existential turn.

2. *The ambiguity of the term* life-world

Profound as these insights are, they have given rise to a proliferation of terms and distinctions in phenomenological philosophy which makes its philosophy of world difficult to grasp and use. This proliferation goes back to the varied vocabulary of Husserl on world and to certain ambiguities in his own writing. Life-world in Husserl's thought is ambiguous because it seems to stand for both a universal a priori structure and a concrete, space-time, cultural environment. In the *Ideas* Husserl used the term, the natural *Umwelt*, to describe the life-world in the sense of the world of everyday life to which we are directed in the natural attitude.[3] Since the immediate world in which we live in the natural attitude is always a particular home-world involving a particular culture, language, and value-system, the term *life-world* can be taken to mean one's concrete home-world. However, if life-world simply means one's actual cultural environment with all its contingencies, it would be a shaky foundation indeed for the sciences. Husserl sensed over and above the contingent content of various home-worlds an a priori structure which enables the life-world to function as the necessary and legitimate substrata of cognitive judgments[4] Nor does he mean by this a priori structure the a priori lawfulness of factual natural laws, but rather a transcendental structure, something which persists after all actualities in the life-world are subjected to a universal epochē.[5] Husserl even distinguishes between two a priori investigations of the life-world, one conducted within the natural attitude and one within the transcendental reduction.

We are left then with the following three senses of life-world, or, one might say, dimensions of life-world. First, life-world is the *1* immediate environment (home-world) in which we live in the practical attitude. Therefore, its content varies with the times and cultures of human history. This is Schutz's "world of everyday life" and Husserl's "home-world" and *Umwelt*. Life-world is also the universal structure of all concrete home-worlds as such, a structure involving intersubjective relations, personal body, lived-space, etc. This compares to Schutz's "structures of the social world" and to Husserl's science of the life-world within the natural attitude. Third, life-world is a universally present and pre-given concatenation of the *3* actual and possible horizons of consciousness-acts. It therefore

3. *Ideas*, secs. 27–28 and sec. 58.
4. *Erfahrung und Urteil*, sec. 9.
5. *Crisis*, sec. 44 and sec. 51.

reaches into the transcendental region, or to express it from below,[9] it is constituted transcendentally and is thus apprehendable in the transcendental reduction.

Phenomenologists after Husserl did not continue Husserl's program of studying the life-world in the third sense of a transcendentally constituted world. However, several kinds of investigations of the life-world did persist. Heidegger formulated "world" in the sense of the existential turn of phenomenology, and world was used to characterize an essential being-in-the-world feature of human existence. Alfred Schutz's researches fall within Husserl's call for an ontology of the life-world within the natural attitude. His program was the study of the essential structures necessarily present in the practical world of everyday life. Otto Bollnow, Merleau-Ponty, Marcel, and others pursued in detail the themes of intersubjectivity, lived-space, and personal body. In these investigations phenomenological philosophy has offered some startling insights, accompanied however by a confusing proliferation of "world" vocabulary.[6]

For the sake of clarity in our use of life-world and its cognant concepts, we offer the following set of distinctions. The main unclarity about the life-world terminology is caused by the fluctuation between the concrete and the essential. Hence, the word *intersubjective* tends to undergo transition from its original Husserlian sense of an essential structure of human consciousness to the more concrete sense of actual interpersonal relations. *Life-world* as a term tends

6. The proliferation of world and its cognates in the phenomenological movement is confusing and results in usages which are often unreconcilable. Heidegger, characteristically avoiding Husserl's terminology, never speaks of the life-world, but does offer a complicated scheme of distinctions of his own. He uses *Mitwelt* to designate *Dasein*'s intrinsic relation with others and *"eigene Umwelt"* to describe one's own nearby environment. *Being and Time* (London: SCM, 1962), pp. 155 and 193. Schutz refines the vocabulary in order to describe the general structure of the social world. He distinguishes *Mitwelt* (world of contemporaries), *Folgewelt* (world of successors), *soziale Umwelt* (world of directly experienced consociates), and *Vorwelt* (world of predecessors) to designate the different kinds of "others" in the social world, each representing a different horizon. *Phenomenology of the Social World* (Evanston: Northwestern University Press, 1967), chap. 4. Ludwig Binswanger, working primarily under Heidegger's influence, uses *Mitwelt* simply as the social world, and adds to it *Eigenwelt* to call attention to distinctive personal and interior dimensions, and *Umwelt* as simply immediate environment. *Being-in-the-World* (New York: Harper Torchbooks, 1967), pp. 31 and 296.

to undergo a similar modification. *Concrete life-world* corresponds *i*
to the first of the Husserlian usages and means the immediate surrounding complex of entities in which human beings live in the
practical, common-sense attitude. It is the world of work, play,
survival, and illness as these occur in a particular cultural and historical situation. *Essential life-world* or *social world* corresponds to 2
the second usage listed above and refers to the essential components
and their interrelations of the concrete life-world. Because these
components involve society in the distinctive human sense, human
life-world is a *social* world. Essential life-world is that structure of
the life-world set forth in Schutz's works. It involves the kinds of
social relationships which everyday activities require and presuppose:
face-to-face consociates, contemporaries, successors, and predecessors. Each side of the distinction between concrete and essential
life-world is naturally an abstraction in that each side is obtained by
temporarily bracketing the other side. When the brackets are removed and the two are brought together, we have a *determinate* 3
social world.

B. DETERMINATE SOCIAL WORLD

Investigations of a determinate social world are absent in phenomenological philosophies of world since they tend to be restricted to the
universal anthropological implications of life-world (cf. Heidegger)
or to the general structures of social world (cf. Schutz). Recalling
the principle of positivity, "essences" obtainable by essence-analysis
or by induction from particular situations always undergo transformation at the level of concreteness. And this transformation includes not simply a move from essence to existence but the addition
of new content. The "temporality" of man as such obtained in
phenomenological analyses is not simply *existing* temporality in the
concrete situation of Buddhist man but is Buddhist temporality. A
determinate social world, combining as it does the concreteness of a
particular life-world and universal structures of social world, presents
to the investigator the special methodological problem of sensing the
way in which the universal structures have undergone modification
and have taken on new content. This is a crucial methodological
issue for any attempt to grasp the situation of faith, since faith occurs

in conjunction with a determinate social world. With this in mind we must look more closely at the strata of a determinate social world, for it is by means of the deeper social strata that faith's apprehensions occur.

1. *Determinate intersubjectivity*

What follows cannot pretend to be a comprehensive anatomy of determinate social world. We want to pursue the matter far enough to at least clarify what a determinate social world is in relation to the various senses of life-world. More specifically we want to distinguish those aspects of determinate social world which we must make use of in uncovering the situation in which realities are present to faith. While this amounts to a social version of religious knowledge, we are not simply describing the transmission of tradition by way of institutional processes. Since our major thesis is that faith's apprehensions occur largely pre-institutionally, our principal task is to differentiate institutional and pre-institutional strata and to show their relationship. The pre-institutional stratum of determinate social world is the stratum of intersubjectivity to which we now turn.

Intersubjectivity was a theme in Husserl's philosophy from as early as his lectures in Göttingen (1910–11).[7] His fullest elaboration of the problem remains the fifth Cartesian Meditation.[8] For several reasons it is not surprising to find intersubjectivity thematized in Husserl's thought. One, any transcendental philosophy tends to solipsism because a transcendental region is intrinsically self-isolating. It could not be "transcendentally founding" if it were not. But if solipsism is the terminus of transcendental investigation, its whole program of the founding of knowledge and science is voided. This problem was in fact the starting point of Husserl's struggles with intersubjectivity. Two, Husserl's early descriptions of "background" and "horizon" in perception led naturally to particular regional ontologies such as nature and human spirit. One of the problems which occurs in such investigations is how the *other* is constituted. Husserl realized how necessary it was to solve the problem of our

7. See *Formal and Transcendental Logic*, p. 243, footnote.
8. On the theme of intersubjectivity in Husserl see also *Ideen* II, secs. 35–47, and *Formal and Transcendental Logic*, secs. 95 and 96.

knowledge of the other as another "mind" when he saw that the constitution of the other preceded and founded all claims to objective knowledge. The very meaning of objective is that an entity is not simply immanent in my own apprehending processes but is in principle apprehendable by a plurality of subjects.[9] It is beyond the scope of our concerns to summarize Husserl's solution to the problem of intersubjectivity or to assess his way of legitimating the knowledge of the other through his theory of empathy.[10] Our concern is to identify intersubjectivity as it arose in Husserlian phenomenology, namely, as transcendental intersubjectivity.

Husserl's proposal was that human beings constitute each other as persons at the same passively pre-given levels in which they constitute themselves or external objects in nature. One moment in this constitution includes the constitution of the sphere of "my own" and therefore a body which is not just a space-time entity which I perceive as a spectator but a personal body which is the locus of my receptivities and which is at my disposal in ways that other bodies are not. To view the other as an other like myself involves intending the other as a sphere of "my own" centered in a personal body. All this occurs pre-reflectively, according to Husserl, and in the everyday world. Intersubjectivity in this sense does not mean then the actual dialogue that occurs between persons, the actual interpersonal relations that occur between two people such as husband and wife, strangers, or fellow members of a small club. It refers to an interpersonal structure which exists *pre-consciously* and which is already prior to any actual relationship or dialogue as their condition.[11] In-

9. *Meditations,* sec. 55.

10. Two excellent analyses of Husserl's argument in the Fifth Meditation are Ricoeur's "Husserl's Fifth Cartesian Meditation" in *Husserl* (Evanston: Northwestern University Press, 1967), and Schutz's "The Problem of Transcendental Intersubjectivity in Husserl" in *Collected Papers,* III.

11. The terms *pre-reflective* and *pre-conscious* occur frequently in these chapters. We use them to call attention to that stratum of consciousness which is "prior to" or "beneath" the actual flow of consciousness in which contents are present in the mode of conscious awareness. A full analysis of that pre-conscious stratum would reveal many strata, some not recoverable at all, some hidden (because of trauma, for instance) but recoverable through psychotherapy, some hidden but recoverable through the transcendental reduction, some resting at the very threshold of the flow of consciousness and easily recoverable through reflective acts.

tersubjectivity in other words is human consciousness in its intrinsically social aspect. It is not produced by everyday acts of interrelationship but is presupposed by such acts. The being of the human being is therefore not merely subjective but intersubjective. Therefore, when we wish to designate the actual empirical relations between persons, we shall use the terms *reciprocity* and *interpersonal relations,* reserving *intersubjectivity* for the pre-given, socially structured consciousness which such presuppose. Here we have a distinction similar to that between concrete life-world (cf. reciprocity) and life-world transcendentally constituted (cf. intersubjectivity).

We are now ready to formulate the concept most important to determinate social world, a concept which, as far as I know, is not taken up in Husserl and Schutz, namely, *determinate intersubjectivity.* Even as concrete life-world and essential life-world are abstractions when separated, so are transcendental intersubjectivity and specific reciprocities. For in the determinate social world intersubjectivity itself is determinate. It retains of course the features which Husserl, Schutz, and others have described, features such as empathetic projection (if Husserl is correct) of one's own-ness sphere and personal body onto the other, or the reciprocity of motives and perspectives (if Schutz is correct). However, in a determinate social world these features are transformed and take on a novel content. In transcendental intersubjectivity there are unconscious or pre-reflective co-intendings between human beings whereby each intends the other as an other, as a center of decision-making, and the like. In determinate intersubjectivity the other is intended pre-reflectively and pre-consciously but he is intended as other mind and personal body in determinate ways.

A marriage relation offers a good example, for although marriage itself is not inclusive enough to be a determinate social world, it is an example of one kind of determinate intersubjectivity in a determinate social world. Marriage is a very suitable example because it involves all the strata of our analysis: conscious interpersonal reciprocities, pre-reflective intersubjectivity, and institutionalization.

Our terms *pre-reflective* and *pre-conscious* do not distinguish these multiple strata but simply point to that total dimension of the consciousness which precedes the flow of awareness.

Furthermore, it seems apparent that an investigation of marriage which restricts itself to simply institutional and reciprocal aspects (as if marriage were simply the institutionalization of conscious sexual reciprocities) has, by omitting its determinate intersubjectivity, left out the distinguishing features of marriage. For instance, if we describe marriage as an enduring sexual relationship between a human male and female, we have not yet apprehended the pre-reflective and enduring intending that constitutes marriage. Although we cannot attempt here a full phenomenology of marriage, the following suggestion may serve at least to illustrate determinate intersubjectivity. Intentionally speaking, human marriage is a sexually oriented commitment between male and female in which there is a mutual acceptance of responsibility for the *possible* offspring of that sexuality. Obviously this does not require the actual presence of children or even the actual capacity or desire to have children. The responsibility which characterizes the marriage relationship is not, like an affair or a temporary sexual liaison, simply one which is limited to the partner. It is a responsibility for whatever larger family unit comes about, either by design or by contingency, as the result of the sexual partnership and the mutual affections and passions which permeate it.

Such a mutual intending toward possible future offspring contains within it a complex structure of sub-intentionalities. "Responsibility for possible offspring" includes, for instance, an intended commitment to solve mutually whatever economic and financial problems are created by the larger family unit. Even the enduring quality of the mutual sexual partnership differs between the affair and a marriage in that the refusal of future offspring implicit in the affair implies that each individual participant sexually desires the other through a certain reservation of his future self; hence, the element of pleasure and gratification, legitimate in themselves, set the tone of the relationship and have a certain autonomy over other elements. These matters become more qualified and more complex when we take into account the different ways this mutual intending occurs in male and female, and when we attempt to set this structure of human marriage in a determinate social world such as eighteenth-century France or a village in Samoa.

The marriage relation is a *determinate* intersubjectivity because it comprises not just the general conditions of consciousness in which any other is grasped as other but the specific conditions of "meaning" the other as enduring mate and possible co-parent. It is intersubjective because the very condition of this act of meaning arises only in a situation of co-intending. It is transcendental in that this intending is not simply the consciously chosen mutual affection or mutual commitment itself but is a depth dimension of such a commitment, rarely formulated or even made the object of reflection. We are not talking about the reflection easily available to introspection in which a person says to himself that so-and-so would make a good father or good mother. We are pointing to the conditions of simply "meaning" the other not just as another personal center with a personal body but whose personal body along with "my own" form the matrix of future children, possible future personal centers as offspring. This matrix of future children is not intended as a mere biological one but as a social, economic unit characterized by qualities of affection, commitment, and endurance. We are aware that, psychologically speaking, these remarks can be almost endlessly qualified. We can imagine endless variants of *psychological* intentions, couples who at the time of marriage desire no offspring at all. Our only point is that the essence of marriage involves a mutual commitment which embraces possible offspring, a commitment which involves pre-conscious, mutual co-intendings. We can imagine of course two people submitting to the legal ceremony without this commitment, in which case something else is being institutionalized than marriage.[12]

12. The point of this example is that beneath the conscious intentions and interpersonal overt behaviors of a marriage there is a pre-reflective constituting or "meaning" of the other as mate. This pre-reflective intention is usually characterized simply as an enduring commitment, prompted perhaps by some sort of deep mutual affection. While not opposing such a view, I would argue that it does not do justice to what is involved in "meaning" the other as a permanent mate. Mere "commitment" to the other says little, and does not describe the way sexuality plays a primary role in the sort of commitment married people have to each other. Yet mere sexually oriented commitment is also a feature of the temporary liaison, and therefore does not account for the intention of the other as a permanent mate. Left out is the way in which futurity, the future both anticipate together, is present in the sexual commitment. The commitment to the other as a permanent mate says in effect, "I wish to share a sexual

Determinate intersubjectivity is not itself a determinate social world since social world is that totality which combines the concreteness of a given society (and therefore its language, customs, institutions, history, etc.) with the universal structures of social world. Determinate intersubjectivity combines that same concreteness with the general structure of intersubjectivity. Marriage is not *the* determinate intersubjectivity of Western civilization but is one among many types of interpersonal situations, the totality of which is the determinate intersubjectivity of the society in view. Actually, this is a misleading formulation since the larger the social unit (e.g., "Western civilization") the less determinate is the determinate intersubjectivity. Hence, we should not let this obscure the fact that determinate intersubjectivity becomes modified in ever more determinate situations. A black youth living in the ghetto of a large American city will participate in a determinate intersubjectivity made up of many interwoven, mutually affecting, and ever-changing interpersonal situations.[13]

2. *The process of institutionalization*

A full theory of institutions is not called for here. However, determinate intersubjectivity may be more clearly delineated by a brief inquiry into what occurs in institutionalization. Institutionalization functions primarily to integrate and thereby order potentially threatening activities and interpersonal relations into the larger society. A by-product of such integration is that the institutionalized activity gains perpetuation over time, usually bridging several generations. The elements of institutionalization through which integra-

present and sexual future with you whatever the outcome of that sexuality." Again, this is not the positive inclination to "have children," but it is an implicit commitment to whatever children may appear in that future as outcomes of the sexual present. This is why the family unit is intentionally present in the constitution of the other as mate.

13. We should clarify that we have simply attempted a philosophical description of determinate intersubjectivity. From the point of view of theology in which anthropology attempts some account of alienation and disrupted historical existence (see Chapter 6, B), determinate intersubjectivity is itself alienated under the conditions of existence. In other words, the effect of radical evil is not restricted to the surface levels of reciprocities, behaviors, and conscious intentions but reaches into and modifies determinate intersubjectivity itself.

tion occurs are symbols, ritual representations, experts or authority figures, and organizations or groups. In our example of marriage the institutional aspect includes symbols (the ring), the ritual (the ceremony), the authority figure (the magistrate, the minister), and the organization (society, church). What happens in the convergence of legal, symbolic, and ritual elements is that society at large approves and integrates into its very structure the marital relation. *What* is acknowledged, symbolized, and legally sanctioned is not simply the affectionate, interpersonal reciprocity of a male and female but their co-intention to bear responsibility for possible future offspring. Hence, any account of institutionalization which begins with human needs and tries to show that such needs are harnessed in institutions passes over the crucial middle ground of determinate intersubjectivity which mediates the need system and social structure.

This is not so much an account of institutions, the definition of which tends to be elusive, as a process of institutionalizing, the integration and thus perpetuation of determinate intersubjectivity into society at large or some unit thereof. To shift our example, competitive play such as baseball (or card games) involves a certain determinate intersubjectivity which has undergone institutionalization in our culture. We have before us then several strata which are always present in any determinate social world, and they range from highly public, visible, and accessible strata to relatively private and relatively inaccessible strata; symbols, rituals, and organizations which bear institutionalization, the acted-out interrelationships (the baseball game itself, the mutual dealings in marriage), the determinate intersubjectivity, and the varied system of bodily and psychological needs which is presupposed by determinate intersubjectivity. In this scheme of strata determinate intersubjectivity is pre-institutional. This does not mean that it can or does exist in society apart from institutionalization but that it is part of that which is institutionalized, and is presupposed by every institutionalization.

C. FAITH-WORLD

The cognates of world (life-world, world of fellow man, etc.) which have proliferated in phenomenological literature are not easily synthesizable, but they do share a common feature. They all attempt to express a stratum of world unified in some way, the unity of which is pre-reflectively intended. For instance, each human being intends a world of interacting fellow human beings at a level prior to acts of conscious inquiry and second-order reflection. In Heideggerian terms the human way of being-in-the-world involves being in the "world" of fellow human beings. We are prompted therefore to adapt this usage of cognates of world in order to call attention to some of the peculiarities of the matrix of faith and to inquire into the relationship between faith and the life-world. Several of the features of the life-world as Husserl described it find exemplification in the realm of faith. Hence, faith does not occur simply in a psyche as a private experience or in an institution as a set of observable stuctures and behaviors but in a faith-world.

1. *The everydayness of faith*

One feature of the life-world which carries over into faith is everydayness. If an act of consciousness or mode of consciousness is our point of reference, we can characterize everydayness in Husserl's term *the natural attitude,* that stance through which we deal with the problems of everyday life. The "scientific attitude" which entered Western history with the Hellenic desire for *epistēmē* or knowledge would grasp the very nature of the world and its components dissociated from the "naïve" acceptances that rule everyday life. In short everyday life has a mode of consciousness or "attitude" which is proper for it. On the other hand, if our point of reference is the "reality" to which this attitude is directed, we notice that everyday life confronts entities presented to it through immediate perceptions and insights. Scientific procedures transform these into mathematical or logical entities, but must also return to them for confirmation. Husserl's way of relating the two attitudes is very un-Hellenic in that he refuses to assign everydayness to "opinion" or *doxa* and the scientific world to "knowledge." His reason is that the mathematized product of post-Galilean science is not the reality itself but a second-order transformation of it, and that the investigations of science presuppose the immediate insights of everydayness. This distinction tends to be a far-ranging one. Lived-space centered in myself is not the physicist's space. Personal body is differentiated from the body studied by the medical student. My pain is something quite different from pain in the sense of objective measurement.

This distinction appears in the region of faith. Faith occurs initially in everydayness. It has a "natural attitude" which is proper to it, namely, the attitude in which the person of faith pursues the activities of faith. And the activities of faith are everyday activities such as attending meetings, worshiping, planning, organizing, sacrificing, and the like. Insofar as faith generates a "scientific" enterprise which desires "knowledge," a similar set of distinctions emerge. The attitude required by scientific investigation differs from the everyday attitudes that propel faith. The attitude of a person who is worshiping varies considerably from the attitude of the person taking the pulse, temperature, and blood pressure of the person who is worshiping. Furthermore, faith occurring in the everyday world is not merely the "opinion" which theology transforms into "knowledge" but plays the same founding role for theology that life-world plays for all sciences. The everydayness of faith does not in itself produce a faith-world. There are many attitudes and activities in the life-world that do not form a "world." It only reminds us that when faith is present at all, it is present in the mode of consciousness proper to the life-world.

2. Faith as having a "world of its own"

A closer look at faith discloses that faith has a "world of its own." We are speaking of course of faith in the determinate sense of a mode of existence which occurs within one of the historical religions. Faith, therefore, not only has activities proper to itself. It possesses a language of its own, ranging from the imagery that permeates its cultus to the conceptuality that dominates its theologically formulated self-understanding. It has a community of its own, including a determinate intersubjectivity plus an ever-changing institutionalization. It has a field of intended realities which presides over its memory, testimony, praise, and reflection. More important, these features of faith's matrix partake of a certain unity. The unity is not merely a logical relationship between the conceptualities of faith's reflection, as for instance the systematic interrelation between creation and redemption. The unity embraces the various strata of the total matrix; the *kind* of intersubjectivity, the sort of institutionalization, the particular activities occurring in the cultus, and the levels of intended realities.

Another way of describing the unity of faith's matrix draws upon Schutz's ingenious combination of phenomenology of the social world and the sociology of knowledge. Schutz's account of common-sense knowledge in the everyday world extends Husserl's notion of appresentation, according to which human beings conduct their activities in the life-world with a minimum of directly apprehended facades and a preponderance of indirectly appresented backgrounds.[14] Schutz's addition is that the appresented or indirectly present aspects are intended by means of typifications. Because these typifications express the typical behaviors and attitudes we can expect in the situation before us, they serve as guides in the perpetual flow of our decisions. According to these typifications, we have certain expectations with which we approach such anonymous figures as a gasoline station attendant and the traffic policeman as well as our closest friends and relatives.[15] The point is that practical acitvity requires a certain constancy present in both nature and fellow human beings. We shall later attempt a detailed formulation of the function of appresentation in faith's apprehensions. Our point now is that a certain constancy characterizes faith's matrix, and this constancy is expressed in typifications which are shared by each member of the religious community.

3. *Faith and the establishment of the one world*

At this point we are tempted to say that in this unity and constancy we have found that which locates faith in a world of its own. If this were the case, faith-world would be a world in the sense of one among many contiguous worlds that exist side by side. The fact that it has its own language, institution, and distinctive activities misleads us into so portraying it. However, two features of faith prevent it from generating such a discrete world. First, faith tends to a /

14. For an exposition of appresentation, see Chapter 8, B.
15. Alfred Schutz, *The Phenomenology of the Social World,* trans. George Walsh, et al. (Evanston: Northwestern University Press, 1967), chap. 4, D.

certain imperialism. Being what it is, faith tends to permeate the total life-world. Almost anything can permeate and color the total life-world given a fanatical and exclusive preoccupation. And faith too can become the occasion for a world-devouring fanaticism. Yet the root of inclusiveness in faith itself seems to give unity to all its strata, its concern with the most fundamental level of human broken-ness, and its repair or, in the language of faith itself, bondage and freedom. Bondage and freedom are so fundamental that they predispose all the attitudes, stances, decisions, beliefs, fears, and life-styles of human beings. For this reason the life-world itself is not just the neutral world of trivial, practical activities, but as the everyday world, it is a network of human strivings, fears, and manipulations. It is shaped and bent by our corporate past. If faith's community, cultus, and language express this fundamental human problem of bondage and freedom, then faith will not be an isolated stratum of the life-world. It will re-form the life-world after its own image. Faith's inclination though not accomplishment is utopian. Through the centuries faith has constantly labored to overcome attempts in its own community to isolate it. Intrinsic to faith is a resistance to restriction to *gnosis* without *agape,* to individual love without societal concern, to emotions without reason, to redemption without creation.

The second reason why faith resists being a separate stratum of the life-world is difficult to formulate, since it concerns a function of faith that almost defies thematizing. Faith tends to be world-creating not merely in the sense of permeating any existing life-world; it calls forth "world" in the very special sense of *the* world, the one world. We recall that in everyday life I am the center of my world, the world whose meanings and furnishings correlate with my purposes and evaluations. But philosophers from Plato to Heidegger have frequently observed that the world of everyday life does not exhaust human being. Mysteries impinge upon the human being impelling him to seek avenues of protection and stimulating his curiosity. If Schutz is correct, a "fundamental anxiety" nurtures and unifies all the activities of the world of everyday life, the anxiety about death. He means by this that survival is the most basic problem to which everyday activities are directed. More profound analyses such as Heidegger's or Kierkegaard's pose the issue of man's transcendence over the practical world by describing the way in which man's being-toward-death generates the larger questions of self-identity and meaning. And Ricoeur has brilliantly portrayed the interrelation between the question concerning the human being, his nature, finitude, and destiny and the question of the nature of whatever it is which is his total background, the cosmos.[16] This interrelation is compounded and deepened by the brokenness of man and history and the question of salvation. What these insights add up to is a built-in refusal on the part of the human being to regard the totality of the various "worlds" which make up everyday life as chaos. This refusal is a transcendental one, as we shall argue in a later chapter, occurring in the very makeup of the human being. In faith, or at least that faith which is addressed to the conjunction of the problem of meaning and the problem of bondage, this refusal obtains an cbject, *the* world. In faith man's bondage and refusal of chaos are referred to a redeeming power which, if it exists at all, requires the power to permeate all of man's "worlds." The cosmological argument is therefore a formalizing of a cosmologizing tendency rooted in faith itself. Because of the world-establishing propensity of faith, the man of faith is directed toward "world" in a far more inclusive sense than the discrete world of faith's own language, cultus, and perspectives. In this sense faith not only has a world of its own but establishes or discloses the foundation of *the* one world.[17]

At this point we shall try to avoid giving the impression that faith, when it exists at all, always fulfills its world-constituting propensities and thus successfully captures any culture in which it occurs. Faith's permeation of the everyday world, its existence in a world of its own making, and its propensity toward the one world are always part of the *telos* of faith and are always only more or less actualized. In Western civilization where secularity has largely replaced the preceding religious world-view, faith is largely unsuccessful in

16. *Freedom and Nature: The Voluntary and the Involuntary,* trans. Erazim Kohāk (Evanston: Northwestern University Press, 1966), Part II, chap. 3, "The Way of Consent."
17. Mircea Eliade has described the cosmologizing effect of the Sacred and the wresting of cosmos out of chaos as a universal feature of religion. See *The Sacred and the Profane* (New York: Harper Torchbooks, 1961), chap. I.

actualizing its own *telos* toward world, and lives in fact in a schiz-
ophrenic state, being impelled to incorporate the very secularity
which is its greatest threat and competitor (cf. Harvey Cox and
William Hamilton). We should avoid so stressing the fragmentation and pluralism of the faith-world in contemporary culture that
we miss the senses in which faith retains a world of its own and is
world-creating. If we limit our review of faith to the level of institutionalization, then fragmentaton seems to be the dominant fact in
faith's situation. From within the determinate intersubjectvity which
persists in the faith-community, fragmentation is not the only or
final fact. The power to grasp the total life-world through the
mythic imagery of faith's stories and the impetus toward *the* one
world seem to persist through the fragmentation.

Chapter 5

ECCLESIA AND LANGUAGE

Things of which we are focally aware can be explicitly identified; but no knowledge can be made *wholly explicit.* For one thing, the meaning of language, when in use, lies in its tacit component; for another, to use language involves actions of our body of which we have only a subsidiary awareness. Hence, tacit knowing is more fundamental than explicit knowledge: *we can know more than we can tell and we can tell nothing without relying on our awareness of things we may not be able to tell.* [1]

Michael Polanyi

The recovery of the faith-world helps partially to correct the usual individualistic treatments of faith, and reminds us that, when faith does occur, it tends to pervade and alter the life-world. This correction, however, omits the very thing that carries faith in its world-pervading and world-creating propensity, namely, a specific human community. If faith occurs in conjunction with everyday activities like worshiping, teaching, and the like, these activities themselves go on within a specific community. If faith-world has components, the components are concretely actual only within such a community. Hereafter, we shall speak of the community of faith as the inclusive entity which serves as the corporate matrix of faith, bearing in mind the various senses in which faith-world refers us beyond that community.

1. Michael Polanyi, *Personal Knowledge: Toward a Post-Critical Philosophy* (New York: Harper Torchbooks, 1964), p. x.

A. The Community of Faith and Its Structures

When Bonhoeffer made his significant but groping attempt to describe the *communio sanctorum,* he learned that the community of faith resists thematization. To be sure, we can describe discrete aspects of it: an incident in its history, its creed, its polity, its sociological elements. Yet something eludes us. Perhaps this elusive something is simply the concreteness of the community, established as it is through an almost unthematizable conjunction of transcendent power and a redemptive alteration. Perhaps it is simply the distinctiveness of the community of faith, involving, as John Cobb points out, an "axial existence" which is a novel form of human existence in history. Furthermore, the community of faith resists thematic inquiry because its "reality" occurs largely in the subterranean strata of imagery and intersubjectivity. This means that our task of investigating the community of faith in its role as the matrix of faith's apprehensions will not get very far unless we can pentrate the formal language of the community to the images beneath it, and work our way through its institutional layers to the underlying determinate intersubjectivity.

What precisely does the term *community of faith* suggest? First, we are talking about an actual community which has had a long historical existence, and which in some sense seems to have persisted into the present. Second, we are focusing on this community not in the most concrete sense of the empirical content of a given sect in a specific time and place, but in the more general sense of whatever distinguishes this community as its essence and *telos.* Third, in spite of this focus on ideality, we do not have in mind an "ideal" community in a utopian or eschatological sense but one that may only partially actualize its own *telos* and therefore reflect in itself the corruption that is an ever-present motif in its own imagery. Finally, stressing as we do the uniqueness of this community, especially at the level of its determinate intersubjectivity, we shall hereafter call the community of faith *ecclesia.* Admittedly, this is merely a verbal trick. Yet the English word *church* carries so much dogmatic and confessional baggage as well as unfortunate connotations associated with the present state of the church that we find the word unusable to designate the community of faith. That which came into history with a life-world altering message, a distinctive imagery, and a novel sort of intersubjectivity was ecclesia.

Unfortunately, we cannot attempt in this inquiry a full eidetics of ecclesia. Instead, we shall isolate those components of ecclesia which bear on the problem of faith and reality. Three things are always present, it seems, in the situation of faith's apprehendings. The first is sometimes expressed in the rather misleading expression *i* *religious language.* Religious language is a catch-all term under which falls everything from formal theological language to ceremonial expressions in the religious cultus. We shall reduce this range and focus on the imagery that is related to faith as faith's intended or meant content. Here we simply remind ourselves that Christian faith involves a depiction of human existence by way of images of human evil, reconciliation, the world, hope, and transcendence. This intended imagery is a constitutive feature of the community of faith or ecclesia. Second, this imagery is not merely a collection of representations in *2* a world-view, but expresses an experiential dimension which is finally unified in the motif of redemption. In other words, one component of the community of faith is an individually experienced alteration of existence toward redemption. Third, the matrix of this experience *3* is a determinate intersubjectivity, a specific structure of co-intentions which makes the faith-community distinctive as a community.

We shall offer the interplay of these three components as the clue to the cognitive or reality-apprehending function of faith. Ecclesia has of course other components: historical, cultic, and the like. However, the reason the reality-claims of the community of faith seem so arbitrary and problematic is that they are usually set forth at overt institutional or psychological levels, that is, in the mode of authority or the mode of conscious individual experiences. Concentration on these modes obscures the pre-reflective apprehensions on which everything else is founded. The present chapter will investigate the imagery of the faith-community in its status as intended or meant, and Chapters 6 and 7 will take up the redemptive reference of this imagery and the determinate intersubjectivity.

B. THE COMMUNITY OF FAITH AS "HAVING A LANGUAGE OF ITS OWN"

Like other communities in a determinate social world, the community of faith does not conduct its business a-linguistically. In fact, its very existence is linguistic since that which establishes it as a distinctive and enduring community are reciprocal relations, co-intentions, and experiences, all of which are present in consciousness through the process of symbolization. To exist as Israel or as ecclesia means to have a certain collective memory, tradition, ritual-istic repetition, and communal *telos,* all of which are borne linguis-tically. Not only is a community of faith linguistic in a general way, it necessarily has a "language of its own." Hence, there is an intrinsic relation between a determinate community of faith and a determinate language. We have already hinted at the reasons.

For one thing, a community necessarily involves ways in which human beings are reciprocally related by such everyday life activities as buying and selling, anonymous services, familial dealings, voting, and worshiping. And these activities involving reciprocal relation-ships are conducted, as Wittgenstein says, by means of the appro-priate language games. Beneath everyday world activities and rec-iprocities are various layers of co-intentions, which range from the most universal one, according to which the other is constituted as a self, to more determinate co-intentions, such as are present in a marriage, business, or church. These co-intentions, existing in the background of everyday world reciprocal activities, are not a-linguis-tic but are also linguistically carried, a point not always acknowl-edged by the restriction of language to language-*games.* We note that language functions differently in these different strata. In the everyday world "speaking" is the paramount mode of language, and since the occasion is usually a practical activity, something to be accomplished, the linguistic units tend to be expressions; verb-noun complexes of words which give commands, answer questions, make suggestions, tell jokes, speculate about the future, recall an incident, etc. But at the level of co-intentions (intersubjective structures), the paramount mode is "intention," an enduring concomitant of the stances of consciousness, and the linguistic unit is the image. For instance, a married couple will come to some agreement in the pur-chase of a house through a continued linguistic interchange involving speaking and expressions, but at the same time the matrix of this everyday activity will be the co-intentionality of their marital relation-ship and the images that direct it. Hence, their explicit dealing with each other in the matter of the house will be guided by ways in which each one acknowledges the other's selfhood and freedom, and this in turn will be present pre-reflectively in the images of the social (and religious) world which they have interiorized.

A second reason why the community of faith has its own language involves the role of language in the community's historical continuity. Communities appear to have a kind of instinct for survival which propels them to a constant self-perpetuation. Hence, in addition to whatever *telos* there is which expresses the distinctive purpose of the community (recreation of a bachelor club, women's rights, a governing order), a secondary structure arises to maintain the community's existence. The rites, symbols, and institutionality tend to serve both purposes at the same time, symbolizing the *telos* and assuring its self-perpetuation. The imagery of a community is an expression partly of the *telos* of that community (for instance, the imagery of black religion in America) and partly of the past history of that community, the memory and recitation of which helps to maintain the community. The language of a community of faith is partly anamnestic. It is a deposit of a "collective memory" which includes its own origins and founding figures, as well as the crises and decisive epochs of its past. Keeping this memory alive is crucial in the community's struggle to perpetuate itself into the future. We are speaking primarily in sociological genre. However, the principle of positivity reminds us that in a specific historical faith-community, memory and its linguistic carriers will express the specific *telos* of that community. For example, the *telos* of redemption in Israel establishes a distinctive attitude in Israel about her own self-perpetuation. The relation between Israel's *telos* and justice in the land establishes a priority over self-perpetuation and revises the function of memory. Israel remembers the patriarchs, the exodus, and the Torah for the purpose of keeping the covenant, not simply for self-perpetuation. When the latter replaces the former, Israel's memory begins to work against her own *telos*. Nevertheless, the general feature is present, the function of memory in the self-perpetuation of the community, making indispensable the role of the imagic carriers of memory.

The third reason why a particular language is intrinsic to a com-

110

munity of faith concerns the role of imagery in the actual modification of human existence. We are presupposing here that redemption
is a dimension of the community of faith, and this sets language
against the background of the structural alienation which characterizes human historical existence. If we grant for the moment that
the redemptive alteration of human existence occurs in the community of faith and that this alteration is an alteration of the alienated
structure of human consciousness, does language play any role in
this alteration? It seems evident that language is an utterly indispensable component of this alteration. Consciousness is never a-
linguistic and this includes alienated consciousness whose explicit
acts and motives rise out of an already alienated familial and societal
matrix. Furthermore, this structural alienation itself is borne linguis-
tically since it involves an imagery of self and other relations, perspectives on the world, life-styles, etc. The human being's refusal
of his own being, his idolatry and self-securing (as in racism, na-
tionalism, and religious idolatry), generate their own imagery. The
explicit worship of a golden calf or an inexplicit fanatical commitment to a nation or state involves images. Insofar as the redemptive
alteration of consciousness effects this bent and alienated consciousness, it involves an alteration and replacement of images. By no
means is this a full or even essential description of redemption. We
contend only that interiorization of images and their subsequent
effect on the imagic world of alienation is involved in redemption.
"Faith comes from what is heard, and what is heard comes by the
preaching of Christ" (Rom. 10:17).

Since the continuity and concreteness of alienated consciousness
occur by means of images, alienation has a proclivity to saturate
the language of the life-world insofar as images are present beneath
the more explicit games played in everyday world dealings. For this
reason, the attempt to limit "religious language" simply to the peculiar vocabulary, images, and language-acts of the community of faith
is unfortunate. In addition to "having a language of its own,"
ecclesia effects the very meaning of having a language at all. For
insofar as structures of alienation are in control, language is no
mere neutral tool of carrying out the practical tasks of the everyday
world. Behind such resides an imagery in the light of which human

111

beings in their alienation co-intend each other, an imagery which expresses relations with reality in the mode of flight and escape or self-securing adulation. Hence, language itself undergoes corruption and becomes a weapon, an instrument of manipulation, the deposit of ideology, the carrier of flight from reality in the form of cynicism about truth. Insofar as ecclesia stands for the community in which these powers are confronted and altered by another power, "religious language" embraces the *way in which* ecclesial man has a language at all, as well as the way in which the imagery of this community infiltrates and alters the images behind the everyday world.

C. Hermeneutics as Intentional Analysis

So far we have tried to disclose the intrinsic relation between the community of faith and a specific language, arguing that ecclesia "has a language of its own" which then spills over into the various languages which operate in its determinate social world. We would now explore this intrinsic relation in a more detailed way.

A religious community in its linguistic aspect is a very confusing item. It presents a linguistic kaleidoscope of constantly changing types of linguistic entities: doctrines, myths, historical narratives, personal stories and autobiographies, images, theological arguments and concepts, and ceremonial expressions. The confusion is extended when the community of faith in a specific historical situation identifies one stratum among these entities as absolutely definitive, for instance, myth. Since fallibility characterizes any given community of faith, such a self-interpretation may be erroneous, obscuring its own essence and *telos*. The purpose of this and the following section is to find a way to identify the more enduring and constitutive dimensions of this confusing linguisticality of the community of faith.

1. *Intended content*

We are familiar with the distinction between an act of consciousness such as perceiving and the object of that act, the perceived. In Husserl's analysis a middle stratum between the two is introduced, namely, the meant-object or *noema*. Husserl's notion of intentionality is that there is a necessary correlative relationship between the

112

act of consciousness and its meant-object. The act of remembering has as its intended object or *noema* a remembered entity. We must distinguish, therefore, between the object itself and the meaning through which the object is grasped in its unity. It is because of this distinction that we can recall an object when it is no longer present to us, or when it has passed out of existence. More important, the meant object is the basis of our capacity to identify an object which we perceive in different appearances as the same object.[2] We are not to conclude from this that the *noema* is the *product* of the act of consciousness. Husserl does argue for transcendental conditions of this capacity to "intend" an enduring entity. But the content of that unity or *noema* is not derived from or produced by the act of consciousness itself. For this reason, Husserl says that the *noema* occupies a different "region of being" from that of a consciousness act. Further, once the object is present to consciousness, its noematic aspect exercises thereafter a certain autonomy or control. Once a certain building is present to me, I cannot in the future recall *that* building and be indifferent to its *noema*. I may of course consciously forget the building, commit errors of memory, or lose its details in vagueness. But in the act of *re*-presenting the building to myself, I cannot by sheer will do that and at the same time mean that building as a book or musical sound. The noematic nucleus and contour exercises a certain control over my subjective inclinations in any attempt of mine to refer to *that* building. We shall call the attempt to review the noematic or meant aspect of an object "noematics of" or noematic analysis. Husserl means simply the propounding of that intended nucleus of meaning through which the object endures for us and thus enables re-presentation.[3]

Noematic analysis would appear to be a potentially fruitful tool in the hands of theologians. If faith involves human consciousness or is in some way an "act of consciousness," it will have *noemata* which can be then propounded. This in fact has been the pre-

---

2. See Aron Gurwitsch's excellent essay on Husserl's notion of intentionality, "On the Intentionality of Consciousness," in *Studies in Phenomenology and Psychology* (Evanston: Northwestern University Press, 1966).
3. Husserl's concept of noesis-noema is found primarily in *Ideas*, III, chap. 3 and in IV, chap. 1. See also the sections on cogito-cogitatum in the *Meditations*, secs. 14–22.

dominant way in which Husserlian phenomenology has been taken over in history of religions, philosophy of religion, and in the phenomenologies of faith in Roman Catholic circles. Noematic analysis has, however, a certain limitation which may create more puzzles than it solves. Except for history of religions, the orientation of these enterprises has been primarily individualistic. This should be no surprise since Husserl's terminology of noesis-noema arises out of his reflection on the individual act of perception. The problem is that faith's individual acts arise out of a corporate participation which precedes them and which itself has a noetic-noematic structure. In other words, these phenomenologies of faith attempt to display the noetic-noematic aspect of faith apart from the role of collective representations and their origin in the faith community. In order to correct this, we shall attempt to uncover the corporate dimension of faith's noetic-noematic structure.

2. *Corporate intentionality*

If the acts of consciousness of individuals involved simply relations between each individual and a set of objects presented in experience, with language simply as a means of naming or dealing with those objects, corporate intentionality would be a superfluous if not meaningless notion. However, if Husserl, Merleau-Ponty, and others are correct, human consciousness is "social," i.e., structured by co-intentions between selves even before it differentiates itself from the objective world.[4] This "before" applies both to psychological history and ontological order. Intersubjectivity, the other-directed structure of consciousness, in which human beings respond to each other in the modes of person, personal body, etc., comes to linguistic expression, and that linguistic expression varies in each determinate social world. For example, the images through which human beings co-intend each other vary greatly between the social world of Arabian nomads and that of a professional football team. The corporate

4. For the priority of intersubjectivity in the psychological development of the child, see Merleau-Ponty's "The Child's Relation with Others," *The Primacy of Perception* in *Studies in Phenomenology and Existential Philosophy,* ed. James M. Edie, trans. Cobb, Williams, et al. (Evanston: Northwestern University Press, 1964).

dimension of human experience ranges from explicit activities such as firemen working together to put out a fire to the pre-reflective intentions which guide more explicit operations such as the images about reality, success, money, and sexuality which prevail in a large corporation.

We are not at this point insisting on some sort of social psyche or even collective unconscious. We do want to say that each determinate social world has a dimension of reciprocal and intersubjective experience which unifies it in ways resembling the unity of an individual consciousness. There is at least an analogy between the stream of experience and consciousness acts of an individual psyche and the cooperative and interdependent activities and co-intentions which characterize a particular social world. Furthermore, and this is the crucial step, the corporate stratum like the individual one is intentional in structure. This means that it too is linguistically carried, that it has meant objects in necessary correlation with its social acts and its depth intersubjectivity. If, for instance, one tribe's cooperative activity is primarily hunting while another's is warlike foraging on surrounding territories, certain intended content will endure in each tribe's memory and accordingly will shape the consciousness of its members. And this content will persist beyond the specific times of hunting or making war. Beneath this level of conscious activities is the characteristic intersubjectivity of the tribe by which the human beings co-intend each other in modes of slavery or freedom, adulthood and children, in sexual relationships, etc. And this largely hidden co-intentionality has noematic content which is socially, not individually, correlated. For instance, an oppressed minority may be governed by co-intentions taken from the majority's stereotyping of the minority, thus the intended corporate noemata through which it interprets itself includes images of slavery, inferiority, and incompetence. On the other hand, the people in an oppressed minority may intend each other as human, free, beautiful, and essentially powerful; images which reflect a very different set of corporate noemata.

Perhaps we are being excessively metaphorical. The serious point here is that there do exist constellations of images which correlate not simply with the individuals of a society but with more unifying cooperative undertakings, societal consensus, self-interpretation, and even the *telos* of that society as a whole. In a religious community the images of worship are the noemata of a corporate activity, not simply the sum of many individual acts, each one solipsistically isolated. This is why there can be a noematics of a social entity, an investigation of the language-imagery necessarily intended by the society's corporate activities and intersubjective structure. In fact, such a noematics is our version of the hermeneutical enterprise. The hermeneutic aspect of a theological program is the investigation of ecclesia's noematic content. Hermeneutics does not exhaust theo-logical reflection because as noematic analysis it does not raise the critical and normative question as to whether genuine apprehensions occur in conjunction with the community's constitutive imagery. Yet it is an indispensable moment in theology because whatever reality-apprehensions occur in ecclesia occur in the interplay of its dis-tinctive intersubjectivity, the experienced redemptive alteration, and the noemata or imagery which are necessary concomitants. Because hermeneutics must reach for the noematic dimension of the com-munity, its task is the complex one of sorting out the community's many types and layers of language. This involves the attempt to penetrate the more explicit strata of claims, expressions, and state-ments to the more constitutive strata of meant-content.

The force of our argument will be diluted if corporate intention-ality is confused with the psychological intentions which occur in individual acts of consciousness. In a particular act of worshiping or repeating a creed, the individual may simultaneously "intend" or mean a multiplicity of matters, a mixture of meant-imagery, myths, and contemporary ideology. All the accumulated layers of language may be intended in this complex psychological act. But the in-tended object of the community correlates with whatever charac-terizes the community as such, its very communality, its enduring corporate experience. In the following section we shall pursue this distinction between the language which bears the corporate intention of ecclesia (story and image) and the language whose function it is to render the corporate intention contemporary and understandable (myth and doctrine).

D. Linguistic Strata of the Community of Faith

We have contended that language is indispensable to reality apprehensions. This is not particularly significant if "language" means the total quantity of linguistic expression in the community which includes reality-denying clichés, Bible quotations, secularized ideologies, naïve and primitive psychologies and mythologies, and antiquated doctrines. We have tried rather to pinpoint a linguistic stratum which carries the community's meant-content without raising the question as to the bearing of that content on truth or reality. We shall attempt to isolate this stratum of ecclesia with the hope of then investigating its role in reality-apprehensions.

1. Story and image: language correlative to corporate intention

In the beginning is the story, or to put it more precisely, a constellation of images unified in a story. At least this seems to be the case with both the Judaic form of historical existence which we are calling Israel and the ecclesial form. Story, a narrative of certain things that happen within a limited scope of time, is the linguistic unit most proper to ecclesia. Ecclesia's witness is to a redemptive alteration of human existence made possible by a redeemer and certain events in space and time. By story, therefore, we do not mean a quasi-existential vehicle of expressing segments of one's own autobiography. With the exception of certain occasions in the Pauline corpus, there seems to be a great disinterest in stories in that sense in the literature of primitive Christianity. We find many stories in the Gospels and in Acts, but none of these is *the* story which is the linguistic correlate of ecclesia. *The* story has two major components, the events and personages with which the events are concerned and a constellation of images. The meant or intended content of ecclesia is neither merely a set of events nor a cluster of images but a synthesis of the two in the form of a narrative. In Israel the story which is the receptacle of Israel's imagery about man, evil, nation, and salvation is simply the story of Yahweh and his people. Even if we find no single ritualistic repetition of this story, it is through this story that Israel understands herself. When ecclesia appears, the story of Jesus both takes over and shatters the story of Yahweh and his people. Most of the imagery is retained with some

117

modification in the altered story according to which Yahweh's redemptive presence to his people takes definitive form in Jesus Christ. What is expanded to the point of shattering is the meaning of "his people." The one thing we stress here is that the imagery of the community of faith does not occur simply as discrete units but in conjunction with a sequence of historical events.

Yet events and personages are not the only meant entities of ecclesia's corporate intentionality. The everyday language of the cultus, even when it addresses itself to events or past historical figures, abounds in images. Image, as we are using the term, resists definition, because the image is the mode in which content is present prior to its translation into definitions. We can at this point do little more than point to certain characteristics and functions of imagery in the community of faith. We shall clarify that what is under consideration are the *constitutive* images, meant correlates of a community's corporate intentionality and not the ever-changing and rich imagery that resides in the rhetoric of the leaders of that community in a given time.

The first characteristic is that constitutive images are not reflec- /
tively produced. If a faith-community does generate a "theological" or critical endeavor, the second-order activity which thereby occurs turns back to and draws on images but is not the origin of such. Hence, the linguistic mode of an image is not a definition or concept, entities which emerge as results of attempts at precise understanding. A "suffering Messiah" is an image but "two natures in one person" is not. Even as the origin of images is not in theological or second-order reflective activities, neither is reflective activity the primary mode in which they are present in the community. These images guide the everyday activities of the religious community, its worship and liturgy, its institutional and canonical ordering, its self-surpassing toward the world through witness and preaching.

Second, constitutive images express situations rather than describe 2
entities. Their content is more like a fact (a conjunction of noun and verb) than a substantive. The images which constitute ecclesia are not such things as color, tree, or altar but entities in a certain relation, situation, or with certain features. The imagery which resides in the liturgy of the cultus or which is appealed to in the

repetition of the story is suffering Messiah who is the ransom for sins, the human being in an inescapable bondage to evil, or Yahweh as loving father.

3 Third, although images are the ways in which *content* is intended, that content is not simply the image itself. This important but elusive issue is the occasion of much misunderstanding concerning religious symbolism. Images (symbols) are frequently interpreted as substitute contents which therefore displace events, facts, historical persons, or ontological structures. In this approach the image displaces all such things and becomes itself the object of belief. Yet it seems clear that in the community of faith, one does not believe *in* images but through them. They represent the mode of presentation of content rather than the object. For this reason images can and do retain different sorts of content: historical, ontological, psychological, and social. The universal network of evil spread over all history that is present, for instance, in Paul's use of the Adam story and also in his imagery of "cosmic powers" is one kind of content. Another is Jesus as the ransom for our sins, embracing as it does a specific historical occurrence as well as an ontic structure. Hermeneutics need not involve displacement of intended realities by intended images unless it assumes from the start their identity or their disproportionality.

4 Finally, the images of the community of faith are to some degree interrelated. This is not because of second-order reflective work which arbitrarily "systematizes" them. Rather, their receptacle is the paradigm story of that community, and they tend to reflect whatever unity the story has. Yet the interdependence of the imagery of a community of faith has a deeper foundation than simply the unity of the events and narrative aspects of its story. We cannot explicate this deeper level apart from the other components of ecclesia such as the redemptive alteration of existence and the intersubjectivity characteristic of that community. Suffice it to say that these components involve a distinctive kind of historical existence and historical community, an insight into the human problem of evil and redemption which unites and interrelates the accompanying imagery. Hence, the imagery of the world dependent on Yahweh's creative act is bound up with the imagery of evil and redemption. It is because of

119

the interdependent nature of this constitutive imagery that ecclesia's "theological" or reflective attempt to understand is inevitably systematic. Contemporary dismissals of systematic theology are unfortunate in that they too narrowly identify "systematic" with system-building and thereby obscure the unity of imagery present in the faith-world which such reflection cannot avoid. One can sympathize with such dismissals insofar as they are prompted by criticisms of Catholic and Protestant attempts to systematize the Scripture or tradition, efforts which are now untenable due to the rupture of the models of authority with which they were operating. But the false intellectualism of an unhistorical approach to Scripture should not obscure the constellation of imagery and the story in which it occurs.

2. Myth and doctrine: the language of contemporaneous understanding

What we have done so far is to place in brackets the confusing amalgamation of words, phrases, and the like which appears as the language of the community of faith in order to isolate a stratum of language which correlates with the enduring and essential corporate intentions of that community. Hence, we focused on the community's story and imagery, not its creeds, doctrines, or apologetic formulations. When we remove the brackets, we find that the story and its images occur in conjunction with more complex linguistic entities. In fact one's exposure to the language of the community of faith might be so dominated by the apologetic and theological accretions, customs and taboos, and cultic expressions that its story and images remain largely hidden.

What is the function of these more visible and everyday world linguistic strata? Why does a community of faith generate a language other than its story and its images? The most obvious explanation is simply that the various activities of the community of faith require linguistic expression. The community of faith thus retains ceremonial language, the language of institutional organization, the language of moral imperative and taboo, and the like.

A more significant clue to the question of the development of language beyond story and image is the perennial problem every community of faith has of "contemporaneity." The problem of contemporaneity occurs because of the inevitable lag between insights, experiences, customs, and institutions which arise and function at one time and the perpetual changes of world-views, cultures, and languages. If the lag were absolute, so that the tradition persisted into the present without any accompanying translation into contemporary modes, its presence would be a mere puzzle, an atavistic residue which had lost all reference to reality. To the degree that a community of faith overcomes this lag, the tradition finds retranslation into the world-view, language, and day-to-day activities of the present. Such a translation is the deeper function of linguistic accretions to the story and its images. Actually this translation begins whenever there are reality-apprehensions and experiential modifications of existence. Because the first generation of a community of faith must make its own experience understandable to itself, this translation process begins immediately and does not wait for a lag between generations. Furthermore, ecclesial existence has a special problem in relation to this lag because its very essence involves a rejection of every provincial and restricted condition of God's presence (cf. Chapter 7). To the degree that translation constitutes ecclesia's very existence, it necessarily contains an impetus to make its story and imagery contemporary through myth and doctrine. The anti-provincial nature of ecclesia makes it intrinsically theological.

Several things are involved in the attempt to make understandable a received tradition whose basal form is story and image. One, the tradition is integrated into whatever inclusive framework or world-picture is dominant. Hence, a cosmologizing of the story and its images occur. Two, the tradition is integrated into institutional structures by which it is preserved and retransmitted to other generations, or, given an evangelical impetus, to other territories. The result of the cosmologizing translation is the *myth*. We recognize that no use of this term could adequately synthesize the disparate definitions and proposals now before us. Our proposal is that myth itself is not the most original layer of religious imagery but the product of an attempt to translate such into the inclusive and objec-

121

tive world-view of a given age. Accordingly, when the image, "Jesus died for our sins," is translated by means of feudal concepts of relationships, we have a cosmologization whose linguistic expression is a myth. When this amalgam of image and myth is subjected to the requirements of truth and knowledge, it reappears in the form of conceptuality which takes on a certain authority in the community of faith. When this happens, we have a conceptualized deposit of image-myth which functions as a measure for institutional loyalty, and this is *doctrine*. When the tradition in the sense of the story and image is translated into the sanctions, principles, customs, and taboos for life and worship in the everyday world, we have *piety*.

These translations are perpetually going on, usually in slow and subtle ways (such as the gradual changes in Protestant piety between 1900 and 1970), sometimes in sudden and dramatic ways (as in the Protestant Reformation or Vatican II). The requirements of contemporaneity generate two processes which work against each other. Story and image are always in search of a myth, a way of being cosmologized into the objective consensus of an age and its world-picture. As this consensus breaks down, the pressure from story and image is toward demythologization. Doctrinalization is ambiguous in that it can both defend or criticize anachronistic myth. If it is ordered toward story and image, the noemata or intentional correlates of ecclesia, it will be more a myth-critique than a myth vindication. This is why contemporary, sophisticated repudiations of "theology" will either contain a hidden theological agenda or else will ironically legitimate religious conservatism and anachronism. This twofold process appears to occur wherever the community of faith exists in the midst of cultural and linguistic changes. For example, the adaptation of the Torah to ever new situations was and remains a perennial problem for the Jewish community. In this case the process of mythologization, demythologization, and doctrinalization cannot be explained simply by the invasion of hellenism, the Greek epistemic orientation. The antithesis of Athens and Jerusalem in terms of doctrinal translation has a certain historical validity, but overstressing it obscures the perennial element of world-view translation and the distinction always found in communities between noematic and adaptive linguistic strata and functions.

The rather sharp distinction between story and its cosmologization in myth for the purpose of contemporaneous understanding threatens to break down when we consider the possibility that a community's story may be a story of the cosmos, and cosmologization may therefore be essential to it. We have in fact already argued that faith itself is inherently world-producing. Its reference is inclusive and total. If this is the case, how can the community of faith's story be distinguished from myth?

The problem lies in the ambiguities resident in the term *world*. Every society has a prevailing world-picture, and its world-picture has a primarily practical function. It is according to this picture that the society carries out its characteristic activities of food-gathering, play, making war, and raising the young. Hence, the world-picture includes ways of ordering these activities into regions such as the region of human beings and the region of gods and spirits, or the two cultures of science and humanities. Whether the society is technological or pre-technological, its world-picture includes a prevailing biology, psychology, and sociology. A world-picture was at work therefore in the biological interpretations of the virgin birth in Tertullian and of original sin in Augustine. While faith tends to permeate and modify world-pictures, the "world" which it establishes is not a world-picture with its attendant regions and categories for interpreting everyday activities. Faith is world-producing in the sense of faith's concern for the ultimate origin and goal, the meaning and destiny of man. "World" in this sense is the ultimate framework of this meaning and destiny, and as such is necessarily founded on the sacred. Given this distinction, the story of the faith-community is necessarily cosmological in the sense of the ultimate framework of human destiny and only relatively cosmological in the sense of a given world-picture. This story may be told in and through the prevailing world-picture of an age, but still represents "cosmologization" for the purpose of contemporaneous understanding. Both world and world-picture are present in the creation narratives of Genesis. The prevailing Babylonian cosmology is appropriated in order to make understandable that the "world" is the setting of the story of Yahweh and his people.

This is not to say that a community of faith is consciously

relativistic about its myths, doctrines, and piety and in earnest only about its story and images. On the contrary, it is the perpetual temptation of a community of faith to displace its more essential but also more elusive story and constitutive images with the more "understandable" myths, doctrines, and pieties which dominate its everyday language and activities. On the other hand, it is evident that myths, doctrines, and pieties have, because of their function of making story and image contemporary, a relativity which the story and its images lack. Or to put this differently, the story and its images, because of their status as noemata, are in closer (correlative) relation with the community-creating experiences and apprehensions than the vehicles which work to render such understandable.

Our stress on the role of myth in making story and image contemporary and the consequent relativity of myth may well obscure the sense in which cosmologizing and myth are not merely relative and dispensable. Such a formulation borders on intellectualism because behind the language of "story in search of myth" is the model of communication. "Translation" becomes a conscious effort on the part of a community to adapt its message, to find a point of connection. Such models have a certain validity in specific situations of communication, but they obscure the relation between myth and man's historicity. We mean by this that man's being and situation are not simply externally related to his world-views, myths, or pieties. In that case man's bondage and redemption would in every age *be* the same but would simply be dressed up in different language (myths). The "reality" would be identical; the expression varied. We would argue, on the contrary, that man's being *is* in some sense his world views, myths, and pieties. How can one formulate, for instance, what it means for Western man to be in bondage apart from the dualistic and alienating technocratic myths? This implies that redemption involves both an incorporation of the story and image into the myth and a breaking of the myth. We would still maintain the priority of story and image over myth, doctrine, and piety as the locus of founding apprehensions. But this should not obscure the essential relation between a specific mythology and cosmology and the alienated consciousness to which the story is addressed.

3. The problem of rhetoric

In distinguishing between the subterranean language of story and image and the cosmologized language which dominates the everyday world of the cultus, we may give the impression that the everyday world language of the faith-community is a mere confusing amalgam of expressions. The question this raises is whether or not ecclesia generates a form of linguistic expression which holds sway over the multiplicity of language acts. In other words, does ecclesia put forth a distinctive rhetoric or rhetorical form? That a community of faith would give rise to a rhetoric which suits it should not be unexpected. For example, a religious faith whose primary activity was transcendental meditation might well generate a rhetorical form able to function as the occasion of meditation, for instance, the aphorism. Since we have not yet propounded the characteristic features of ecclesia, our question is somewhat premature. If ecclesia does have a rhetoric of its own, it would express, it seems, not all of its activities (inquiring, meditating, marriage and burial rites, organizing, etc.) but the activities expressive of its essence and *telos*. Provisionally, we would suggest the following.

Ecclesia not only has a story which is the correlate of both its corporate experience and individual experiences of the modification of existence, but it is a form of historical existence in which the two are connected. The perpetuation of that story is somehow the occasion of the modification of existence toward redemption. While both Catholic and Protestant forms of ecclesia share this conviction, they differ in that classical Catholicism perpetuates the story in sacramental mode while classical Protestantism perpetuates it in preaching the Word. Both Catholicism and Protestantism have undergone corruption at this point, although the corruption was present in seed form from the very beginning. In Catholicism the perpetuation of the story is displaced by the sacrament which comes to have a certain autonomy over the story. In Protestantism the story is diffused into Scripture so that what is preached are the authoritative writings themselves which come to have autonomy over the story. In both cases something besides the story becomes the occasion of redemption.

If the perpetuation of the story is essential to ecclesia as an occasion of the redemptive shaping of consciousness, we have an activity in ecclesia which is paramount over other activities. And this activity is more central to the very survival of ecclesia than the many activities with which the actual community might occupy itself. Furthermore, if the story has to do with certain happenings in history coupled with a constellation of images, a rhetorical form is created which is proper to it, namely, the message. The reason a message is the paramount rhetorical form of ecclesia is that "Jesus died for our sins." A multiple vocabulary expresses this rhetorical form in the literature of early Christianity: good news, the kerygma, the message which was received, testimony and testifying, proclaiming, and the like. And this is what early interpreters appeal to as normative and authoritative (the received message), and the content of the message provides the framework for their polemical and pastoral admonitions. In this message, which has the character of both an announcement and a testimony, we have a rhetorical vehicle of ecclesia's story and imagery which resists attempts to translate the language of ecclesia into totally different forms. Hence, other linguistic activities which occur in ecclesia in order to serve its purpose (second-order inquiry, meditation, interpersonal consolation) have as their reference point the story present in this paramount rhetorical vehicle. Hence, any attempt to replace totally the paramount form with aphorisms, speculative arguments, autobiographical stories, or poetry will probably be unsuccessful. Such forms may serve but not displace the message.

Chapter 6

ECCLESIA AND REDEMPTIVE EXISTENCE

Human life as a specific entity, which has stepped forth from nature, begins with the experience of chaos as a condition perceived in the soul.[1]

Martin Buber

Phenomenological theology's aim is to locate the immediate and founding apprehensions which accompany faith. Generally expressed, our thesis is that faith's apprehensions occur pre-reflectively and by means of an enduring participation in a form of corporate, historical existence which we are calling ecclesia. Specifically, we submit that the major clue guiding our search is provided by a nexus of interaction and interdependence between certain components of ecclesia. In Chapter 5, we looked at one of those components, language, and tried to locate that stratum of language which was a correlate of ecclesia's corporate intentionality, namely, story and image. But what is ecclesia? Although we shall take up the question explicitly in the following chapter, we need now a provisional indication. Theologically expressed, ecclesia is that form of corporate historical existence whose origin and continuation is made possible by Jesus Christ. Since Jesus Christ is the redeemer, ecclesia is both his instrument of redemption and the extension of his redemptive presence. In early Christian literature Jesus' titles and names involve a vocabulary of redemption (redeemer, Lord, saviour,

1. Martin Buber, *Good and Evil* (New York: Charles Scribner's Sons, 1953), p. 125.

Messiah, Son of Man); the metaphors describing his ministry and work are metaphors of redemption; and the portraits of ecclesia and human life in ecclesia are portraits of redemptive existence (love, freedom, justification, spirit, and life). Participation in ecclesia means, therefore, a modification of human existence toward redemption. This is the most general way of expressing it, and the term *modification* is not used here to exclude more specific descriptions such as justification. We use the expression *toward redemption* to indicate the incompleteness and therefore the eschatological dimension of redemption in ecclesia. In the next chapter we shall explore ecclesia's corporate structure. However, that structure (its co-intentionalities) is based on the redemptive modification of existence, to which we now turn.

If founding apprehensions of reality occur through participation in ecclesia, is not individuality replaced by collectivity? Does this not simply eliminate *existence* in the Kierkegaardian sense from the situation of faith? Again, we recall that ecclesia is the corporate matrix in which an alteration of *existence* occurs. If this component is passed over, the other components of language and intersubjectivity make little sense. We shall attempt two things in our consideration of the existence component of religious knowledge. First, we shall try to understand how *existence* is part of the situation of faith. Second, we shall attempt a noematics of redemption, an exploration of the nature of the modification of existence as it occurs in ecclesia.

A. The Transcendental Origins of "Existence": The Religious A Priori

More than any of the categories with which we are working, existence resists thematization. Because it suggests the life of consciousness in its most concrete and historical sense, existence embraces all those uniquely personal contents and structures of an individual. When a human being senses his own "existence," he senses his own utter uniqueness, but not in the rationalistic sense of apprehending an essence which is differentiated from other essences in a rational act. Existence, it seems, can be apprehended in several dimensions. When we grasp concretely our own flow of consciousness, we are closer to existence than to essence. When we experience our own for-itself dimension, according to which our being is never simply a given content but is always a possibility to be actualized through acts of freedom and creativity, we are closer yet to existence. And when we experience ourselves in the mode of certain built-in refusals (of death, of external manipulation) which reveal themselves in the form of persistent emotions, we may be as close to existence as we can get. Existence of course is not these apprehensions themselves, the condition of which is always a certain distance from the existence which we are. The mode of existence is existence itself, and that mode is transformed in these "distancing" acts of apprehension.

Why does redemption or redemptive modification affect existence? Even a brief answer to this question requires an excursion into philosophical anthropology and fundamental theology. Here we can only hint at what deserves extensive elaboration. We begin by distinguishing between transcendental and historical existence. Transcendental existence means the transcendental conditions and grounds of existence. Transcendental existence is portrayed in the form of universality, a universal, constitutive structure of man as such. In this sense it resembles an essence, except that this "essence" has the peculiar function of being the condition of man's essence-transcending novelty, incompleteness, decision-making, and creativity. It is transcendental because it is a constitutive feature in man which, like other transcendental structures, serves to make possible the acts, feelings, and activities through which man is related to the world. The depiction of existence in the transcendental sense is very much in the line of the anthropologies in Greek philosophy, and, strange as it may seem, the "existence" in Heidegger's thought is transcendental existence.

In man's concrete historical situation, existence is not merely transcendental existence. The universal features of being-for-itself, of being-toward-death, of despair are ontological structures, not an individual of flesh and bone. Historical existence is what happens when these universal and transcendental structures combine with a historical situation, which includes the actual phase of human development, a determinate social world, and the biographical situation. If we grant for the moment that man's being is being-toward-death, this rises into existence in a different way in Israel of the eighth century B.C. than in the urban setting of modern technological culture. The distinction between transcendental and historical existence may help uncover the ambiguity which usually attends depictions of existence as alienation or bondage. There is a certain validity in arguing that bondage accrues to man's transcendental structure, that man's death-ridden being and its residual despair are a kind of bondage. On the other hand, man does not experience alienation simply in the form of this universal structure but in and through the positivity of a historical and biographical situation. Hence, the imagery of alienation does not express merely the universal ontological structure but a determinate historical situation wedded to it.

1. *The transcendental refusal of chaos*

The distinction between transcendental and historical existence is important for our purposes because the redemptive modification of existence is distributed over both transcendental and historical dimensions. When we say that the transcendental makeup of the human being has a part to play in man's redemption, we join ourselves to the Augustinian tradition of a religious a priori. Far from being a concern for a "natural knowledge of God" in competition with revelation, the impetus behind this tradition is theological. More than theological, ecclesia's intended imagery itself requires it. We mean by this that ecclesia's redemptive imagery presupposes its creation imagery and vice versa; hence, all heteronomous versions of the relation of redemption to the essential structure of the human being shatter ecclesia's imagery. The religious a priori required by this imagery does not entail a "natural knowledge of God"; it does imply that the "knowledge of God" in redemption is natural (fitting, proper) to man. Expressed negatively, redemption does not destroy the human being in order to save him. Whatever else it is, salvation is a salvaging of what is proper to man. The religious a priori means that man is so constituted that knowledge of God is essential and proper to him.

For this reason the issue of the religious a priori should not be confused with the issue of the power or capacity of man to know God or to receive revelation. Whether or not God's Word and redemption correspond to man's essential humanity is a different issue from man's inherent capacity or incapacity to hear that Word or respond to redemption. The most radical descriptions of man's incapacity do not displace that correspondence. For this reason the motifs of the knowledge of God and the religious a priori should be distinguished. On the other hand, their connection is disclosed when we ask the question whether or not the knowledge of God is possible without that correspondence. There are those who claim that the knowledge of God is totally a matter of God's initiative to which man contributes nothing but his own sin. I find this an essentially gnostic formulation because it places redemption completely outside the structure of an originally good but corrupted creation, making redemption solely a matter of the "divine." Because redemption is an alteration of existence which is not essentially evil, that existence in its essential ontological structure is a "condition" of that alteration in the sense of a *sine qua non.* The religious a priori is not, however, itself the knowledge of God or even the positive power of apprehending God outside of God's redemptive act. Therefore, the investigation of the religious a priori does not establish or demonstrate God's existence.

In the fullest sense the purpose of the investigation of the religious a priori in theology is to show that redemption and revelation correspond to what is essentially human, and that without them, man remains in a bondage which distorts and arrests his own being. Our concern now is slightly different. We want to call attention to the religious a priori in order to show why the redemptive alteration is an alteration of *existence,* and therefore why the imagery of ecclesia refers back to existence.

In that which follows we can do little more than assert and describe, hoping that the assertions have the power of evoking certain immediate self-apprehensions of the reader. We begin with a question. If we assume that the redemptive alteration of existence offers to man a world-unifying, ultimate reference and that it addresses what can be called human evil, do these offerings pertain in any way to the way man is constituted *qua* man? Are they in any way anticipated (intended?) by transcendental existence which serves as a condition of their possibility?

The first part of the question is, does a world-unifying ultimate reference correspond to the way man is transcendentally constituted? If the following four steps are founded in genuine insights, we must answer affirmatively. First, we shall regard as axiomatic those recent fundamental ontologies which portray man as self-transcend- *1* ent, a being whose "being" is always partly future and which is perpetually being brought about through the projective plans and decisions of the will. Kierkegaard, Nietzsche, Berdyaev, Sartre, and Heidegger each has his version of self-transcendence and what it means for a human being to "be." Second, self-transcendence has as an inevitable concomitant the self-apprehension of non-necessity. *2* Although no existent is "necessary," human existence apprehends this about itself, and the result is a structural insecurity. Death may *a* be, as Unamuno and Heidegger contended, the paradigm event of this non-necessity or insecurity. Yet the insecurity is not directed simply toward the physical cessation of one's being, but toward the non-necessity of the being we become through our decisions. In- *b* security, therefore, pertains to who or what we are, a question symbolized in the human being's search for himself.

Third, this ontic insecurity is accompanied by a *refusal* which *3* finds specific expressions in emotions of fear, anxiety, and outrage and which Augustine portrayed in his description of man as *inquietus,* suggesting the driving, insatiable nature of historical existence. We are following here Unamuno's portrayal of a built-in refusal of death, a refusal in the face of all rational considerations which prompt us to "realism." Even though death is the paradigm occasion of structural insecurity, this insecurity appears indirectly in ciphers connected with other occasions. At this point non-technological man seems to have more perceptive equipment than technological man. For non-technological man senses the presence of threat, the element of insecurity, in cross-road situations of human life: birth, marriage, puberty, going on a journey, entertaining a stranger. He senses the unpredictable element in such things, the unfathomable future course which life may take from these occasions. Because of this unfathomable element, death and destruction rise to the surface in these occasions. Technological man with his incredible success in medical sciences and environmental manipulation brings certain aspects of these situations under relative control (such as death from the complications of birth). His very success preoccupies him with the technological aspect of these occasions and masks the sense in which they contain an unfathomable and unmanipulable dimension pertaining to the course of future events. Sensing this dimension, pre-technological man bathes these occasions in symbolism and protective rites, while technological man stocks his medicine cabinet and reads about the psychology of puberty. Which of the two is more superstitious would be a difficult question to settle.

Finally, this refusal built into man's transcendental makeup carries with it a certain intentionality and therefore a *noema*. Since it is a refusal of that which threatens man's life, that which would dissipate his very nature, the refusal has as an intentional correlate *whatever it is* that would end such a threat. This intention is negatively expressed in the form of a complaint, an indictment against the world as man knows it. If the world is a mere multiplicity of inter-acting events, the pluralistic makeup of the world is responsible for insecurity. Of course in everyday life, insecurity, pain, and death are present through specific agents like disease, accidents, or demonic social systems. But the refusal to abide by the effects of these agents generates an overall indictment, "What kind of world is this?" "How can such a thing happen?" And at this point the cosmos has come into the picture. The *noema* of the intentionality which has its beginning in man's structural insecurity and his refusal of that situation is *cosmos*. What we are calling the religious a priori, at least in this first aspect, is a refusal of *chaos* as the ultimate frame-work of man's endeavors. This says nothing at all about whether or not the most inclusive context of our being is in fact chaos or cosmos. Nor does it mean that the noema of this refusal is God. The noema is simply a meant-object, a *whatever,* capable of sup-porting this refusal against the threat of chaos.

2. *The transcendental refusal of external determination*

The second part of the question concerns human evil. The redemption which ecclesial man experiences is a modification not just of human finitude but of human evil. Is there any transcendental structure witihout which such an alteration would not be possible?[2] All human civilizations as we know them, technological and pre-technological, distinguish between human behavior which is preferable and non-preferable, right and wrong, good and evil. All human groups have taboos and prescriptions which attempt to order human behavior. And as Freud and others have shown, a minimal ordering of instinctual animal behaviors is necessary to the existence of any society. If we grant that valuational ordering of human life is universal in human history, is this ordering nevertheless a mere historical contingency without any positive relation to the human being in his humanness? Is that normative or valuational structure of human communities which restricts man's aggressiveness and orders his mating, his play, and his survival-oriented activities such as hunting and possessing in any way a reflection of the transcendental makeup of man? Are good and evil simply something which is fastened onto man by man himself out of the arbitrary customs of society, or does it arise with the emergence of a creature like man?

We shall begin with a thesis. *The capacity to distinguish good and evil is a constituent of a self-transcending being.* In the previous section we allied ourselves to that philosophical tradition which in various ways has described the "structural openness" (Bonhoeffer) or self-making of man. Following Kierkegaard, Heidegger, and Unamuno, we argued that structural insecurity is a necessary feature of self-transcendence. In addition to insecurity which pertains to one's own future existence and destiny and the refusal of chaos as the ultimate framework of that destiny, human self-transcendence contains within itself a second refusal, the refusal of *external determination.*[3] To be self-transcending means that the "being" of the human being is perpetually coming into being, and that the will plays a decisive role in this coming into being. We acknowledge of course that aspect of the human being called the in-itself (Sartre) or the involuntary (Ricoeur), and the important role it plays in man's

2. Ricoeur's *Fallible Man,* trans. Charles Kelbley (Chicago: Regnery, 1965), is the most inclusive attempt available to set forth the transcendental conditions of evil.

3. A more explicit version of this thesis can be found in my article, "God as Dominator and Image-Giver: Divine Sovereignty and the New Anthropology," *Journal of Ecumenical Studies,* vol. 6 (1969), 354–375.

perpetual coming-into-being. Yet, because man is a self-transcending being, the involuntary itself is not simply an efficient "cause" of the will, a factor in the will's decisions and self-actualizations. We do want to avoid giving the impression that self-transcendence is merely a quantity or essence which characterizes man in the same way that three angles characterize a triangle. Because of its very nature of *self*-determination, self-transcendence has the peculiar capacity of self-repudiation. Under the pressure and pain of the experience of non-necessity, the human being can attempt to transfer his fundamental structure of self-determination into the mode of being-determined-by. We shall pursue this point in more detail at a later time. We only want to say that self-transcendence is an aspect of historical existence and occurs in the mode of more or less. One major point, however, is that self-transcendence calls attention to *the* most distinctive thing about human being; namely, human being is being-in-process in which the being brings about its own being by way of the will. Human being is a being who can will to be this or that kind of being, do this or that kind of work, be this or that kind of person, and then repudiate that particularity for something else, which can in turn be repudiated. Bringing-about-one's-being is that about the human being which discloses a built-in refusal of external determination. "To be" in the human mode involves a perpetual resistance to be in the mode of mere thing-ness, the mode of being-brought-about, or of having one's being determined by another.

Because of this structural openness, the human being has a self-continuity or identity in a very distinctive sense. The "I" of a self-making being is not simply a content or quantum like a color or number, because it includes the possibility of future decisional alterations. It is always an "I can," "I refuse," "I agree." In short, the human "I" is always a will. The human being has "developed" from the past to what it is now through the will, and what it shall be in the future will occur through the will. Therefore, part of the human "I's" self-awareness is a sense of its own indispensability or importance. The indispensability we are talking about is not the indispensability of a separable ego for the body. The human "I" is a corporeal or bodily "I," for the "I" or "I can" involves psycho-

135

physical powers of actualization. "I can purchase a car" is a possibility to be actualized by a corporeal "I." Indispensability means that the embodied self has a crucial role in determining what my being is, the bringing about of my being. This ontological indispensability of the embodied self is the basis of a pride which is constitutive of a structually open being which is responsible for its being and is aware of its own uniqueness and importance. Since the "I" is a corporeal "I," this pride extends to the body, not in the superficial sense of being proud of one's body, but in the sense that what is unique and important is my total bodily sense.

This makes possible our next step. A self of this sort is violable, vulnerable. We argued previously for an insecurity which constitutes a self-transcending being. Over and above insecurity, a self which attaches importance and uniqueness to itself (ontic pride) is vulnerable not so much to external things that pose as threats to its existence such as death but to attempts to violate that uniqueness and importance. A self-surpassing self is vulnerable on two fronts as it becomes the object of two kinds of destructive external intentions. The first, *manipulation,* is the attempt to transform another's self-determining mode into the mode of being-determined-by, or thingness in a behavioural situation. The second, *ridicule,* is the attempt to violate another's pride or uniqueness-sense by transforming that novel existence into some fixed and at the same time negative category. Ridicule is always both a reduction and a negation. Ridicule, to be distinguished from disagreement, correcting mistakes, prescriptions, or even commands, attempts to rob the human being of his future-oriented and self-transcending powers by *fixing* the human being into some undesirable characteristic. There is an infinite qualitative difference between "you made a mistake" and "you are stupid"; between "you should not act like that" and "you are just a *woman!"* We are not saying that ridicule necessarily accompanies these expressions since, like all expressions, they are susceptible to different intentions. To express ridicule they must carry intentions to fix the other into a feature which determines and exhausts his being, thereby violating the novelty which founds his pride. Manipulation and ridicule are obviously closely related. It could even be said that ridicule is a form of manipulation. We distinguish them

136

in order to call attention to the difference between attempting to determine another's behavior or being (manipulation) and the more linguistic and attitudinal way of relating to the other (ridicule).

Human beings as self-determining beings are constituted to resist both manipulation and ridicule. One might say that a human being is this resistance and the potential violence which it triggers. In the final step of our argument we are presupposing the essential interdependence between individuality and sociality. The kind of self-transcendence just indicated has as an indispensable condition a social matrix of co-intentions. Whether the reader agrees with this or not, he will agree at least that historical man is a social being. His self-bringing-about, embodied "I," his built-in pride and sense of novelty, exists in relation to other human beings. Each individual's bringing-about-his-being occurs in reciprocal interaction with others who also are bringing-about-their-being. The result is that a certain normativeness presides over the social situation and establishes its basic structure. This normativeness is generated out of the transcendental region, out of the human being whose very being is constituted by a vulnerability and resistance to ridicule and manipulation. Given this kind of "I," mutual pride and resistance will preside over the reciprocities of the tribe, the family, the gang, or the nation.

Mutual resistance to ridicule and to external determination founds a mutual ordering. The most primitive and dramatic manipulation of the other's corporeal "I" is murder. Even as death is a paradigm event which gathers up and symbolizes man's structural insecurity, murder plays a similar role in the social world.[4] The prevention and punishment of murder is a society's most basic act of protecting self-determination. Built on this primary act and vastly extending it, the customs and taboos of society develop toward more inclusive ordering of ever wider areas of possible inter-manipulation. For instance, societal structures and laws restrict the attempt to determine another person by possessing his possessions, possessions being an extension of his corporeal "I," a field of "things" in which he exer-

4. The primacy of murder as an issue in philosophical anthropology is expressed by Albert Camus in *The Rebel* (New York: Alfred A. Knopf, 1969), "Introduction."

cises his will and actualizes his being. In the field of sexuality, rape is the paradigm manipulation, and this field also is subject to customs and taboos which attempt to protect the corporeal "I." Societal order also moves into the region of human speech and limits the possibilities of linguistic violation. In situations of cultural conflict or minority oppression (i.e., black-white relations) these protective customs break down and terms of ridicule arise as instruments of oppression. Much of this ordering tends to be unwritten, yet is a powerful limit on murder, rape, theft, and insult, and we find such ordering from the most primitive tribes to sophisticated urban culture.

Our thesis about the transcendental origin of good and evil should now be clearer. The transcendental region itself generates a normativeness which distinguishes good acts and evil acts, good men and evil men. The evil man is the man who ignores this normativeness and violates the self-determination and the pride of the other. Furthermore, human existence as we know it always appears *within* the distinction of good or of evil not as a pure exemplification, but as a reflection of both. Historical human being never completely abandons his resistance to insult and manipulation. On the other hand, historical man never completely grants self-transcendence and pride to the other. Hence, this transcendental structure has a certain ideality which historical existence only approximates. This ideality finds a clearer expression in society than in the individual, in constantly broken *laws* which would limit man's propensity to violate the other and in *myths* of a golden age at the beginning or a utopia at the end. These laws and myths are not simply the arbitrary or accidental inventions of specific cultures; rather they express a structure which is constitutive of human, that is, structually open being. They express corporate conditions proper to the mode of "to be."

We described the refusal of chaos, the inclination toward cosmos, as a religious a priori. Is this refusal of external determination part of the religious a priori? Here the ambiguities of "religion" and "religious" threaten to make the question meaningless. If religion simply means some reference to the "infinite" or "ultimate meaning," our second motif appears to be excluded. However, that which is before us and which is our concern is a determinate historical faith whose story concerns alienated historical existence and its redemption. Since the religious a priori means the transcendental conditions that dispose man to the actualizations of faith, it seems that the transcendentally grounded resistance to manipulation and ridicule is a part of the religious a priori. Without vulnerability, man would not be the kind of being whose being could be disrupted, susceptible to the distinction of evil and good, bondage and freedom, alienation and redemption. Like the refusal of chaos and "God," the refusal of external determination does not demonstrate the existence and validity of redemption itself. The story and imagery of redemption are not "implied" in this constitutive normativeness. Nor is this refusal a "power" or capacity to redeem oneself or even to cooperate in the process of redemption. Instead it characterizes what man is, the mode of his "to be," and therefore redemption is redemption of *man* and not of something else.

We began this section asking if the imagery of the community of faith pertained to (human) existence. We propounded our "fundamental theology" (the two refusals) partly in order to answer the question. Although the two refusals are located transcendentally, they reappear under the conditions of historical existence as the clues to the peculiar sense in which man's being is "existence." Human life occurs in the situation in which our "to be" (our nature, destiny, meaning) is constantly at stake. Man lives constantly with the possibility of not-being, not just in the sense of physical death but in the sense of not-being himself. And this makes the human mode of *existence* unique. Further, the situation of threatened existence pervades all the levels of man's psyche and social life; his subconscious, his emotions, his everyday acts, his reciprocities with others. This is why any faith which addresses these refusals of man, refusals which found this peculiar existence, must be apprehended or internalized in the mode of existence.

B. Disrupted Historical Existence

The purpose of this chapter is to propound the existence dimension of ecclesia. We have contended that "transcendental existence," the transcendental conditions of human existence, disposes man toward matters which are actualized in faith. We risk this easily misunderstood term *transcendental existence* in order to call attention to the insecurity and vulnerability which constitute man's transcendental makeup and which predispose his actual existence to the more conscious affective and linguistic levels such as the "search for meaning" and resistance to demonic authorities. Technically speaking, transcendental existence is not existence, since existence connotes the concrete and actual mode of individual life. Therefore, man's participation in ecclesia is not "existential" simply in the sense that these transcendental structures find some expression. Intervening between these transcendental structures and ecclesia is human history in all its variety and determinateness. Furthermore, historical man is not simply the set of possibilities, conditions, and idealities which in an abstracting (or bracketing) analysis we portray as transcendental. However we account for it, historical man is non-coincident with his own ideality. According to the old myth, he lives in exile from his original home where he enjoyed the immediate presence of God, lordship over the earth, and harmony with his own kind. Hence, we must sharply differentiate the transcendental conditions of insecurity and vulnerability and the refusals which accompany them from the modification these undergo in history in which man's being becomes alienated being. Vulnerability to external determination and to ridicule is not itself an alienation, a disruption in the self, but a structure characteristic of any self-transcending being. Something must happen to this constitutive vulnerability and insecurity before it is alienation. When we attempt to thematize this something, we immediately confront the hermeneutical problem. How is man's own alienation present to him, if in fact it is present at all? On the one hand, it appears to be universally apprehended, insofar as the split between what we are and what we could be or should be dominates everyday world endeavors. A fundamental discontent characterizes human life everywhere and this discontent is not entirely unconscious. No one can live in the everyday world without being aware of the failure of the other to fulfill our expectations. The world of everyday life is filled with accusations, feeling guilty, hoping, trying to do better, failing, regretting an action, resisting manipulation, giving up and starting again, and all of these occur under the non-coincidence of man with his own ideality.

On the other hand, one of the marks of alienation is that it blinds the consciousness to its own reality. Alienation like the structure of the transcendental region is too close to see because we "see" by means of it, that is, through a consciousness already modified by it. Alienation, therefore, is seen clearly only when it itself is undergoing modification toward redemption. This is why the portrayal of aliena-tion is a hermeneutical problem. Our best access to it is through redemption. And we best grasp redemption not in the contingencies of an individual autobiography but in the intended imagery of the redemptive community. This community has experienced redemption in a certain determinate mode and has expressed that redemption in its imagery. Redeemed existence, therefore, is the path to that alienation which is apprehended outside redemption in an unfocused and vague discontent. Alienation itself is a modification of essential human nature and its transcendental basis, and redemption is a modification of that modification. We have, therefore, a mode of existence in ecclesia which is alienation-in-transition-to-redemption. This transition occurs at the level of existence and has an intended imagery, a constellation of noemata which expresses both alienation and redemption. Our access to alienation, therefore, is by way of an examination of this imagery. We hope that such an inquiry will further clarify the nature of participation in ecclesia and the sense in which existence is a necessary component in faith's situation. Although the order of insight is from redemption and its imagery to alienation and its imagery, we shall begin with the imagery of alienation since we wish to examine how alienation modifies man's transcendental makeup and how redemption modifies alienation.

We are omitting an account of our method of obtaining these images. We can say briefly that they are part of the story of the community of faith, always presupposed and sometimes explicit. These images persist through all periods of ecclesia and do not stand or fall with various mythologizations and doctrinalizations of them. Beyond this we shall rely on the reader's acquaintance with this historical faith for confirmation of our inquiry. Furthermore, what follows is not an exhaustive treatment of the imagery of alienation in this historical faith. There are images which express the depth and universality of human evil which we shall not pursue. There are many specific images of redemption (e.g., justification) which we omit. Our purpose is to set forth the intended imagery of the transition to redemption in order to indicate sufficiently the part this transition plays in ecclesia. For our next task will be to portray ecclesia itself in anticipation of our over-all task of discovering how these components form the matrix of reality-apprehensions.

1. *Idolatry*

Bonhoeffer is quite right in his observation that we who live in the "middle" of time can never directly apprehend the events of the "beginning."[5] We would also agree with him that these inaccessible beginning events contain the mysterious origin of man's disrupted historical existence. We see no way to get to this origin or even settle the difficulties which accompany the two major alternatives that "explain" the transition from ideality to disruption; one which describes the transition as itself a perennial occurrence expressive of the intrinsic makeup of man and the other which assigns it to the evolution of man. Like Kierkegaard we see a connection between pre-alienation insecurity and alienation itself, a connection which is not, however, an explanation or cause[6] The insecurity which constitutes man includes a refusal of chaos as man's ultimate context. This refusal persists even when man's world picture is thoroughly secular and when there is an *intellectual* resignation to chaos. Human consciousness is structured by a proclivity toward the anti-chaos, whatever that is.

Along with this general impetus, human life is not only made up of many specific needs such as hunger, sex, and companionship, but it is always surrounded by entities which promise satisfaction of these needs, entities which are pleasurable, alluring, and attractive. Besides serving to fulfill actual needs, they offer themselves as candidates for allaying the fundamental insecurity. This candidacy is based partly on their capacity to obliterate the "death-sickness" and partly on the promise that a given entity such as a family or nation may itself be the anti-chaos and thus the true *telos* of man's being. Such

5. *Creation and Fall* (New York: Macmillan, 1959), p. 9.
6. Soren Kierkegaard, *The Concept of Dread* (Princeton: Princeton University Press, 1944), pp. 41 ff.

is the connection between insecurity and what we shall call idolatry. The connection does not account for the actualization of idolatry but does give us a clue as to its nature. Idolatry is the attempt on the part of man to secure himself against refused chaos and to transcend his vulnerability by means of something in his environment. Therefore, anything can serve as an idol, including the divine apprehended in the mode of something in the surrounding world.

Idolatry as a motif appears in the story of Yahweh and his people in the command to worship Yahweh alone, in the prohibitions against image-making, and in the constant critique of all unqualified loyalties to king, nation, and cultus. In both the experience and the testimonies of Israel, idolatry is always a destructive force. We offer the following demythologized account of its destructive power. If *idol* means something we intend as the solution to the fundamental problem of our being, serving as the ultimate and most powerful context which displaces chaos, it will unify human life and organize all its relations, eliciting the response of unqualified loyalty. From this flow many consequences. The human being becomes defined, so to speak, through that object. His *being* is reduced to the *telos,* purposes, features of the idol, as for instance when a political party becomes absolutized. Second, the mode of consciousness required for an idol is certainty rather than doubt. Since one's very destiny and salvation is at stake, the idol cannot fill its insecurity-eliminating function and at the same time permit doubt in its own powers. To function successfully as the anti-chaos, the idol must be invested with perfections, powers, and marvelous attributes. It must in short be de-historicized. Intellectual processes must then be generated which preserve these perfections from relativity and criticism as well as our non-doubting relation to them. This is why dishonesty and fear are essential ingredients of idolatry. We must constantly bend reality to make the idol which is itself threatened by chaos into the anti-chaos. And since the meaning and destiny of his very being depends on the idol and on maintaining its adequacy, the idolator lives constantly at the edge of a precipice.

We would not give the impression that in everyday life idolatry always occurs toward an obvious and discretely identifiable entity. Because of structural insecurity, alienated historical existence is marked by idolatrous relations with everything in the surrounding world. Alienated man intends the whole content of his surrounding world in the hope that any or all has the capacity to replace chaos. Idolatry, therefore, modifies one's transcendental consciousness and becomes a way of being temporal, a way of living one's personal space, and an ingredient in all motivations and decisions.

Is God an idol?

2. Flight

Idolatry expresses only one aspect of disrupted historical existence, the response of finitude to its own non-necessity and its reduction of the anti-chaos (transcendence) to the surrounding world. In addition to the refusal of chaos is a refusal of external determination which is the transcendental condition of the intersubjective conditions proper to man's being and therefore of the distinction of right and wrong. Like the refusal of chaos, this second refusal functions as a transcendental condition of human alienation. This universal structure of "rightness," of what is proper to man's existence, freedom, and communality, appears in the story of Israel in the motifs of the good creation, the covenant in which man's obligations are established, and above all in Torah. The refusal of manipulation and ridicule generates specific forms of mutual protection and obligation in the community, and this is the essence of covenant and Torah. In its negative role, Torah guards human beings in their vulnerability (their bodies, families, possessions) from rapaciousness. Positively, it expresses the obligation to acknowledge the other's refusals of manipulation and ridicule. The concrete bearers of Torah are language, both imagic and legal, institutional structures, and interpersonal loyalties.

This makes clear a second aspect of the disruption of human historical existence, based, however, on the first aspect. The first aspect, idolatry, is the unwillingness to live with our refusal of chaos and the willingness to translate that refusal into fanatical loyalties. But this attempt to secure ourselves in the mode of loyalty occurs in dialectical relation with an opposite style, utter repudiation of the world, its events, furnishings, and relations. This world-repudiating response of self-securing finitude is *flight*. Transcendentally expressed, it is the attempt to ignore our own constitutive normativeness,

144

to find solace for our insecurity by pretending to be contentless; unmanipulable by any other, invulnerable to ridicule, and without need of communal or intersubjective structures of protection and obligation. In the language of Israel flight is the attempted repudiation of the obligations expressed in Torah. We repeat, idolatry and flight exist in dialectical relation to each other. For example, when human beings turn to sexuality as the power that removes chaos (idolatry), they repudiate simultaneously those structures of sexuality which their own vulnerability to ridicule and manipulation require (flight). Every idolatry is a flight because it displaces the structures of being in the idol with the idealized features of perfection.

This brief exposition cannot pretend to exhaust the images of alienation. We have here little more than suggestive hints. A fuller analysis would treat the imagery in the story of Israel in which alienation is a corruption of something essentially good, something universal and corporate, and which involves a corrupted response to Torah itself (self-righteousness). We hope that these hints are sufficient to indicate the difference between the "existence" concern which ascends from the transcendental region (given its insecurity and its vulnerability) and disrupted historical existence. In disrupted historical existence the transcendental region undergoes a modification. Its structural insecurity and vulnerability are not lost but are transformed. In one sense structural insecurity's search comes to an end insofar as it secures itself in the idol. On the other hand, the insecurity is compounded and is transformed into fanaticism and fear and the willingness to do anything to oneself, the other, or to the world out of loyalty to the idol. Vulnerability to ridicule and resistance to external manipulation are also transformed. In flight and idolatry resistance to external manipulation can become a mere succumbing to such determination. In this case resistance persists only in the mode of hidden resentment and discontent. Or the resistance can attempt to transcend the mutuality of co-determination and dominate or manipulate the other. These transformations are the matrix of actualized evil, of evil plans, acts, and emotions. Furthermore, these disrupted transformations of the human being find linguistic, social, and institutional expression.[7] Such is disrupted his-

7. Hoping not to sound too outrageously general, we would maintain that

torical existence, and since the apprehensions of faith are made possible in part by an alteration of disrupted existence, we cannot get very far in our attempt to explore the problem of reality-apprehensions without keeping this mode of existence in view.

C. REDEMPTIVE EXISTENCE

Ecclesial man never experiences disrupted historical existence simply in itself but in conjunction with his own modification toward redemption. Alienation is grasped and symbolized from within this redemptive modification. For ecclesial man redemption not alienation is the paramount thing. A comprehensive treatment of redemption in ecclesia would be necessarily Christological. Our purpose here is simply to illustrate the existence level of faith's situation; hence, we shall abstract redemption from its inclusive Christological context and focus on its discrete imagery.

1. *Freedom*

The imagery of redemption like the imagery of disrupted existence is not present in the language of ecclesia in the form of easily identifiable units. There is of course a language of redemption made up of stories, parables, metaphors, and titles. However, we must penetrate this plurality of linguistic forms if we are to discover the noemata of redemptive existence. We shall focus on the redemptive imagery which correlates with the two motifs of disrupted existence. Even as idolatry and flight are interdependent (with idolatry as the founding act), so are freedom and obligation interdependent with freedom having a certain priority. We mean by freedom the modification of idolatrous existence toward an existence whose feature is a certain power over one's self-securing and its idols. Several things are involved here. First, the breaking of the power of idolatry cannot mean simply a return to structural insecurity and its undesignated and unfocused object of a "Whatever," an "ultimate context," or

different forms of cultural existence tend to be weighted more toward idolatry than flight or vice versa. Hence, the repudiation of essential transcendental human structures tends to take the form of idolatry in Western culture, while flight is the classical Eastern mode of relation to those structures. Such a generalization is naturally subject to many qualifications.

an anti-chaos. The connection between this transcendental condition and idolatry is so close that once the transcendental thrust is fulfilled by the idol, a mere undesignated object cannot replace it. The *problem* is the refusal to live with a vague and undesignated ultimate context. That which can break the power of the idol can only be that which the idol pretends to be and is not, the transcendent itself. This is why the transcendent is not simply an arbitrarily introduced entity in this story but its very foundation.

Second, the dialectic between self-securing or idolatry and flight produces a strange, even paradoxical, bondage. The human being sets up idolatrous relations with the cultural and religious expressions of his normativeness (Torah, society, religion) and in so doing he secures himself by means of Torah and cultus. In Paul's letter to the Galatians the law played this role in Judaism and the cultus in hellenism. The result is the most radical understanding of freedom imaginable. Freedom must be freedom toward the expressions of man's own transcendental requirements and toward the instruments of redemption itself. Unfortunately, in the Western form of ecclesia's cultic and doctrinal tradition, the motif of radical freedom is treated within a narrow juridical framework. Hence, justification has come to mean a way of obtaining pardon (along with attendant psychological benefits) from a legally valid accusation. The demythologized translation of divine accusation to self-accusation is hardly an improvement. Needless to say, this obscures the idolatrous structure of disrupted existence and the power of freedom to overcome it.

Third, freedom is not simply the granting of the longed-for security which constitutes the human being. In one sense the human being is secured insofar as his life takes place before the Word and presence of God. He is not secured, in that freedom is also a power to live in the mode of courage and responsibility toward an indeterminate future which man neither knows nor controls.

2. *Obligation*

If redemptive existence were restricted to freedom, the result would be a creative but directionless and contentless power. Both the experience and imagery of redemption refer us back to the normative aspect of the human being. Our stress on the origin of this aspect in self-transcendence and our focus on an inviolable self-determination and on a self-respect which is sensitive to ridicule may sound misleadingly individualistic. We recall at this point that this normativeness is part of the transcendental foundation for human sociality. It founds, one might say, the set of obligations necessary for the protection and promotion of self-determination. Even as this provides a clue as to the meaning of alienation, namely, a flight from that normativeness and the sociality necessary to it, it also suggests a second aspect of redemptive existence. We could call it simply the other side of freedom. Redemptive existence is obligatory existence. Obligation, like freedom, can appear under the form of alienation. When this happens obligation loses the flexibility and relativity which concrete situations of obligation require, and becomes a mere instrument for self-securing. In this case conformity to rules displaces obligation. The resistance to the distortions of legalism, itself a symptom of man's inherent refusal of self-determination, yields what seems to be a freedom from all obligation. Such a freedom is illusory because self-determination, self-respect, and the power over self-securing all have intersubjective conditions and involve an acknowledgment of the other's vulnerability and self-determination. The language of ecclesia that describes redemptive existence as obligatory or responsible existence includes *nomos* or law and its content as well as the moral vocabulary of mutual forgiveness and *agape*.

To summarize, the imagic language of ecclesia refers back to human existence in several ways. First, the human being is so transcendentally constituted that the mode of his being is *existence*. His very meaning is constantly at stake as he lives his life. Because the imagery of redemption refers back to this transcendental structure, its import is "existential." Second, when we consider the human being in his concrete historical existence, we find a disruption which bends and tears his very being. Third, when we view the human being in the mode of ecclesial man, we find an actual modification of disruptive existence toward redemption. This redemptive modification is in one way a protection of his constitutive and transcendental refusals of chaos and external determination, but it goes beyond this insofar as it concerns the transcendent and insofar as it concerns a concrete moral content such as agape. Redemptive existence, then, even in the mode of irreducible individuality is an indispensable element in the situation of faith. The intended imagery of faith and the nature of ecclesia are simply not understandable apart from the redemptive alteration of existence. And this existence dimension permeates all the acts characteristic of ecclesial man as well as their accompanying imagery. Praying, reconciling the unreconciled, instructing children, and resisting tyrants are all connected with the ultimate threat in all our situations, with our disrupted existence which remains a part of us, and with the redemptive power constantly at work. This threefold structure of existence pervades the imagery and sociality of ecclesia and, as we shall later argue, founds its apprehensions.

Chapter 7

ECCLESIA AND INTERSUBJECTIVITY

> However, we may assume that we are deceived by the most obvious appearances when we hypostatize, treat as a self-enclosed, independent reality what is perhaps only the land of a certain undefinable realm whose submerged areas and underwater outcroppings can only be identified by accident or by sudden illumination.[1]

Gabriel Marcel

Chapters 6 and 5 dealt with two abstractions in the sense of abstracted components of ecclesia, the transition to redemptive existence which modifies the individual and the language which accompanies this transition. In the present chapter we perform another abstracting act by focusing on the intersubjectivity of ecclesia, keeping in mind that all of these components are inseparable in ecclesia itself. The general thesis guiding our inquiry is that faith occurs in a faith-world, a social matrix whose concrete corporate form we are calling ecclesia. Any attempt, therefore, to inquire into faith's "cognitivity" will go astray if it bypasses this matrix. The reason is that faith's apprehensions occur in accordance with a consciousness shaped and rendered determinate in this matrix.

Because this matrix itself holds the clue to faith's cognitivity, theological prolegomenon in the sense of phenomenological theology cannot avoid being in some sense an ecclesiology. The principle of positivity requires that methodological and pre-methodological issues

---

1. *Creative Fidelity* (New York: Farrar, Straus & Giroux, 1964), p. 92.

be faced in conjunction with determinacy, in this case, with the determinate nature of the community of faith and its redemptive existence. Does this mean that we are offering here a "theology of the church"? Insofar as a theology of the church means a description of the distinguishing historical and essential features of ecclesia, we must say yes. On the other hand, a full theology of the church involves necessarily a *theological* account of the church's origin and existence. And this cannot be done apart from Christology and theological exploration of God and the world. Therefore, the treatment of "material" theological themes in phenomenological theology still occurs within brackets, and these themes must be taken up again without the brackets and by means of theological method proper which attempts to grasp how each motif interacts with others.[2]

What do we mean by ecclesia? Few people would deny that the Christian faith marked the appearance in history of a new form of historical corporate existence.[3] Even if we agree that there is such a thing, we nevertheless face a terminological jungle in which we can easily lose our way. We hear of church (visible and invisible), *Communio sanctorum*, holy Catholic church, community of faith, *koinonia*, and Christian existence. Whatever the vocabulary, it is usual practice to employ a term for the total corporate entity with its institutional aspects like polity, organization, law and doctrinal tradition, and a restricted term for an essential and distinctive faith-

2. The same holds for our treatment of redemptive existence. Our description of religious a priori, disrupted existence, and redemption retain an abstract character precisely because they are dealt with apart from theological method proper, which would necessarily include working in and with "authorities," and therefore would in some sense be a symbolics of redemption. Our work with material theological themes in this initial stage of phenomenological theology, while it is unavoidable, is ordered toward the purpose of phenomenological theology, the displaying of reality-grounding in this historical faith. In other words phenomenological theology is not dogmatics.

3. John Cobb calls this new form "Christian existence" and he sees it as one of several forms of "axial existence" which have emerged in history. *Structures of Christian Existence* (Philadelphia: Westminster Press, 1967), chap. 10. John Knox calls it simply a "new community." *The Early Church and the Coming Great Church* (Nashville: Abingdon Press, 1955), p. 45. Gordon Kaufmann's term is "Christian existence" which he defines as a "transformed existence within a new community." *Systematic Theology: A Historicist Approach* (New York: Charles Scribner's Sons, 1968), p. 480.

community. As we have said previously, we are adopting Emil Brunner's convention, using ecclesia to mean the distinctive, corporate existence characterized by the presence of Jesus Christ, and church as our inclusive term.[4] Although ecclesia means a distinctive form of corporate existence, it is not easily identified with any one form of human sociality. It is not an exclusive form of social organization such as a nation or tribe, a determinate social world, a "finite province of meaning," a sub-culture, or even a local face-to-face community. It does, however, involve a determinate intersubjectivity. We recall that determinate intersubjectivity is the transposition of the universal structures of intersubjectivity (intending the other as self-transcending other, as personal body, etc.) into the specificity required by a particular relationship. Thus the everyday conscious reciprocities of a marriage relationship presuppose an intersubjectivity in which the partners intend each other as mates and possible parents. Although in its concrete, everyday actualization, ecclesia involves interpersonal relationships and reciprocities which occur in conjunction with its characteristic activities such as worship. These reciprocities presuppose an intersubjective structure in which participants constitute each other as believers.

Our thesis is that the closer one gets to this determinate intersubjectivity, the closer he is to ecclesia. Like individual human-consciousness, human sociality exists in more or less accessible strata. The church (the inclusive entity) as a type of sociality presents itself by way of surface and depth strata. At the surface is the visible institution; its activities and structures; for example, the Roman Catholic Church in its cultic activities and its hierarchical order. Also at the surface are the characteristic reciprocities which are necessary to these activities; e.g., reciprocities between clergy, between priests and laymen, reciprocities occurring in connection with the confessional or the Mass. Slightly below the surface, but nevertheless conscious, are what Schutz calls typifications. Typifications are ways human beings intend each other in order to deal with each other in the everyday world. Laymen therefore typify the clergy in that they deal with them on the basis of certain expectations.

4. Emil Brunner, *The Misunderstanding of the Church* (Philadelphia: Westminster Press, 1953), p. 6, pp. 10–12.

Typifications are conscious in that one *consciously* expects certain attitudes and behaviors from the typified person. They are beneath the surface in the sense that these expectations are not themselves direct objects of the acts of consciousness in which we behave and feel toward these persons. For instance, the layman who is taking communion does not consciously focus on the various typifications he has of the officiating clergyman. The direct objects of focus are the physical and symbolic elements of the communion itself. Presupposed by all three layers is the determinate intersubjectivity of this community, the largely pre-conscious co-intentions in which each one constitutes the other as "with him" in this community. This differs from typifications in that typifications guide our behavior toward another's behavior, and thus are tied to specific acts. Determinate intersubjectivity expresses the inter-human structure characteristic of the community as such, hence correlates with the *telos* of that community, its story, and its constitutive imagery.

Even as determinate intersubjectivity is distinguishable from institutionality, so is ecclesia to be differentiated from its institutionalized levels. We do not suggest that the institutional aspect is unimportant or dispensable, a problem which we shall take up later. We only want to clarify that ecclesia is a form of corporate existence, and in its social dimension is a determinate intersubjectivity. When we recall that the modification of existence toward redemption is the unifying feature of this corporate existence, we can say that ecclesia is that intersubjectivity made determinate by transition to redemptive existence.

What follows is an attempt to gain access to this determinate intersubjectivity, the intersubjective structure of redemptive existence. This means that it is a very limited enterprise, omitting most of the motifs which are present in a full theology of the church and of ecclesia. We are not investigating the levels above determinate intersubjectivity. Hence, we are bypassing those motifs which dominate treatments of the church such as the means of grace, the Word, the ministry, and the sacraments. We are also bypassing a general morphology of ecclesia, which, if pursued, would have to investigate its distinctive collective memory, its relation to past and future, the way it is constituted by events in its history. And finally, we are not attempting an explicit theological account of the origin and nature of ecclesia. That motif becomes thematic when ecclesia attempts to express its own self-understanding. It either sees itself in salvation history or it does not. It either speaks about God and his Word or it does not. It witnesses to the presence of the Spirit within itself or it does not. Such questions occur within the criteriological framework which occurs after and on the ground of phenomenological theology. Our attempt is the much more limited one of portraying what we need to clarify the situation in which faith is directed toward realities.

A. THE WAY FROM REDEMPTIVE EXISTENCE TO ECCLESIA

How do we obtain to the depth dimension of ecclesia's intersubjectivity? The traditional imagery which bears ecclesia's self-understanding is not particularly helpful. Phrases and metaphors like the body of Christ, "in Christ," the Apostle's *koinonia,* the vine and the branches, *agape* for one's brother, presuppose but do not themselves reveal its constitutive intersubjective structure. This is because they tend to be limited to the relation between ecclesia and Christ, or they serve as models for conscious interpersonal relations and acts. In addition these metaphors do not disclose the constellation of images actually at work when participants in redemptive existence constitute each other as believers. The distinctiveness of the ecclesia's intersubjectivity will continue to elude us until we grasp the connection between determinate intersubjectivity and redemptive existence. To explore this connection defines the phrase, "the way from redemptive existence to ecclesia." The statement stands for a procedural, not an ontological, order. We would not want to give the impression of a chronological sequence from the one to the other.

It seems universally acknowledged that redemptive existence involves a sociality of some kind. The reasons for this connection, however, vary and are frequently ill-founded. We note three views prominent in the reflection of the church about itself. The first, which we shall call the *supernatural* view, explains the sociality of Christian existence in terms of the divine presence. This not only means that God himself established the church, but that its sociality is procured by Christ's continued lordship and presence. The entity

154

which entered history as ecclesia was a supernatural co-inherence between Christ and believers. Believers are together a form of sociality because Christ so forms them, indwelling in them, and thereby relating them to each other.[5]   A second view, reflecting classical Protestantism, adds a sociological dimension.   While not denying that the church is founded on an act of God and continues as the mode of Christ's presence, this view points out that the sociality of redemptive existence arises necessarily as a "means" by which that existence takes place, namely, in the preached word and in the sacraments. Since preaching is the specific mode in which God chooses to address man, a gathered community is thereby required.   We call this *sociological* because of its resemblance to secular accounts which contend that the survival and transmission of any faith requires community consensus, organization, and the means of bridging generations.   A third view, reflecting pietism and its stress on individual experience and conversion, sees the sociality of the church as secondary to *individuality* and created out of the similarity of individual experiences of conversion which prompt individuals to a common life and cultus.

We find the clue to the relation between redemption and the sociality of ecclesia in the nature of redemption as a *modification of existence*.   We can expose this clue by a question.   What precedes this modification?   What is this "existence" which undergoes modification?   In Chapter 6 we displayed the existence that precedes redemption in the motifs of a general transcendental structure constitutive of man as such and disrupted historical existence.   We now observe that an intersubjectivity attends both of these dimensions. One of the significant contributions of phenomenological philosophy, if not its unifying thread, is its world-oriented and other-oriented anthropology, its view of the human being as in-the-world-being and as being-for-the-other.   In Husserl's view this interpersonal structure has its origins in the transcendental region itself.   Or to use the terms of our present argument, the human being is not only self-determining in the sense of bringing about his own being and acknowledging

5. While Bonhoeffer's total portrait is much more complex than this, the supernatural view is his dominant emphasis.   See *The Communion of Saints, a Dogmatic Inquiry into the Sociology of the Church* (New York: Harper & Row, 1960), pp. 106 ff.

that the other is also structurally open; he is self-determining in his refusal to be determined by the other. In our view there is nothing disruptive or evil about this general intersubjective structure of all human consciousness.

However, under the conditions of disrupted historical existence, this general feature of human intersubjectivity undergoes modification. Under the conditions of self-securing, all other entities including the other human being are intentionally altered. They become possible instruments of the victory of chaos over man, possible occasions therefore of suffering, catastrophe, and death. The other human being is a special instance of threat because he can attempt to impose his own effort to manage the world on me. Furthermore, he can establish his own meaning and self-identity by contrasting it to mine in the fashion of ridicule. The consequence of this altered status between human beings is that general transcendental intersubjectivity becomes a disrupted or alienated intersubjectivity. More specifically this means that human beings constitute or "mean" each other through the modes of their own alienation, the modes of self-securing and flight. Suspended is that normativeness of human self-transcendence on which depends the mutual acknowledgment of freedom. Instead of being one whose acknowledgment of me is a condition of my own welfare and self-realization, the other is intended as one who, like me, is in the world in the modes of idolatry and flight. Thus a distinctive intersubjectivity arises with disrupted historical existence. Because self-securing and flight are perpetual and insatiable pilgrimages, the status of the other undergoes perpetual change. As an external dominator and source of ridicule, the other's status is that of an enemy. As one of the attractive objects in the environment, the other is a potential idol. Idolatry and flight, therefore, constitute the other in this unstable fluctuation. Insofar as the other is part of the total environment which poses itself as a threat, the other is someone from whom to flee. When the flight characterizes the way the other is "meant," the particular stances toward the other are indifference and the refusal of responsibility; stances which dominate the intersubjective world of technocratic society more than the competitive constitution of an enemy or the adoring constitution of an idol.

156

This then is what precedes the modification of existence toward redemption. The existence which precedes this modification is an intersubjective existence. We are prevented therefore from describing the rise of ecclesia as the generation of a sociality out of mere isolated individuals. This raises an important but difficult problem. Does not alienation reflect disruption in the human community and redemption restoration of community?

At this point we must acknowledge Bonhoeffer's claim that disruptive historical existence has a certain individualizing or isolating effect. Isolation is apparent in the previously mentioned motifs which set forth the status of the other as enemy, idol, or anonymous neuter. The relationships which accompany these ways of constituting the other are all modes of isolation. Competitiveness, aggressiveness, and protection describe the stance toward the enemy. Idealization, placing at a distance (on a pedestal), and dehistoricizing describe the stance taken toward the idol. And callousness, depersonalizing, and forgetfulness describe the relation to the other in the mode of flight. We conclude that insofar as societies and face-to-face communities reflect disrupted historical existence, they are permeated by these forms of isolation. Insofar as alienated existence is modified by redemption, these forms of isolation are modified. To this extent redemption is a community-creating power. On the other hand, in spite of the presence of isolation, disrupted historical existence retains its own intersubjectivity, that is, its own characteristic ways in which human beings intend each other in pre-reflective acts of consciousness.

What this amounts to is that *human intersubjectivity itself is alienated or disrupted.* Alienated intersubjectivity is not merely our invention or speculation but implicit in the imagery of the community of faith itself. This imagery is usually received in mythical and doctrinal receptacles; that is, in formulations of Fall, hereditary sin, and imputed guilt. Yet it is clear that this imagery portrays human consciousness not individualistically but as mutually interdependent and bridging the generations. What a human being *is,* his very *being,* cannot be separated from his participation in history, the people who are his people, and the culminations of evil and redemption which have shaped them and defined their sociality. Although this approach does not exclude supernaturalist interpretations of ecclesia's origin, it bases ecclesia's sociality on the fact that ecclesia involves a modification of disrupted intersubjective structures which preceded it.

B. THE CO-INTENTIONALITIES OF REDEMPTIVE EXISTENCE

We enter now upon the most difficult investigation of this chapter, the description of the intersubjectivity which accompanies redemptive existence, the co-intentionalities characteristic of ecclesia. The question is difficult because of the resistance° of ecclesia to analysis, because of the depth° to which this structure pertains, because of the mass of materials in the theological tradition which purport to describe ecclesia's sociality, and because we are adopting a way of reflecting about ecclesia which is somewhat foreign to our customary approaches. The intersubjectivity of redemptive existence is more apparent, more accessible to us, as a plurality of co-intentions. What first comes into view when we turn our reflective attention to ecclesia are a number of ways in which the other is intended within redemptive existence. More difficult because it is more hidden is the unitary structure these co-intentionalities share. Our overall thesis is that the distinctiveness of ecclesia's intersubjectivity derives from the strange way in which the human being who is not a participant in ecclesia is present to those who are participants. To put it differently, ecclesia's intersubjectivity has something to do with the peculiar sense in which "mankind" is apprehended° in the co-intentionalities of ecclesia's participants. Although we shall not develop this motif until the next section, we mention it now in order to explain the course of the inquiry.

The issue can be expressed by means of an overly simple typology. When theology portrays the community of believers, it tends to fluctuate between two options. Fearful of losing contact with the tradition, the Scriptures, or the church, it describes this community strictly in terms of intercommunity relationships. These relationships (the most prominent one being agape) constitute° this community, and their presence differentiates it from other communities. On the other hand, conscious of the relativity of all historical communities, concerned about the difficulties of a *heilsgeschichtliche* approach, and wanting to do justice to all types of religious faiths, theology describes Christian faith wholly in terms of the appearance of existentials like faith, wonder, justice, hope, or freedom, which appear here and there in history but apart from a definitive community. The decisive issue which these options pose for the task of portraying the depth sociality of ecclesia is the interrelation of provincial and non-provincial elements. In the present section we shall set forth ecclesia's *provincial* aspect, co-intentionalities which are possible only within the imagery, the shaped consciousness of this redemptive existence. In the following section we shall try to indicate the incursion of a non-provincial element upon these seemingly provincial co-intentionalities.

We have described ecclesia as a form of determinate historical existence, founded in a redemptive modification of existence, borne by its own story and imagery, and marked by a distinctive intersubjectivity. It will be evident that ecclesia's redemptive existence provided the point of departure for our account of disruptive historical existence. It is crucial at this point to remember that redemptive existence "modifies" but does not simply replace transcendental and disrupted existence. Therefore, the mutual intendings (intersubjectivity) of redemptive existence, whatever they are, will build on and modify the intersubjective structures of general transcendental intersubjectivity and disrupted or alienated intersubjectivity. This is simply a complicated way of saying that in ecclesia believers intend each other as human beings and therefore as self-transcending beings marked by the refusals of chaos and of external determination. And they intend each other as participants in disrupted existence, and therefore as retaining in some sense the modes of self-securing and flight and their intersubjective expressions. Thus, the religious a priori and the images of idolatry and flight are present in the co-intentions of ecclesial man. But these sets of co-intentions are always present in and are modified by redemptive existence.

1. *The intersubjective dimensions of freedom and obligation*

What are these co-intentions which arise with redemptive existence and which found the sociality of ecclesia? By "co-intentions" we mean intentions which describe intersubjective structure, and as such are interdependent. Looked at from the side of individual consciousness, each one has a double object; I intend the other in X manner, and I intend him as intending me in X manner. If existence is modified toward redemption, then human beings intend each other not only as embodiments of transcendental refusals which have been disrupted but as embodiments of the redemptive modification of this disruption. In the terms of our analysis, ecclesial human beings constitute° each other as existing in the mode of freedom, which modifies self-securing, and obligation, which modifies flight.

What is involved when I pre-reflectively intend the other as free toward self-securing? First, I "mean" him as one who is free from the impetus to secure himself from chaos and its threats by attachment to some entity in the environment. Negatively expressed, I constitute him as consistently iconoclastic, as one whose refusal of chaos expands into a refusal of all idols. Concretely, this means that the participant in ecclesia takes it for granted that his brother in ecclesia will not give unqualified allegiance to a god, to the nation, the tribe, to nature, the world, a cause, to himself, to ecclesia, or to me who intends him. And I will deal with him in everyday life through typifications which presuppose this negative constitution of him as believer. Positively, it means that I intend him as directed toward the idol-breaking power, the sacred itself. In the language of the tradition, this means that I take for granted that my brother worships God and God alone, and a mutual impetus is present which impels us into the cultus. We intend each other as living before the transcendent and refusing all forms of self-securing.

Second, because I intend him through the image of freedom toward self-securing, I intend my ecclesial other as directed toward me in certain ways. If he is free toward me, I will not function as his idol. If he intends me as free, I will not be for him the enemy. For I will not manipulate him as an instrument of my needs system. If I am free toward him, I will not need to establish my own meaning and destiny by ridicule of his person or violation of his pride. In other words those in ecclesia do not intend each other through the images of idols or enemies; hence, their specific stances toward each other are not simply competitive or worshipful. Ecclesia thus involves an intersubjectivity of freedom *from* the other.

What happens to intersubjectivity when obligation replaces flight? We recall that the transcendental basis of this modification is the human being's refusal of all external determination and ridicule plus the structure of mutual welfare generated as the condition necessary to this refusal. Negatively, this means that when this refusal is mutually honored, human beings do not prey on each other in murder, cannibalism, torture, or rape, nor do they appropriate each other's possessions (the extensions of personal body) by violence. These negative agreements tend to be not only minimal conditions of human social survival but the foundations of positive intersubjective human needs. I need the other not only in the negative sense of *not* murdering me, but in the positive sense of help in surviving in the face of hunger, disease, and violence. Furthermore, a self-transcending being is more than a physical organism. He has social and psychological needs which pertain to his social and emotional survival. Therefore, I need the other as a source of support and concern for me, and this generates subtle and enjoyable features of human interaction such as humor, play, sexuality, and the cooperative pursuit of tasks. But self-securing and flight and the constitution of the other as enemy and threat involve a rejection of this mutual obligation which in turn wrecks the intentional structure of mutual concern. It is this structure which redemptive existence restores. And we cannot stress enough that it is an *intersubjective* structure, not merely one which is individual and existential.

In ecclesia, therefore, I constitute the other not in the mode of flight but in the mode of obligation, and *Torah* or *nomos* is the concrete expression of this co-intention. The other is the one who is obligated toward me, and who intends me this way; hence, I typify him as a source of responsible acts in both negative and positive senses. But the reverse is also true. The other is the one for whom I am responsible, and he typifies me (expects from me) as the source of responsible acts. The particular attitudes, feelings, and stances which obligatory intersubjectivity creates are interest in the other, compassion, delight, etc. We cannot stress too much that obligation is not merely placing the other under a law but has its roots in the acknowledgment of the *self-determination* of the other, and therefore of his essential vulnerability and the inviolability of his psyche and personal body. Redemptive existence creates therefore a freedom *for* the other as well as a freedom *from* the other.

161

2. The retention of alienated intersubjectivity in redemptive existence

We said before that the co-intentions of redemptive existence gather into themselves the "preceding" intersubjective structures of man's essential transcendental makeup and his disrupted historical existence. This has important effects on the way in which human beings "mean" each other in ecclesia. Because redemptive existence remains under the conditions of our disrupted history, it is mixed with disrupted existence. And this introduces into the intersubjectivity of ecclesia those images which are so prominent in the literature of primitive Chistianity, the image of our continuing evil and our perpetual need of forgiveness from each other and from God.[6] In other words to intend the other as redeemed is neither a sheer *demand* nor a perfectionist expectation. The mutual expectations of freedom and obligation are qualified by expectations of their disruption. In this situation the inclination to the other's good takes the form of forgiveness. Second, the presence of the transcendental makeup, the two refusals which comprise the religious a priori in the co-intending of redemptive existence is absolutely indispensable because it establishes redemptive existence as that which is proper to the human being. Without the religious a priori, redemption is sheer heteronomy. Because of the persistence of the transcendental dimension into redemptive existence, I view my own evil and my brother's evil as a foreign invader, something improper and alien to our essential makeup. We are not arguing that this transcendental dimension ought to be present. In ecclesia it is present in the form of the imagery of creation. Even when that imagery is not explicitly mentioned in Johannine, Pauline, or other literature, it is always presupposed even as disrupted historical existence is presupposed. What we are calling attention to is that this imagery reaches into the deepest intersubjective structures of ecclesia.

---

6. Joseph Haroutunian made the mutual forgiveness of sins the prominent feature of the communion of saints. In this view the major sign of the presence of Christ is the faith of Christians whereby they forgive each other. Haroutunian (along with John Knox) was one of a few twentieth-century theologians who saw the "knowledge of God" mediated through the kind of sociality embodied in the *communio sanctorum*. Hence, I am deeply indebted to both Haroutunian and Knox for this emphasis. See Haroutunian's *God with Us* (Philadelphia: Westminster Press, 1965), especially the essay, "The Knowledge of God in the Church."

The transcendental or essential makeup of the human being plays another role in ecclesia. Redeemed existence does not simply leave behind or repudiate but presupposes that man is constituted by his refusal of chaos as the ultimate context and destiny of man. Ecclesial man is still man who in his everyday life suffers pain, worries about things, and walks a weary way toward death, that most prominent cipher of chaos. Futhermore, these sufferings appear in the prominent times of human life in which the mystery of being and the threat of chaos are especially apparent; birth, death, marriage, illness, separation, home-leaving, and home-coming. If the intersubjectivity of ecclesia is an intersubjectivity of freedom and obligation *for* the other with its attendant concerns of justice and compassion, then these special times will receive cultic and mythic attention in ecclesia. In other words the festive celebrations of birth and death are not merely accidental cultural accretions to ecclesia but are rooted in the religious a priori itself which redemptive existence presupposes. This is the basis of ecclesia's continuity with other religious faiths, especially primitive religions where the ciphers of chaos are handled through mythology and taboo. Our point is that because the intersubjectivity of ecclesia contains the transcendental refusals, ecclesia as a form of historical existence celebrates (usually by ritual and symbol) the paramount traumatic occasions of human life. The very nature of ecclesia prevents it from ignoring these occasions or relinquishing them to other communities of the determinate social world. When these cipher-occasions of chaos are in fact left to other communities, it symptomizes the diffusion of ecclesia or the substitution of essential human matters by authoritarian, ideological, or heteronomous concerns.

3. *Individuality and promise*

So far we have focused on the plurality of co-intentions in ecclesia, their ordering toward the dimensions of alienation and redemption. Still confining ourselves to the quality of interpersonal relationships within ecclesia (to the provincialist formulation of ecclesia), we now pose the question of the individual and his status in ecclesia. Although "individualism" and individualistic formulations of religious knowledge are the chief targets of our proposal, we would not leave the impression that ecclesia is a mere collective in which individuality is surrendered. In our opinion the "isolating" effect of disrupted historical existence is not individuality but the repression of individuality. The reason is that the more a human being exists in the modes of self-securing and flight, the more he is subject to determination by external forces; by deities, idols, nations, other persons, etc. On the other hand, redemptive existence effects self-determination. In ecclesia we have the seemingly paradoxical situation of the human being whose self-determining freedom increases with the interdependence marked by freedom from and for the other. Augustine exemplifies this in that he is both "individualistic" (as in the *Confessions* and the anti-Pelagian writings) and ecclesiological (as in his anti-Donatist writings).

If we grant that individuality is promoted and not repressed in ecclesia, what place is there for the concerns of individual existence for meaning, survival, integrity, and the like? If these concerns are retained, what is their relation to the intersubjectivity of ecclesia? This question discloses a co-intention at work in ecclesia which is more fundamental than those we have thus far treated. If we return to our previous example, the unifying co-intentionality of marriage has the character of a promise which is not simply a commitment to the mate, but to the possible offspring which may be forthcoming. The promise is that, whatever happens, we shall be mutually responsible for the offspring of our sexuality. We cite this example in order to call attention to a parallel element in ecclesia. In ecclesia the sphere is not sexuality but the more indeterminate sphere of *existence* and the built-in refusal by human existence of chaos and external determination; in short, the issue of human meaning and destiny. Participation in ecclesia resembles marriage in that it too involves a commitment toward the future. "Whatever happens," I promise to pursue the life and death issues of my very destiny within the framework of certain intentions directed to me by the other. You intend me in the mode of freedom and obligation, and I trust to these intentions my very humanity. Before you, the plural you, I will pursue my salvation. In ecclesia one's salvation is placed in the hands of the other and vice versa.

The most obvious rejoinder at this point is that the promise which marks the entrance to ecclesia is a promise to God or to Christ. We do not object to this. However, we are not describing all the components of the participation in ecclesia but its intersubjective stratum. If we ask how God is present in ecclesia, how he accomplishes his saving work, what "belief" in Jesus Christ specifically involves, we are quickly referred to God's establishment of means of grace such as preaching and sacraments. What we have done is to pursue these "means" to a deeper level, proposing that the creation of ecclesia itself with its co-intendings is *the* way in which redemption occurs. The traditional "means" of grace function to build up ecclesia. Intersubjectively speaking, to trust oneself to God in this sense, the sense of Christian faith, means to promise to pursue one's salvation in the matrix of this intersubjectivity. The individual says, in effect, to the other(s) in ecclesia, in your hands I place my very destiny. Compared to this intentional stratum, loyalty to the institution in which ecclesia embodies itself is a far more external and relative matter.

C. The Self-Surpassing Nature of Ecclesia's Intersubjectivity

The aim of this chapter is to describe the intersubjective stratum of ecclesia. In Section B we set forth co-intentionalities which arise with redemptive existence, thereby confining ourselves to descriptions of relations within ecclesia which have no essential referent beyond ecclesia. Yet these immanent or provincial co-intentionalities do not convey the strange novelty of ecclesia as a form of corporate historical existence. In our view this novelty resides in ecclesia's peculiar way of referring beyond itself and its own faith-world to the stranger, the strange other. And this we must now investigate.

1. *Ecclesia as the abolishment of salvation-history*

So far we have conducted our descriptions of redemptive existence by way of an abstraction. We placed in brackets so to speak the whole question of God and with it the issue of the role of God in bringing about redemptive existence. Now we must remove the brackets, not to set forth systematically the theme of God, but in order to explicate the peculiar novelty of ecclesia. The Christian faith like other religious faiths is not a humanism. The modification of existence toward redemption is experienced in relation to the divine presence. This seems to be evident simply from the nature of the problem of self-securing, the endless series of attempts to locate a securing and secure object. Only the transcendent itself breaks this idolatrous power because the transcendent is the only non-idolatrous alternative to chaos as the ultimate context of human life. Assuming that the divine presence is redemptive, the decisive issue becomes the locus of that presence. It would be of little help at this point to propound a typology of the options which world history reveals. With the exception of natural theologies which claim that the divine is present in some a priori way in the constitutive nature of man, most historical faiths resemble each other in claiming to possess necessary institutional conditions of God's redemptive work. In mythopoeic religions the perpetuation of the original divine work of creation occurs through the seasonal and ritualistic performances of the cultus.[7]

In Israel the divine presence is necessarily tied to institutions which God himself establishes. He does not judge and redeem simply through meditative or mystical disciplines or through relations established with individuals. He is present to a people which he himself establishes and with whom he makes a covenant. Individual visions and dreams which occur in this historical faith are received in this covenant framework. God's presence is not only a presence among his people; particular forms of sociality mediate that presence and are necessary to it. In earlier times the "people of God" existed in tribal form, eventually developing into a nation occupying a settled geographical territory. In connection with this national and geographical locus grew institutions of God's presence. The definitive locus of divine presence was Zion, first in the sense of the city of David and then in the more restricted sense of the temple. Other holy places, altars, shrines, and the like became subordinate to the holy city as the definitive locus of God's presence. For it is the people which obeys or disobeys God and from the holy city, with its king and temple, the people are theocratically governed. This locat-

7. Mircea Eliade, *The Sacred and the Profane* (New York: Harper Torchbooks, 1961), chap. 2.

ing and focusing of God's presence is not abandoned in the dispersion. The hope of dispersed Israel is expressed in the imagery of return to the land, the restoration of the nation, the perpetuation of Zion.

To be sure, along with this nation-city-land way of locating God's presence are elements which go beyond this framework. God is not tied to his people and their institutions in the way that the presence of sacred power is tied to the cyclical rituals of animism or totemism. The freedom of God and the historical interpretation of the expression of his freedom combine to make it conceivable that he transcend his own institutions. This suggests that the nation-city has only a relative status as a condition of God's presence. God's universal power and presence make it possible for him to work among other peoples, and his righteousness makes him willing to oppose, even destroy his own city and nation. Although universalism of a sort was a possibility in this historical faith, it was not actualized in the rise of Judaism. Judaism like Israel has remained a closed religious society, not because conversion to Judaism is inconceivable, but because the presence of God remained tied to an ethnic, linguistic, and historical tradition.

Both Jews and Christians will readily agree that the discontinuity of Christian faith from its own historical matrix in Israel is due to the centrality of Jesus in the new community. From the Jewish side this new element means at the worst a new idolatry, a sophisticated polytheism, and at best, a new dogmatic requirement, an intellectualist transformation of *Emunah* into *pistis* or belief.[8] Christian theologians traditionally characterize the novelty and discontinuity represented in Jesus as a deepening or fulfilling of the faith of Israel. To this end they emphasize the radical view of human evil in the teachings of Jesus, reaching into the hidden region of motivations, the need for Torah to be supplemented by grace, and especially the fruit of all this in a new quality of human and interpersonal life, agape, the unique feature of which is the seeking of the other's good regardless of his merit and which seeking rests in the very depths of

8. For instance, Martin Buber, *Two Types of Faith* (London: Routledge and Kegan Paul, 1951).

a transformed human spirit rather than in a moral obligation.[9]

The history of the doctrinal and cultic development of Christianity tends to confirm the Jewish interpretation on both counts. Jesus has been worshiped in idolatrous and quasi-polytheistic senses, and faith has been intellectualized. In our view these distortions adhere to contingent historical pieties and brands of Christendom rather than ecclesia itself. While we would not disagree with the traditional accounts of the discontinuity and novelty introduced in Christian faith, we think they are misleading insofar as they obscure the issue of bounded or provincial conditions of the presence of God. The most striking thing about ecclesia is that the presence of God has absolutely no existing social or ethnic conditions. Ecclesia presupposes no land, no holy nation, no holy city, no geographical center, no central temple, no particular language. In ecclesia Zion is abolished.[10] The breaking of necessary connections between the divine presence and divinely established (or permitted) societal structures, always a possibility in Israel, is actualized in ecclesia.

This being the case, the "people of God" in the sense of ecclesia no longer means the people of a determinate history with its determinate language, social institutions, and religious traditions. Ecclesia in fact replaces the people of God in the sense of a chosen people. This does not mean that ecclesia has no special relation to Israel. Israel is ecclesia's past and matrix. The God of Israel is the God of ecclesia. The Torah of Israel in the sense of an expression of man's transcendental obligation and freedom for others remains the Torah of ecclesia. The imagery of ecclesia concerning evil and redemption, freedom and obligation, occurs in certain ways in Israel. But this continuity is broken insofar as Israel stands for a determinate *ethnic* and national way of remembering God and pursuing his Word. Accordingly, in ecclesia "salvation history" is broken and transcended. *Heilsgeschichte* in the framework of Israel is necessarily the history or story of God's relation with a determinate historical people. Its background is the election of that nation; its con-

9. See Nels F. S. Ferré, *The Christian Fellowship* (New York: Harper and Bros., 1940), chaps. 2 and 3; John Knox, *The Early Church*, pp. 60 ff; John B. Cobb, *Structures*, chap. 11.

10. Zion is retained in the imagery of Christian theology and hymnody but as an eschatological rather than a historical reality.

tinuing basis is his covenant with that nation; and its eschatology with its motifs of restoration and fulfillment is an eschatology of that nation and its enemies. Accordingly, Jew and Gentile is a different kind of distinction from Christian and non-Christian. "Gentile" is the stranger dwelling outside the ethnic and socially bounded tradition. If ecclesia does not refer to any one social unit such as a nation, "non-Christian" or the stranger beyond ecclesia takes on a very different status. To develop this we must now explore specifically the way in which the stranger is present in the co-intentionalities of redemptive existence.

2. *The transformed status of the stranger*

The key to this strange abolition of social and institutional conditions of God's presence is found in the co-intentionalities of redemptive existence. We have provincialistically described these co-intentionalities as occurring within a determinate community. Yet the modification of existence toward redemption is not experienced as an arbitrary adaptation to the customs of a society but as a recovery of what is truly human. If this modification remains true to man's essential or transcendental makeup, its status will go beyond a provincial theology or provincial ethic. Even though the other whom I constitute in these co-intentions is present to me in a concrete social and cultural situation and along with me is shaped by this situation, nevertheless this other is replaceable by *any* human other from any other concrete cultural situation. The only conditions for participation in ecclesia are the religious a priori and disrupted historical existence. When I intend the other through the imagery of redemptive existence, I intend the human as such and therefore the stranger who can replace him or join him. The stranger, the other whose being does not reside in this determinate faith-world, is intentionally present in the intersubjectivity of ecclesia.

But we can take this a step farther. In ecclesia the very being of the person is his modified intersubjectivity of redemptive existence. Ecclesial man is not someone to whose being is added a capacity to perform certain acts such as forgiveness or agape toward others in ecclesia with whom he is in reciprocal relation. Insofar as the power of self-securing is broken and modified by freedom from the other and for the other, this power defines the very being of the participant of ecclesia. Thus, while the matrix of that power is ecclesia and its intersubjective structure, that toward which that power can be directed has no bounds. The new freedom is freedom for the other as such, not simply the other in ecclesia. The new obligation is for the other as such, not simply the ecclesial other.

This is why ecclesia involves a transcending of a provincialist religious community and a startling redefinition of the status of the stranger. In communities dominated by the fear and pride of disrupted historical existence, the stranger is always a threat and potential enemy. Israel, reflecting its own redemptive existence, could see the stranger as one who needs aid on his journey through Israel. If the stranger himself grasps God's redemptive Word, he must enter Israel in the full ethnic sense of the word. Where ethnic and national traditions are necessary to God's presence, the stranger either remains unredeemed or he must be ethnically translated from his own ethnic home-world to the provincially religious home-world. In ecclesia the stranger is appresent not as one who, to be redeemed, must abandon his own home-world but as a potential participant in ecclesia simply because of his disrupted humanity. For in ecclesia the stranger is constituted as one who embodies the transcendental refusals and the suffering of disrupted historical existence. Since interest, delight, and compassion for the other are marks of freedom for the other, the stranger's status is that of fellow-sufferer and potential participant in redemptive existence. The specific effect of this is that contact between ecclesia and strangers beyond ecclesia occurs through freedom-from and freedom-for intentions. Another effect is that, because of the obliteration of salvation-history and provincialist ethnic conditions of God's presence, ecclesia adapts its social and institutional form to the home-world of the stranger and not vice versa. In short participation in ecclesia cannot mean ethnic conversion.[11]

11. The far-reaching effects of the emergence of ecclesia permeate the literature of primitive Christianity. One indication is the resistance to applying the language of messianism to Jesus, either on the part of Jesus himself or early stages of Palestinian Christianity. The problem was that Jesus was not the Messiah in the sense of an ethnically bounded redeemer of Israel. The ecclesial shattering of salvation-history shattered the Messiah of salvation-history. Early Christianity did proclaim Jesus as

Contact with the stranger may or may not occur by means of explicit strategies of evangelization. The intentions themselves are of such a nature that they set up reciprocities which begin to shape the consciousness of the stranger and draw him into the orbit of ecclesia. And no type of human being is excludable, no race, life-style, age group is disqualified. Even the persecuting stranger is intentionally present in ecclesia itself. This is not meant to be a description of the way in which ecclesia spreads or the way in which individuals become a part of it. The point is that the boundary of ecclesia is not that of a provincial religious community, defined by a social unit such as a tribe or nation. The intentional presence of the stranger, the perpetual drawing in of the stranger simply in the reciprocities of everyday life, and the absence of definitive institutional conditions make the boundary of ecclesia unformulatable. The peculiarity of ecclesia is that it is a determinate religious community without boundaries. This is part of the mystery of ecclesia and it accounts for the difficulty of locating and identifying it. Ecclesia is perpetually permeating all the reaches of whatever determinate social world it is a part. For this reason the permeations of the Roman empire by the Christian religion could not have been possible by rabbinical Judaism.

This strange way of relativizing definitive social conditions of the presence of God is also apparent in the specific means through which spreads the religion connected with ecclesia. Since there is no definitive social unit required by ecclesia, it can spread easily across all national, cultural, and linguistic lines. It is no accident that ecclesia can spread simply through testimony. Ecclesia does not require holy wars, massive acculturation, or the transposing of one social unit over another. Paul expresses this when he says that faith comes by hearing. Furthermore, it was Paul who first followed out the logic of ecclesia's strange universality when he insisted that one could be drawn into ecclesia (and faith) without first appropriating

the Messiah but had to mean by Messiah the one whose sufferings and resurrection *universalized* Israel. Further, the new vocabulary for this new historical existence is indicative. Ecclesia itself meant a gathering in which Jesus alone (or his Spirit) was the condition of redemptive existence, hence it cut across all nations and cultural boundaries. The *hagioi* were no particular kind of people but could arise within any class, culture, race, or nation.

the religious and ethnic tradition of Israel. And when early Christianity attempted to account for its own spread, it simply spoke about testimony and the work of the Spirit. We must admit that much of New Testament literature formulates ecclesia provincialis- tically. This is partly because its writings were letters and tracts meant to be circulated among particular congregations whose situation was the focus of the tract. But in spite of these descriptions of *agape* between the brothers (I John), the *charismata* of the Spirit which structure the church organically (I Cor. 12), and the apostle's *koinonia* (Acts 2), the *telos* of ecclesia was always something beyond its present boundaries. As long as the stranger continued to suffer and struggle in the web of human evil, the koinonia of the apostles could not be simply an end in itself. The apostles of Acts 2 enjoyed their koinonia with one eye cast on Asia Minor.

We cannot stress enough that simply immanent relations between participants do not characterize ecclesia's novelty. This is why ecclesia is not simply the community of agape. In fact the peculiar nature of agape in ecclesia is obscured by the stress on its unmotivated capacity to seek the other's good regardless of any quality or merit he may have.[12] Agape in this sense could still be confined to the provincial or closed religous community. Agape's radical character is disclosed only when it is coupled with the repudiation of all determinate social units as conditions of God's presence. In that framework agape's depth, interiority, and disinterest in merit becomes a bridge to the stranger. In agape the stranger is intentionally drawn into ecclesia.

Only now are we ready to recall the traditional language which purports to express ecclesia's uniqueness, the language of "belief in Jesus Christ." I suspect but am not prepared to verify the notion that elements in the ministry and teaching of Jesus anticipate ecclesia. The message of the kingdom of God is so cast that it transcends the salvation-history framework of the holy nation and the holy city. However this turns out, it seems clear that, in primitive Christianity, to "believe in Jesus Christ" meant to enter into a new form of corporate existence, and with that entrance began participation in its co-intentionalities which are directed beyond itself to the stranger. However we account for it, Jesus himself replaced indispensable

---

12. Haroutunian's essay, "The Problem of Love," in *God with Us* offers a powerful polemic against the interpretation of agape as a selfless, self-sacrificial, and unmotivated pursuit of the other's good.

social units of God's presence. To testify to Jesus' Lordship, to confess him as *Christos,* to assign to him such apocalyptic names as Son of Man, were acts signifying his destroying and fulfilling role with regard to the conditions of the divine presence. To put it as bluntly as possible, Jesus replaces Zion as the condition of God's presence. To say that Jesus is universal Lord means that God's Word and presence now crosses all linguistic, racial, and cultic boundaries. We would not, therefore, formulate the decisive features of the new community as grace replacing law or agape replacing external piety and legal conformity. Ecclesia retains Israel's story and imagery with respect to essential human structures and the universal presence of evil. It is true that both agape and grace are stressed in different ways in the kerygma of the new community, but the context of the new emphasis is the redefinition of the stranger. I am not sure how close we have come to isolating and portraying the intersubjectivity of ecclesia, because, as we said before, it is easier to grasp the pluralities, the specific co-intentions, than the unifying motif. Our proposal is that ecclesia means the coming into existence of a corporate, intersubjective consciousness shaped by the co-intentions of redemptive existence in all three of its dimensions and marked by its inclusion of the stranger without imposing ethnic conditions.

The following observations connect this proposal with our present situation. From the very beginning ecclesia's concrete existence is always under the conditions of persistent disrupted historical existence. In Chapter 1 we alluded to the cultic background of reality-loss, calling attention to the present crisis of the social and institutional forms of the church. This crisis appears to be a crisis of ecclesia itself for the following reason. Ecclesia is endangered whenever its participants exchange their freedom for the stranger, for mankind as such, for provincial and immanent communal relationships. This threatens ecclesia in every age because the sociality and provincialism necessary and proper to man's existence (his loyalties to family, nation, race, social class, and the like) are constant occasions of self-securing and idolatry. The irony of the church is that it becomes the basis of a new idolatrous provincialism whereby the stranger is again typed, judged, and excluded. Furthermore, the capacity to intend the stranger in the way proper to ecclesia is tested in concrete ways in different times and places. In Paul's lifetime that test and temptation presented itself in the form of subjecting all men to the tradition and cultus whose reference point remained Zion.

While the following may appear far too general to many, I am convinced that history is now testing the American religious community's capacity to transcend itself toward the stranger by presenting to it one dramatic instance of the stranger in his midst, the oppressed black man. What it means to be ecclesia in any time is the envisioning of the stranger (the weak, suffering, oppressed other) through the imagery of redemptive existence. But what this means in our day is the capacity to envision the oppressed black man in this way, the specific results being the lack of a boundary around the church at this point. More than doctrinal purity, individual moral integrity, or cultic vigor, the status of the oppressed black man is *the* test of whether a church embodies that form of historical existence which we are calling ecclesia. It may not be too farfetched to suspect that the church's role in legitimating slavery in America marked a decisive step in the loss of its ecclesial character, its definition of itself along racial lines. Such is our version of the present crisis in the church, and as in every age that crisis is a moral one.

The church is not above occasionally taking its own pulse, and it does sense that something about itself is wrong. Accordingly, the church is responding to the crisis of its own life in ways that endanger ecclesia even further. One response is the deliberate pursuit of *koinonia* or fellowship. Ironically, such koinonia is an antithesis and perversion of ecclesia because it means the church's attempt to bracket the stranger and enjoy immanent interpersonal relationships pursued in small groups, staged in church gatherings, reclaimed by attempts at "preaching the Bible" or retaining the "pure Gospel." A second response is that of the liberal wing of the church, which, agonizing over the massive corruption and injustice of our society, proposes activist strategies for social and political change. Worthy and necessary as these strategies are, the liberal program ignores the strange intersubjectivity of ecclesia and its self-transcending impetus toward the stranger through the co-intentionalities of redemptive existence. In both cases the church legitimates itself and mollifies its conscience at the expense of ecclesia.

D. ECCLESIA AND INSTITUTIONALIZATION

We have hitherto confined ourselves to a stratum of the church which is pre-institutional, namely, determinate intersubjectivity or ecclesia. Our focus obviously eschews individualistic formulations of the situation of faith which interpret redemption wholly in psychological and existential terms. At the same time, are we not in danger of another form of romanticism also popular in our day, the romanticism of an interpersonal community over against institutionalization which is at best arbitrary and at worst the work of the devil. Although we do give a certain priority to determinate intersubjectivity, we do not see institutionality as an intrinsic corruption. This raises the complex problem of the relation between ecclesia and institutionality. In the following remarks we shall argue for the relativity of specific forms of institutionalization to ecclesia, and at the same time maintain that ecclesia itself retains minimum social features. In the light of these comments we shall indicate why some kinds of institutionalization do not serve but distort ecclesia.

1. The indispensable status of institutionality

"Institution" and "institutionalization" are not the clearest of terms. In Chapter 4 we offered a brief interpretation of institutionalization as the process by which an inclusive social grouping integrated into itself certain human enterprises and their distinctive intersubjectivities. Our example was the integration of marriage into the more inclusive unit of the nation. In addition to the institutions of the inclusive society, sub-groupings in a society also tend to imitate institutionalization. We mean by this that social groupings tend to develop forms of social order needed to guarantee their survival and to implement the purpose of the group. An impetus toward institutionalization exists in any group which wishes any kind of permanence and effectiveness. Because a given group would scarcely retain any continuity apart from repeatable and visible repetitions, it tends to originate customs, rules, organizational structures, rites, and symbols which express and maintain the purpose or purposes of the group. We find institutionalization in this sense in groups as divergent as a suburban fire department and a motorcycle gang. It is this sort of sub-group institutionalization which we have in mind in what follows.

Whatever else it is, ecclesia is a specific form of corporate existence. A certain determinate intersubjectivity is its unique feature, but this intersubjectivity occurs concretely in conjunction with a specific corporate entity. In some sense of the word ecclesia means a specific community. Because this is the case, ecclesia is itself

175

marked by certain social features over and above its intersubjective structure, and it bears in itself an impetus toward institutionalization which necessarily finds some actualization. We are distinguishing, therefore, between the features intrinsic to the sociality of ecclesia and the ever-changing forms of institutionalization which ecclesia undergoes.

A full treatment of ecclesia's intrinsic social features goes beyond our present purpose. I would indicate three such features in order to illustrate our point and to provide a basis for assessing forms of institutional corruption of ecclesia. Most essential to ecclesia is a feature which marks any genuine community; face-to-face reciprocities. Determinate intersubjectivity, the shaping of intersubjective consciousness, takes place primarily although not totally through enduring face-to-face behaviors and relationships. The determinate intersubjectivity of ecclesia is both formed by face-to-face activities and it also determines the quality or tone of these activities. Face-to-face reciprocities comprise a more visible and conscious stratum of ecclesia's sociality than intersubjectivity, reflecting as they do the specific ways human beings are together in the cultus (in cooperative endeavors, in mutual consolation, in teaching and transmitting).

A second feature of ecclesia's sociality, that is, its existence as a specific human community, is *memory*. This motif has become a common one in recent biblical and theological studies.[13] With regard to the complexity and depth of the problem, these studies represent only the beginning stages of possible research. Because ecclesia's historical continuity as well as its meaning in any given present depends upon the retention of its originating events and its originating person, Jesus of Nazareth, memory is a structural aspect of its sociality. More difficult to grasp is the distinctive sense in which memory functions in this community with its specific determinate

13. Walther Zimmerli, "Promise and Fulfillment," in Westermann, *Essays on Old Testament Hermeneutics* (Richmond: John Knox Press, 1963); John Knox, *Jesus: Lord and Christ* (New York: Harper & Row, 1968), pp. 61 ff; Dietrich Ritschl, *Memory and Hope* (New York: Macmillan, 1967); James Gustafson, *Treasures in Earthen Vessels* (New York: Harper & Row, 1961), chap. 6; H. R. Niebuhr, *The Meaning of Revelation* (New York: Macmillan, 1946), pp. 110 ff.

intersubjectivity. This raises the issue of the sense in which ecclesia is constituted by its own "social time."[14] I suspect that the often made distinction between *kairos* and *chronos* is at this point not particularly helpful.

The decisive issue appears to be how memory functions in a religious community whose intersubjectivity has abolished salvation-history. The tendency of recent writers is simply to propose a parallel between the founding events of Israel and the founding or paradigmatic events of ecclesia. This parallel glosses over the fact that Israel's paradigmatic events serve to found a bounded ethnic and national unity. "Memory" in Israel therefore means the persistence of these events within this ethnic bounding. Israel's story is the story of the holy nation even when that nation is dispersed. But the story of ecclesia is not the story of any one societal unit, and therefore its memory is of an unusual genre. To "remember Jesus Christ" is a different act than to "remember the Exodus" or by the waters of Babylon to "remember Zion." To be sure, both are acts of remembering the founding events of a historical faith. But the memory of Exodus is the memory of the event which established the bounded religious community, the holy nation. It is therefore memory from within a faith whose unity has a geographical element. To remember Jesus Christ does not mean remembering the event which established a bounded community but one which disestablished that community and broke all ethnic conditions of God's presence. Therefore, it is not memory from within conditions with a geographical element but from within a universal community. For this reason Jesus remembered as the Christ and as the Lord is not a "founder" of a bounded religious community, and therefore is not a founder in the usual sense of the word. Another difference between remembering the Exodus and remembering Jesus Christ is revealed when we consider that what is remembered are not just the founding events themselves but the subsequent history of the community. In ecclesia the subsequent history is one of ever-changing ecclesial boundaries, fluid

14. For the concept of social time, see Georges Gurvitch, *The Spectrum of Social Time* (Dordrecht, Holland: Reidel, 1964), which is a study of varying forms of social time.

177

interaction with the world of the stranger. To remember Jesus Christ means also to remember this, the continued process of universalization.

A third feature of the sociality of ecclesia is what students of the history of religions call *sacred space*. This too remains for the most part an unexplored area of ecclesia's uniqueness. It seems evident that ecclesia will not simply contain sacred space in the indeterminate sense of phenomenological studies of religion. Because ecclesia involves an intersubjective consciousness in which co-intentions of redemptive existence spill over into the world of the stranger, the provincial way of differentiating the home-world from the alien-world is altered. In one sense ecclesia abolishes sacred spaces insofar as they refer to indispensable and fixed social conditions of the presence of the sacred. The sacral nature of the community is somewhat relativized by the intentional presence of the stranger in ecclesia. This is why ecclesia can permeate so many different social regions without worrying about profanization. The temple, cathedral, or church building is not, therefore, *the* space of ecclesia. Ecclesia's space is more the space of ever-changing boundaries than discrete regions of divine mediation.[15]

Face-to-face reciprocities, social memory, and sacred space are not themselves institutions, but as features of ecclesia's sociality, they do incline ecclesia toward certain kinds of institutionalizations and away from others. As such these features represent only a very general and abstract description of ecclesia's sociality. Insofar as ecclesia refers to a form of historical existence in which the conditions of God's presence are denationalized and universalized, we can say that previous institutional forms are replaced. If nation, land, ethnic people, holy city, and temple served as institutional forms through which God was present in Israel, what replaces them in ecclesia? Since universalization occurs through the death and resurrection of Jesus, it can be said that Jesus replaces Zion as the place of God's presence. Redemption occurs not through the institutions which are

15. Two exceptionally intriguing works on personal space (lived-space) which might be fruitfully employed in pursuing this investigation are Otto F. Bollnow, *Mensch und Raum* (Stuttgart: Kohlhammer, 1963), and Gaston Bachelard, *The Poetics of Space* (Boston: Beacon Press, 1964).

bound up with land, ethnic people, and temple but through Jesus. But how does this effect the cultus itself? How is it that God continues to be present "through Jesus"? Theologically speaking, there is a variety of answers to these questions in primitive Christianity itself. But socially speaking God is present through Jesus by means of witness or testimony to Jesus. And this testimony is extended in the creation of special ordinances through which believers enter the universal community, and by which they remember Jesus, and appropriate the redemption available through him. What it is, therefore, which binds together the general social features of face-to-face reciprocities, social memory, and sacred space are the specific corporate acts of testimony (Word) and sacraments. Are these then definitive institutions of ecclesia? We defined institutionalization as the production of forms of social order needed to guarantee the survival of a group and to implement its purpose. In this sense testimony and sacraments are not pure institutionalizations because their primary function in ecclesia is salvific. Intentionally speaking their function as means of corporate survival is secondary. For this reason they must be distinguished from the ever-changing institutionalizations which do arise to maintain the corporate group in a time of change and crisis such as hierarchical ecclesiastical governance or the store front church.

In addition to these features of sociality which are intrinsic to ecclesia is a complex institutional dimension which occurs when the impetus toward institutionalization generated by ecclesia is actualized in a concrete historical situation. Our term for the totality which combines intersubjectivity, ecclesia's sociality, and institutional structure is *church*. There is in ecclesia an impetus toward institutionalization because of the nature of its intersubjectivity. Redemptive existence and the intention of the stranger create the desire to expand and transmit the Gospel, the need for cultus, and for a ministry of consolation and edification. For these reasons institutionality is not a dispensable appendage to or intrinsic corruption of ecclesia. Nor has ecclesia ever existed apart from some form of institutionalization. In certain periods the institutional form of the church undergoes crisis, disruption, and displacement by new institutions. Therefore, we cannot seriously entertain the view that ecclesia's time of authenticity was in the halcyon days of the disciples and Jesus, or the brief "communist" period after Pentecost following which it corrupted itself by developing institutional forms. Needless to say, institutionalization is dialectically or reciprocally related to the determinate intersubjectivity of ecclesia. Hence, the actual quality of the co-intentions, reciprocities, and face-to-face activities is different in the monastic order, the sect group, the suburban church, and a denominational bureaucracy.

2. The relative status of institutionality

Having observed that ecclesia has certain intrinsic social features and that it continually seeks and actualizes institutional embodiment, we now pursue in more detail the relation between ecclesia and institutionality. Our general thesis is that while ecclesia requires some institutionalization, specific forms of institutionalization are not intrinsic to ecclesia as such. This relativity is qualified to the extent that some forms threaten or tend to destroy ecclesia while others are more adaptable to its purposes. Such adaptability depends on the extent to which the institutional form retains the features of ecclesia's sociality.

We begin by recalling that ecclesia as a form of religious existence abolishes all inclusive social and ethnic units as necessary conditions of the presence of God. This means that ecclesia's relation with these units is first of all non-competitive. Built into ecclesia's very nature and *telos* is the refusal to be an inclusive social unit; hence, the refusal to attempt to displace the inclusive units of government, leisure, etc. Furthermore, because the redemptive existence which it bears addresses the problematic of man as such, it eschews any attempt to displace those institutions which meet some specific human need; education, family, etc. Institutional imperialism is foreign to ecclesia. On the other hand, ecclesia's constitution of the stranger as disrupted and potentially redeemable existence produces another sort of imperialism. As a determinate intersubjectivity ecclesia tends to infiltrate and thereby modify all the institutions of its particular social world.

When we consider ecclesia's own institutionalizing propensity, we find a utilitarian relation between ecclesia and institutional embodiment. These embodiments are solutions to problems which ecclesia itself has (survival, continuity, transmission) in a particular time and place. Both the problems themselves and the available institutional materials change from one historical period to the next. Hence, the problem of survival and transmission was a very different one in the early Middle Ages than on the American frontier. Also different were the available "materials" for institutionalizing. The history of the church confirms this relativity. Its constant search for new institutional embodiment has resulted in a plethora of institutional forms all the way from the monastery to the circuit rider. These institutionalizations are relative not only because they reflect a specific historical situation but because of their distance from the social features intrinsic to ecclesia. For example, face-to-face relationship is more intrinsic to ecclesia than monastic organization, a denominational committee structure, or a Sunday school.

The only relation we have observed so far between ecclesia and the institutionality which it generates is a utilitarian one. Ecclesia makes use of available institutional forms to implement its own purposes. We must now qualify this twofold analysis of intrinsic social features and relative institutionality. Because ecclesia involves redemptive existence and an openness to humanity at large, certain forms of institutionalization can enter ecclesia only at the price of conflict and tension. For instance, institutionalization which results in a closed and provincial society, excluding the stranger on the basis of the stranger's race or ethnic heritage, imperils if not destroys ecclesia. A positive version of this essentially negative formulation is that ecclesia tends to transform those features which are present in institutionalized social groupings. It is a step forward when theologians acknowledge and defend the inevitability and appropriateness of such institutional features in the church as political power.[16] But one receives the impression from such accounts that politics is drawn into the church from the society at large without being affected by the *telos* of ecclesia. Since ecclesia is not simply an ideality but reflects disrupted historical existence, it can and does tolerate institutionalizations which conflict with its own *telos*. For this reason

16. Gustafson, *Treasures,* chap. 3.

there is empirical confirmation for these perspectives. However, this interpretation ignores the tendency of ecclesia to transform what it takes from the larger society. Accordingly, the typical interior political activities that occur in the church may not have the nature of negotiations between party caucuses insofar as the purpose of the institution is guided by a universal reference to mankind. Even if something like parties, caucuses, even *coups,* arise in the church, their status tends to be provisional, and the impetus from the depths of ecclesia's intersubjectivity is to displace them for more appropriate modes of political power.

3. *Ecclesia in peril*

Our interpretation of ecclesia as a perpetually open community leaves us with an obvious yet terrible problem, one which we can raise but are not prepared to resolve. Ecclesia names an actual historical existence, not a mere ideality. Could it be that ecclesia aborted at the time of its birth? If so, ecclesia is more the *telos* of the church, toward which the redemptive existence and its imagery disposes the church but which disrupted existence has so far prevented. If this is the case, ecclesia is an eschatological dimension of church. Or is ecclesia an ever-present hidden dimension of church, whose presence is responsible for cycles of church renewal? Whichever alternative we choose, it seems evident that disruptive historical existence persists in redemptive existence. The specific symptom of this is the church's temptation in every age to settle for or pursue something other than ecclesia and to exchange ecclesia for other modes of sociality. This exchange has taken two major forms, one primarily ancient (institutionalism) and one distinctively modern (individualism).

Individualism, the contemporary form of the church's repression of its ecclesial dimension, is so close to us, so very much a part of us that it is almost beyond thematization. A major feature of contemporary historical consciousness, it is one of the few features shared between contemporary Christendom and its "alienated" theologians. Most present-day theologies are individualistic and seem to be becoming more so. Hence, they all share with each other at least one common characteristic, the omission of ecclesia in the formulation of the situation of faith and the pursuit of theological themes.[17] In the light of this almost universal omission, we should not be surprised that frustration, alienation, career-change, scholarly disillusion, and virulent anti-theology characterize so many theologians themselves. Nor should it be necessary to demonstrate the reigning individualism of Protestant life and piety. Nothing could be clearer than that the institutionality of present-day Protestantism is ordered toward the individual, his sins, guilt, grief, and misery. Such is the thrust of Protestant preaching, both conservative and liberal. The least serious product of this is that everything about the Christian faith undergoes a strange distortion within individualism. The very meaning of evil and redemption are transformed out of the structure of interdependence, presupposed by the imagery of faith, into individual, moral situations. The most serious product of individualism is that it is the one element in Protestant piety most responsible for the demonic role of specific Protestant congregations in the decay of our civilization and in the real moral issues that demand clear-cut decisions. Protestant individualistic man is a specific kind of human being which has arisen in history. Individualism is the background of the two most prominent features of this historical man, biblicism and legalism. This human being sees sin and guilt in wholly individual terms and also redemption. Unable to grasp the way in which human corporateness shapes the consciousness in evil and good, he responds to the cries of the American ghetto, the Third World, and the poor in terms of individual initiative, desert, and guilt. Having lost sight of his own corporately shaped evil and ecclesial redemp-

17. John Cobb's *Structures* attempts to restore the ecclesial element to the theological enterprise, but this is not typical of the Whiteheadian theologies. The lack of interest in the communal dimension of experience on the part of linguistic, existential, and radical theologies is too prominent to need documentation. The result has been a concern for "religious language" but without ecclesia, existence without ecclesia, and "understanding" without ecclesia. Ecclesia is present in some way in one strand of contemporary Protestant theology, the contextualism of H. Richard Niebuhr and Paul Lehmann. While ecclesia may be the central concern of these two theologians in their version of the "context," it tends to drop out of sight in the "contextualist ethics" which they inspired, being replaced by an amalgam of individual decision-making and its morphology and the everchanging cultural situation. For the most part Protestant social ethicists and sociologists of the church seem largely unconcerned with pre-institutional forms of faith's corporate existence.

tion, he responds to the moral issues raised by oppressed peoples through a callous and desensitized conscience.

The second way ecclesia's birth is aborted, its reality hidden, is the lust for institutional bounding. Hardly had ecclesia appeared in history when its participants were working overtime to establish a new Zion, a new definitive geographical center of God's Word and presence. The result was the claim that the new and definitive corporate entity which entered history as the matrix of redemption was not ecclesia but a new institution, the existence of which was the absolute and indispensable condition of faith and redemption. An irrefutable apologetic defended this new institution by legitimating and sanctifying it from its own tradition which is traced to God himself. This is why the most serious distortion of faith that arose in the early centuries was not "hellenization" or even the rise of a central authority, but the return to redemption conditioned by and mediated by a definitive institution. With the rise of this institution, the depth levels of both faith and ecclesia tended to be lost. For the institution claimed for itself the power to define faith's articulations and ecclesia's necessary institutionalizations. Although the Reformation was in part a protest against this self-appropriated status, its biblicism coupled with traditional understandings of authority drove it to search for a definitive institutionalization founded on the Bible. It failed to notice therefore the utilitarian relation between ecclesia and its institutional forms. Hence, in both Catholic and Protestant forms of Christianity ecclesia itself tended to remain hidden and vulnerable to the strange distortions with which we have become accustomed.

The central distortion is always the exchange of ecclesia for a closed and provincial religious community. Insofar as this occurs, the church can reflect but hardly challenge the repudiation of the stranger which is characteristic of nations, ethnic groups, or social clubs. It is customary to observe the church's conformity to the general culture at the point of legitimating its affluence, war-making, and racism. Our point is that one root of such conformity is the identification of church with definitive and ancient ("biblical") social forms, thus losing sight of the distinctive intersubjectivity which is ecclesia. This is the central displacement which threatens if not

184

disperses ecclesia's intrinsic social features. Face-to-face relation is displaced by the anonymity of the large and economically successful (non)congregation. Individual piety and religious experiences replace collective memory. Provincial space and concern for fellowship replace the space perpetually drawing in the stranger.

It should be evident that the view of ecclesia in this chapter involves both Catholic and Protestant elements. In our interpretation ecclesia is *the* saving entity, that which God introduces into history by means of which redemptive existence transcends the bounds of a determinate culture. With Cyprian we would say that outside ecclesia there is no salvation. But our formulation is Protestant in that we think the doctrine of the definitive institution transfers what is definitive from the dimension of ecclesia to the relative dimension of institutionalization.

Chapter 8

THE SOCIAL MEDIATION OF REALITY

Individual Experience, therefore, must abide with us to the very end of our quest, as one principal and fundamental source of insight. But it is one aspect only of Religious Experience. We shall learn to understand and to estimate it properly only when we have found its deeper relations with our Social Experience.[1]

But so far as such communities both exist and are distinctly recognisable as religious in their life and intent, they form a source of religious insight to all who come under their influence. Such a source acts as a means whereby any or all of our previous sources may be opened to us, may become effective, may bear fruit. Hence, in this new source, we find the crowning source of religious insight.[2]

Josiah Royce

Having characterized the matrix of faith as ecclesia, a determinate community with a language, existence, and intersubjectivity of its own, our next inquiry concerns the function of ecclesia as the mediator of realities. Our inclusive contention is that the realities to which faith is directed accompany the shaping of a consciousness toward redemption, which shaping occurs by virtue of participation in that kind of intersubjectivity we are calling ecclesia. This presupposes that realities can be "socially" mediated, that, in fact, the phrase,

1. Josiah Royce, *The Sources of Religious Insight* (Edinburgh: T. and T. Clark, 1912), p. 34.
2. Ibid., p. 276.

"the social mediation of reality" makes sense. The social distribution if not determination of reality appears now to have almost universal acceptance. Our thesis, however, goes beyond this consensus. We are not simply presupposing that reality is "influenced," distributed, or conditioned by society, but that determinate social forms of human existence actually mediate reality. The ecclesial mediation of the realities of faith is not restricted to ecclesia alone but is an instance of something that happens throughout the human community. We shall attempt in this chapter to explicate this phenomenon, trying to clarify and justify the phrase *the social mediation of reality*.

Reality apprehension has a twofold structure. Content which is directly intuited, be it a space-time object, a mathematical formula, or a consciousness-act, always "appresents" other aspects of itself and its context. Grasping a presented object always involves grasping in some way or other its appresented aspects and field.[3] We shall organize our exploration of the social mediation of reality according to these two aspects. We shall explore the function of a determinate sociality in mediating directly grasped realities and shall then propose our own version of how a social entity involves appresented realities. We must do this because, in our opinion, the reality mediations of ecclesia involve this very structure. In fact apart from the presentational and appresentational functions of ecclesia, we miss the distinctiveness of reality apprehension in the community of faith.

A. THE SOCIAL MEDIATION OF "REALITIES AT HAND"

1. *The problem beyond the problem of the sociology of knowledge*

Today, a corporate interpretation of knowledge is an invitation for misunderstanding, not because of the rarity but because of the abundance of such interpretations which range from sensitivity groups to the sociology of knowledge. We may better clarify our proposal by contrasting it with the sorts of insights offered by the sociology of knowledge. The term *sociology of knowledge* retains a certain ambiguity because it connotes both the social explanation of *what is taken for* knowledge in a society and the investigation of social conditions

3. See Section B of this chapter for an exposition of appresentation.

necessary to genuine knowledge.[4] In the latter approach sociology of knowledge in the pre-Scheler sense tended to vindicate the prevailing relativism and its by-product of skepticism. Insofar as knowledge is servant of ideology and the struggle for power, it is accounted for by something other than its own nature and object. Insofar as sociology of knowledge takes seriously the critique of relativism, it hesitates to claim to be an "explanation" of genuine knowledge and falls back to the more modest program of the social background of what is given the status of knowledge in a society. The problem ceases to be that of the corporate conditions of genuine cognitive acts and becomes the sociological problem of how that to which a society grants the status of knowledge obtains that status. What are the social conditions of whatever it is a society takes for granted as true? What are the social processes behind a society's cognitive consensus? Because the actual truth or falsity of this consensus is not an issue, a more accurate term for much of this literature would be *sociology of belief*.

In the work of Alfred Schutz the sociology of knowledge takes a slightly different turn and becomes the investigation of the social dimensions and conditions of *everyday* knowledge, knowledge which is taken-for-granted in the life-world. Drawing heavily on Husserl, Schutz describes everyday knowledge as occurring through typifications according to systems of relevance. These elements are found in every determinate social world, and a religious community is no exception. Certain basic axioms pervade the cognitive consensus of the religious community which are presupposed by its more visible beliefs, customs, and taboos. These axioms are rarely if ever subjected to critique since they found and guide the critique which occurs in the community. In the light of Schutz's refinement, we reformulate the problem. Do the taken-for-granted typicalities (what is *taken* for knowledge) of a social world necessarily involve genuine

---

4. The ambiguity reflects a divergence in the literature between the early relativistic treatments of the social background of knowledge as in Marx, Nietzsche, or Dilthey, in which sociology of knowledge is a social and psychologistic relativizing of knowledge (psychologism) and Scheler's *Wissenssoziologie* which attempts to overcome such relativism. Cf. Peter L. Berger and Thomas Luckman, *The Social Construction of Reality* (New York: Doubleday and Co., 1966), Introduction.

apprehensions? Because these typicalities include a mass of arbitrarily embraced claims, some of which like racism are expressions of disrupted historical existence, the answer must be negative. How then can the genuine and the spurious be differentiated in what is taken for knowledge in a determinate social world? Contemporary Western man has of course a ready answer and one which expresses one of his own typifications. Repeated practical confirmations refined by experimental methods separates the spurious from the genuine. Since typifications of what Schutz calls the paramount reality of everyday life serve as the presuppositions of every science and all verification, this answer does not directly confront the question. We recall Husserl's argument that the sciences are based on the life-world and its immediate insights rather than the other way around.

The primacy of the life-world in knowledge has a theological counterpart. Although theology may engage in critique of spurious religious beliefs which occur in the faith-world, it is like the sciences in that its insights by which it engages in critique originate in the faith-world. If these insights or apprehensions are themselves established as genuine by theology, then the academic or intellectual dimension ends up founding itself and serving as its own object. It seems clear that we have a problem before us which cannot be solved within the framework of the sociology of knowledge. Sociology of knowledge inquires into the conditions of what is taken for knowledge in a specific social world. Our problematic pushes us to ask, how does the depth stratum of a social world (determinate intersubjectivity) mediate realities, playing therefore an indispensable role in reality-apprehension? Our thesis is that the faith-world like the life-world contains typicalities rooted in apprehensions, and these apprehensions occur in conjunction with the pre-reflective sociality of the faith-world. We must now determine what this means.

2. *Two levels of the social mediation of reality at hand*

We emphasize again that the problem of this exploration is neither the transcendental intersubjective conditions of knowledge as such (Husserl) nor the social conditions of what a society happens to

189

regard as cognitive.[5]   Our general thesis is that determinate social worlds mediate reality in ways unique to themselves.   We find a hint of this in one of the few passages in which Husserl takes up determinacy.   "Each man understands first of all, in respect of a core and as having its unrevealed horizon, *his* concrete surrounding world or *his* culture; and he does so precisely as a man who belongs to the community fashioning it historically.   A deeper understanding, one that opens up the horizon of the past (which is co-determinant for an understanding of the present itself), is essentially possible to all members of that community, with a certain originality possible to them all/and barred to anyone from another community who enters into relation with theirs."[6]   Husserl's point is that actual participation in a concrete or determinate social world is an indispensable condition of apprehending that world in its concreteness.   Schutz presupposes this axiom in his insightful descriptions of the problem faced by an immigrant to a new culture and also a war veteran returning to an altered home-world.[7]

In the correlation between special insight and social determinacy our thesis finds partial illustration.   According to this interpretation a determinate social world does mediate reality, namely, the reality of its own determinateness.   In a determinate social world with its determinate intersubjectivity we do have something unreducible to anything else.   Being, one might say, takes this shape in this time and place.   In this sense a native of Micronesia, a Wall Street broker, and a member of a submarine crew all exist in (possibly overlapping) determinate social worlds whose reality is imbibed simply in the continual decision-making, the exercise of skills, the obeying of taboos, and the internationalization of language patterns.   We reject, therefore, the claim that social determinacy falls outside of being and is "unreal."   Instead of being a mere perspective on reality, social

5. The social and interpersonal conditions of knowledge as such have been a frequent theme in phenomenological literature.   An elaboration of Husserl's position is found in Remy C. Kwant's *Encounter* (Pittsburgh: Duquesne University Press, 1960), especially chaps. 2 and 3.   Kwant argues for the priority of interpersonal relations to knowledge of the world.

6. *Meditations,* p. 133.

7. "The Stranger: an essay in social psychology," and "The Homecomer," in *Collected Papers,* III (The Hague: Nijhoff, 1966).

determinacy is itself a way in which historical being has come to be. There is no reason to give reality status to the determinate regions of nature and deny it to the human being. We suspect that the reason for the denial is the special hermeneutical problem which social determinacy presents, the problem of *Geisteswissenschaften*.

Our example of the interpersonal aspect of marriage is corroborative. The participants in that relation prehend through their continuing relationship the peculiar and ever-changing features which characterize their co-intendings of each other. In this sense a religious community involves apprehensions which accompany pre-reflective participation in that community, namely, the apprehension of the novel, social determinacy of the community itself including the form of interhuman existence present in it. This is the weakest sense in which a determinate social world mediates reality.

A second and stronger sense in which apprehensions accompany participation in a determinate social world involves the power of a social world to bring into existence unique *perceptivities*. Such a statement presupposes that human consciousness is not merely a retainer of memories but acquires an ever-accumulating shape or structure. This accumulating structure is not merely the general structure of all human consciousness because through time it becomes more and more concrete, more and more itself out of the memories, experiences, and decisions of the determinate social world in which these occurred. This accumulation of experience into an ever-enlarging structure makes the temporality of human consciousness not unlike other entities in process. Because of the particularity of this accumulating structure, consciousness is predisposed in some ways and not others. Gradations of importance are built into it which ground specific acts of evaluating, deciding, rejecting, changing one's mind, etc. This concrete predisposing-toward makes consciousness perceptive (Whitehead's term is *prehend*) in and through its determinate shape. We are using perceptivity here to mean a power or capacity in the consciousness to prehend or apprehend, a power which varies with the particular structure of consciousness.

How does a consciousness shaped by the combination of self-transcending freedom and a determinate social world serve as the locus of perceptivity? Although a full analysis is not appropriate here, two suggestions should suffice for our purpose. First, the particular social world effects in consciousness what Schutz would call *1* the systems of relevance, that is, grades of importance and interest. When a persisting interest combines with the reception of facts, information, and typifications of experience, the result is the capacity to bring into the foreground what otherwise remains amorphous, hidden, or entangled in the complex interweaving of the background. In this sense ornithologists, politicians, and poets have special perceptivities.

Second, interpretations of human consciousness perpetrate a mis- *2* leading abstraction when they ignore what Ricoeur describes as the "fault" running through historical human being. Accordingly, the operations and powers of human consciousness are marked by a rift which separates the human being from his own ideality. In the language of the Hebrew-Christian story, human life occurs between Fall and eschaton and is characterized by both disruption and hope. We must add to this the rather obvious fact that a universal disruption will effect man's perceptive powers. In short the powers of perceptivity are dulled by human bondage. The predispositions which would open up reality or dimensions of reality become themselves at the mercy of those deeply rooted inclinations of man to secure himself at all costs, to render himself and his home-world beyond criticism, to establish himself by sheer power, authority, manipulation, violence, and ridicule toward the other human being. For example, racism, that most prominent expression of the fault in American life, is characterized by a certain imperceptiveness in which the black man is the invisible man. This racial imperceptiveness begins with the incapacity to "see" the black man, but eventually permeates the life-world, creating religious, moral, and political imperceptiveness. Conversely, insofar as a determinate social world includes traditions, imagery, interpersonal relations, and laws which express its attempt to address human bondage, it creates new powers of perceptivity. Or to return to our earlier expression, a consciousness is shaped in which new predispositions begin to modify the old bondages.

How does the effecting of new perceptivities differ from the weaker sense in which a determinate social world mediates reality? In the weaker sense the modification of consciousness in a determinate social world opened up an otherwise hidden region of reality, namely, the determinate social world itself. But when new perceptivities are created, they range beyond the social world in which they are effected into various alien-worlds, their objects, structures, and symbolic systems. An alien-world can be another contemporary determinate social world, geographical region, a former historical time and people. In order to see how the powers of perceptivity transcend their own determinate social world, we must recall our distinction between the determinate social world and the ontological features of the human being which are present but hidden within it. For instance, the human being is a structurally open being, a self-transcending being, even if he lives in a social world as a slave. And whatever the social world, the human being is constituted in some way by awareness of his own finitude and eventual death. In the weaker sense of social knowledge, one might grasp the concrete nuances of the particular culture which is divided into slaves and freemen but remain unaware of certain of these ontological features which constitute his own reality. In fact the social world's very determinacy may effect an interior bondage which obscures these features. Therefore, a slave may simply interiorize the society's legitimations of slavery and see nothing about slavery which contradicts his being, missing entirely the self-transcending center of his being. Conversely, a determinate social world may also so shape the consciousness that a perceptiveness is effected which is able to sense certain ontological features of the human being. For instance, the determinate intersubjectivity of a small primitive village may create "antennae" which are sensitive to those universal ontological features which comprise the transition from childhood to adulthood lost sight of in a more sophisticated civilization. Scheler claims for instance that human historical development toward "higher" stages of civilization also involves a loss of certain capacities. Animals and primitive man as well as children have a certain power of grasping the identity of an alien pattern of life, a power which atrophies in adults and in more advanced stages of civilization.[8]

8. *The Nature of Sympathy,* trans. Peter Heath (London: Routledge and Kegan Paul, 1954), pp. 30–31.

B. Toward an Intersubjective Theory of Appresentation

It should be clear by now that our concern has not been with "knowing" in the sense of deliberate reflective or investigatory acts but with reality-apprehensions which necessarily precede such acts, on which they build and to which they must always refer. Accordingly, faith's apprehensions are more akin to perception than reflection, inference, inquiry, or clarification. In the previous section we tried to indicate that the situation of faith does involve the direct or originary apprehension of certain realities, realities which are "at hand" and which are susceptible to direct confirmation. Perception, however, even in the narrowest sense of the word, is not simply originary apprehension. Husserl's most significant contribution to the philosophy of perception is the insight that directly presented objects of perception include *appresented* references. We shall argue in Chapter 9 that the cognitivity of faith retains this double structure of presentation and appresentation. Anticipating this argument, we must first set forth appresentation in its original Husserlian form and in its application by Alfred Schutz.

1. *The genesis of appresentation in Husserl's early philosophy: appresented aspects of perceived objects*

The term *appresentation* occurs in English translations of Husserl's works in the fifth Cartesian Meditation in connection with Husserl's empathy theory of the knowledge of other minds. Nevertheless, both the term and the concept come from earlier periods of Husserl's writings.[9] The concept functions in connection with two different philosophical inquiries, the nature of perception and the problem of other minds. Husserl developed the concept in his

9. The concept first occurs in the *Investigations* (vol. II, Invest. I, sec. 23; Invest. VI, 3d sec., secs. 4 and 5) in connection with Husserl's treatment of apperception, and it is found in various passages throughout his works on the theme of perception. The terms themselves, *Appräsenz, Kompräsenz,* and *mitpräsentieren,* occur in *Ideen* II, written in the same pre–1913 period as *Ideen* I, and in connection with the constitution of other psychic lives and personal bodies. (See *Ideen* II, secs. 44 and 45.) Although it is difficult to ascertain exactly when the various segments of *Erfahrung und Urteil* were written, collected as they were by Landgrebe after Husserl's death, the section on the horizontal structure of experience (sec. 8) is also pertinent to the concept of appresentation. These passages plus secs. 50–54 of the *Meditations* are our sources for this interpretation.

analysis of perception and used it in his attempt to solve the problem of the knowledge of other minds, a development which may have created more confusion than clarity. In the early works the *idea* of appresentation enters in connection with Husserl's altered interpretation of apperception, and even in the *Meditations* he tends to use apperception and appresentation interchangeably.[10] We shall begin our exposition with a brief review of the term *apperception* in order to see how Husserl modified it for his own purposes. Although apperception comes from a French verb used by Descartes (*apercevoir*), its first technical use occurs in Leibniz who needed a term to show that our grasp of our own inner states is a different sort of act than ordinary perception.[11] The theme of apprehending our own consciousness-acts is prominent in British empiricism, but it was Kant who made apperception a major operative principle. Furthermore, Kant introduced the important distinction between *empirical* apperception, in which the ordinary and constantly changing acts and contents of consciousness are apprehended, and *transcendental* apperception, in which we grasp the unity and structure of the consciousness which is necessary to and the condition of our grasping of any presented object whatever.[12] The consensus which ruled from Leibniz to Kant was that external matters of fact and "inner states" appear in different modes, namely, through perception and apperception. In the *Investigations* Husserl departs from this consensus by rejecting the identification of perception with the perception of externally presented entities and apperception with the grasp of inner states. The traditional view, according to Husserl, obscures the way in which apperception is a necessary structural aspect of perception itself. At this point enters Husserl's modification of apperception toward appresentation.

10. Meditations, sec. 53, sec. 54.

11. See Leibniz, "Principles of Nature and Grace," sec. 4, in *The Philosophical Works of Leibniz,* trans. George Martin Duncan (New Haven: Tuttle, Morehouse & Taylor, 1890).

12. *Critique of Pure Reason,* trans. N. K. Smith (London: Macmillan, 1961), pp. 135 ff. Husserl follows Kant in sharply distinguishing psychological (introspective) re-presentations of the consciousness and transcendental reduction, but he does not use the Kantian terminology of empirical and transcendental apperception.

In order to describe this modification we must at least briefly touch upon certain aspects of Husserl's philosophy of perception. For Husserl perception differs from mere sensation partly because perception always involves grasping an object as an intended totality or noema which can then be subject to *re*-presentation and, if perceived again, be perceived as *that* object. That this is possible not only requires certain continuities in the object itself but a certain accomplishment on the part of consciousness by which the disparate aspects of the object are gathered together into a unity. To perceive an object is to *mean* a unity of some sort. To perceive a red ball is therefore not merely to receive sensations of red color, of spherical shape, of plastic material, each sensation unrelated to the other and unsynthesized. An ant crawling over a red ball does not perceive a red ball. In other words a meaning-conferring act is necessary to perception.[13] Involved in this view of perception is the intentional structure of consciousness-acts which Husserl later elaborated in his doctrine of noesis-noema, the noema being the *meant* unity of the object which could be retained whatever that object's empirical fate.

What does meaning-conferring have to do with apperception, i.e., appresentation? For Husserl part of the essence of perception is presentation, *something* is presented. But the object in its actual totality and unity is never presented. In our actual visual apprehending, only a portion of the total object is presented. We see the face of the object but not the sides, back, or interior. Seeing a red ball is not a simultaneous grasping of the uniform red surface covering the total object. Yet when we perceive something, we do not identify what is perceived with simply the facade of the object directly viewed, as if perceived objects were like the fabricated towns of western movies. We view directly a facade, but we *intend* a total object. We fill out, in an analogizing act which owes its possibility to the imagination, the yet un-sensed portions of the object before us. These un-sensed portions are not directly presented but are appresent. They are present in the mode of appresence. It is only because of appresentation that, when one hears certain sounds, he hears them as sounds of a *symphony orchestra*. Furthermore, ac-

13. See the *Investigations,* vol. II, Invest. I, chap. 2 for Husserl's inquiry into meaning-bestowing acts.

cording to Husserl, appresentation (or apperception which was his term in the *Investigations*) occurs both in external and inner perception; hence, apperception cannot be restricted to either empirical or natural objects or to transcendental consciousness.[14] Although Husserl has in these analyses altered the traditional meaning of the term *apperception,* our focus is less on terminology than on the new dimension of perception which Husserl's inquiry has disclosed.

2. *Appresentation and the problem of other minds*

Although appresentation originally had to do with perception, Husserl sensed that it might help overcome the solipsism which tends to threaten all transcendental philosophy. In *Ideen* II, "phenomenological studies in constitution," Husserl explores the way in which the human being "bestows meaning" upon and constitutes spheres of nature, psychic reality, and spirit. In this work we find the early stages of an argument elaborated later in the *Meditations.* He begins by differentiating *Urpräsenz* and *Appräsenz.*[15] *Urpräsenz* means what is before us in an originary or immediate way. He means by this simply a directly presented entity, be it a tree before my eyes or some inner feeling of which I am aware. *Appräsenz* is that which is only indirectly present, co-present to what is directly present. In a second step Husserl differentiates two kinds of originary presence. In the first are entities which in their very nature are potentially present to *any* and *every* subject in an originary mode. The most obvious examples are space-time objects. And this provides Husserl with the clue as to how man constitutes *nature* as a distinctive region, namely, as a realm of space-time objects able to be present in principle to a multiplicity of subjects. But there is a second kind of originary presence. The temporal flow of an individual consciousness is present in an originary way (*Urpräsenz*) to the person himself, but it is not and can never be present in that way to another subject. This peculiarity discloses the distinctive nature of the whole sphere of subjectivity, animal or human. The mental states, consciousness-acts, the immediate experience of one's own personal body, the noematic correlates of consciousness-acts are all origi-

14. Ibid, vol. I, pp. 309 ff., and vol. II, pp. 859–60.
15. *Ideen* II, no. 44.

narily present to the subject himself and only appresent to other subjects.

It is at this point that Husserl's notion of appresence undergoes expansion and development although not without certain difficulties and obscurities. Appresented aspects of a space-time object present themselves in the mode of *possible* confirmation. This suggests that while presence is self-evident, appresent entities require confirmation ‒ before they can found judgments. If this is the case, the appresent seems to be no different from what is presumed or hypothesized. This in turn implies that the grasping of the appresent is in a predominantly intellectual act of inferring. At this point Husserl seems ambiguous. He fluctuates between describing appresentative apperception as a genuine intuition and as a presumption yet to be confirmed. If the latter is definitive, appresentation represents little more than the discovery of the way analogy is present in the very heart of perception itself. Husserl's description of apperception as an "analogizing transfer" seems to confirm this.[16] In the *Investigations* Husserl argued that sense-contents provided the analogical building material which founds the act of meaning which goes beyond it.[17] In the *Meditations* he describes the apprehension of another's body as a living organism like our own as an "analogizing apprehension." This reflects his view that we first constitute the sphere of our own living organism and subjectivity and transfer this analogically to another. On the other hand, Husserl explicitly denies that apperception is an act of *inference* from analogy.[18] It is an intuition "at a glance" as when a child apprehends an object on the table as a pair of scissors. The condition of this direct apperceptive reception is that prior to this a meant-object, scissors, was constituted. This seems to place Husserl's argument on a solid basis because the initial constituting of a sense object would have involved an exploration of various aspects of the object, each of which was originarily present when explored.

This assessment, however, misses the thrust of Husserl's argument. An object's "reality" or "being" is never simply the sum total of

16. *Meditations*, p. 111.
17. *Investigations*, vol. I, p. 310.
18. *Meditations*, p. 111.

directly experienced aspects. We never directly experience all the aspects of any object, and yet we do "mean" a unified entity when we perceive it as, let us say, scissors or red ball. Apperception is, therefore, not simply a term for one's presumption that other experienceable aspects of an object which we have directly experienced at some time or other are part of that object. In that interpretation appresence is intended only to the degree that it once was in the mode of presence. Most of the aspects of an object are never directly experienced (its molecular structure, the constant flow and collisions of its microscopic particles, its perpetual molecular interchange with molecules in the air making its boundary an indistinct and ever-changing one).

Apperception is that act in which we actually intuit components of an object which are co-present with its directly grasped facade and which are necessary to meaning or intending the object as a unity. This statement is elusive because it speaks of an actual intuition which is nevertheless indirect or mediate. The issue at the heart of this ambiguity is, Can there be a "mediate apprehension"? When I perceive a red ball, I do not directly intuit its interior. Therefore, the specific features of that interior remain unknown and subject to hypothesis. Do I conclude from this that there might possibly be no interior at all? Insofar as I have directly perceived by touch and sight enclosing sides, an interior-less ball is inconceivable. Although I do not in any way perceive the interior of the ball, I do intuit it as something *necessarily* co-present to the aspects which I am directly sensing, necessary to the kind of facade before me. While my judgment about the content of the interior (hollow, solid, plastic, etc.) may have the status of hypothesis to be confirmed in the future, my judgment that this object has an interior is not a hypothesis which could possibly be disconfirmed. That is, given this kind of object, there must be an interior co-present with its enclosing sides. The object so to speak "demands" its appresented aspect. Hence, appresentation differs from mere associations or "pairings" made on the basis of repetitive exposures to two things because of a strange a priori element. My pairing of a banker and personal wealth is an association but not a true appresentation. An impoverished banker is at least conceivable even if unlikely. On the other hand, the banker appresents to me a human physiological interior, a conscious self, and a "field" which includes vaults, deposits, loans, and the like, all of which I may have grasped by way of experience, but which are related to the banker in an a priori way. Insofar as appresentation involves grasping this a priori structure, it is more like an intuition than a hypothesis or inference.

However, the application of appresentation to the problem of solipsism (how the other is constituted) involves showing how one kind of entity can appresent an entity or sphere of reality *on a different level from itself*. We find this line of thought as early as the *Investigations* in Husserl's argument that language and its signs function in appresentative ways. At one level a spoken word is simply a physical object, a production of sound waves. However, it is not that physical object to which we attend but that to which it refers. When Husserl took up the problem of how human beings constitute the other as a living organism and conscious subject, he applied appresentation not in the restricted sense of appresented aspects of perceived objects where the appresented aspects were of the same level of reality as the presenting aspects, but in the sense of one level of reality appresenting a sphere which transcends the presenting level. Thus, the heard speech, bodily movements, and gestures of the other person appresent to us a personal body and consciousness like our own. In one sense the situation resembles our grasp of the appresented interiority of the red ball. We become directly familiar with a certain kind of reality, namely, our own sphere of subjectivity and body (own-ness sphere). We directly apprehend ourselves not as mere "bodies" in the sense of the external things which we move or touch but as psycho-physical unities. Touching ourselves, therefore, involves a double sensation at both points of touching fingers and touched surface. When we confront the other human being, we apprehend in the originary mode of *Urpräsenz* a body which displays marks and behaviors different from the space-time objects which are around us and at our disposal. The other's body displays characteristics which we know immediately in our own psycho-physical sphere. This other body appears then as the kind of body which we know ourselves to be. Although we do not have direct access to the "own-ness" sphere of the other, it is appresented to us in and through the kind of body and bodily behaviors which we know directly in ourselves. This instance of appresentation differs in one important respect from appresentation in the perception of space-time objects. That which is appresented, the lived-experiences, the inner bodily experiences of the other, are never susceptible to *Urpräsenz* or direct presentation.[19]

3. *The appresentation of "background" realities*

We have discussed appresentation as a dimension of perception and as the way in which non-present features of other selves are appresent with their presented bodies and gestures. Appresentation occurs in yet a third sense in phenomenological literature. This third meaning of appresentation originates in Husserl but is elaborated by Alfred Schutz. The situation of perception remains the occasion of the analysis. In our exposition of Husserl's notion of world, we traced the way in which intentions buried in perceptions always spilled over into the background against which the perceived object was viewed. In this situation of grasping objects against their "field" or background, we have an instance of appresentation. Perception not only involves appresented aspects of the object before us but appresented aspects of that object's environment. To perceive is to focus upon, to pay special attention to an entity which formerly was part of the background and which is now in the foreground. The background of that object, however, does not simply disappear but continues as the intended background even though it is not an object of focus and even if it is totally out of view. I perceive a given tree not as an isolated monad floating by itself in a vacuum

19. Almost all phenomenological philosophers find difficulties in Husserl's "empathetic" solution to the problem of other minds. See for instance Schutz's essay, "The Problem of Transcendental Intersubjectivity in Edmund Husserl," *Collected Papers,* III. Scheler also rejects the empathetic solution for a more direct emotive apprehension occurring between selves (*The Nature of Sympathy*). Merleau-Ponty's essay, "The Child's Relation to the World," *The Primacy of Perception* in *Studies in Phenomenology and Existential Philosophy,* ed. James M. Edie, trans. Cobb, Williams, et al. (Evanston: Northwestern University Press, 1964), argues that the relation with the other is prior to and is the condition of the differentiation of one's own self. This more psychologically oriented essay may not actually contradict Husserl's thesis. Our concern is not to defend Husserl's solution, but to trace and illustrate his theory of appresentation.

but in connection with its field. We should make clear at this point that we are not talking simply about sensation, the mere impinging of colors or sounds, but perception as it includes meaning-conferring or intentional acts. One cannot perceive a tree as a tree (conferring on it the sense *tree*) without at the same time intending the "field" necessary to a tree, in which roots grow, on which weight rests, etc. Therefore, if I perceive only the branches of a tree outside my third story window, I fill out what remains in a twofold way. I complete aspects of the tree itself which are not directly presented to me, and I complete the context or field which tree requires.[20]

It is especially this third meaning of appresentation, the appresenting on the part of a presented object of an order of objects beyond itself, which Schutz develops in a somewhat perplexing scheme. Husserl had already seen that appresentation occurred not simply in sense-perception but in every kind of apprehension (mathematical objects, one's own consciousness, the other self) and that the appresenting object may refer to appresented entities which are of a different order than that object. Schutz extends these insights in his notion of several orders present in any appresentational situation.[21] Without setting forth the details of Schutz's elaboration, we would say that his treatment illustrates how appresentation can be present in any apprehending situation and also how appresentation can vary with the situation. He points out, for instance, that the kind of consciousness-act involved in appresenting or "pairing" the

20. Because appresentation in this third sense expresses man's structural relation to the world, it is one of the keys to Husserl's central philosophical theme, worldly transcendental intersubjectivity. Man is "worldly" through inner and outer horizons which refer beyond themselves. The metaphor of horizon sets forth the situation of perception as involving possible further experiences of other aspects of an object or its field. Horizon suggests both the unity of these appresented aspects, their open-ended yet undisclosed nature, and the possibility of discovering them by a change of position. As a clue to the relation between man and world, appresentation has a metaphysical import, for it is a feature of the mode of presence of all worldly being. In *Urpräsenz* and *Apprasenz* we are approaching the very nucleus of Husserlian phenomenology.

21. Schutz's essay, "Symbol, Reality, and Society" in *Collected Papers*, I, pp. 287–357, propounds a theory of how symbolization occurs in the social world by applying Husserl's notion of appresentation. See pp. 297–300 for Schutz's elaboration of the four kinds of schemes present in any appresentation.

presented and appresented objects can vary. Pairing a symbol and the symbolized, the front side and back side of an object, an entity and its field, and a set of visible behaviors with a conscious self are different *types* of pairing. We mention this in anticipation of our own thesis that appresentation is part of the very structure of the apprehensions which accompany faith.

C. The Social Mediation of Appresented Realities

In Section A, 2, of the chapter we propounded two ways in which realities at hand were mediated through a determinate social world. The more difficult question is whether a determinate social world can mediate realities which are not simply that social world itself and are not simply new perceptivities which open up possible insights into the various spheres of man and world. This question forces us to consider the most significant but also the most elusive way in which a social world mediates reality. It is elusive because it involves two pre-reflective, pre-conscious dimensions of human life, namely, transcendental intersubjectivity and appresentation. Although we have already expounded both of them, a brief recapitulation is in order. Transcendental intersubjectivity combines that which Husserl sets forth as necessary to human beings constituting each other as conscious selves and personal bodies with the specific forms these take in a determinate social world (co-intentions of obligation, evil, the freedom of the other, etc.). Both are "transcendental" in that they involve the ways in which human beings "mean" each other and which meaning actually structures the consciousness prior to the specific reciprocities and behaviors of the society. Appresentation is that aspect of any apprehension in which those aspects of the apprehended object or its field are "required" by the very nature of that object but which are not originarily present in the apprehension itself.

Our thesis is that the intersubjectivities of a determinate social world itself bear certain appresented realities. This presupposes that the co-intentionalities which we have in mind carry with them certain insights, prehensions, which are simply present and do not require deliberate acts of investigation. To participate with the other in mutually determining co-intentionalities is to have certain insights and prehensions. Our point is that these insights themselves appresent realities, and this carries us beyond the three kinds of appresentation which we previously outlined to a theory of social or intersubjective appresentation. We must now illustrate this almost totally elusive depth process.

We have already said that a particular social world involves specific determinations of the universal features of transcendental intersubjectivity. We select as an example the way in which personal body is grasped in the two very different social worlds of a religious, monastic order and a secularized bachelor club oriented toward the Playboy philosophy. In the monastic community the human beings constitute each other as mutual participants in a discipline whose *telos* is the ultimate destiny of the soul. Since the ultimate framework of this discipline is a cosmic lawfulness to which the soul must conform, conscious, rational control is more the mark of what is proper to man than unconscious needs or impulsive acts. Personal body, therefore, is present in this scheme as a threat. This situation makes available genuine insights into personal body: its finitude, its function as the fountain of certain needs, and its capacity to be controlled through discipline. Appresented to such insights may be possibilities for human evil in human sexuality, or the way grief in the face of death can be assuaged by ritualistic and symbolic interpretations of the bodily dimension of the human being.

In the bachelor philosophy human beings consciously relate to each other as objects of temporary, mutual bodily pleasure. Prereflectively they intend each other primarily as the occasion and stimulus of the self's desires and secondarily as a recipient of the self's capacity to give pleasure. While this sort of heterosexuality has been much criticized in the traditional Christian sex ethic, it is not without its insights. Because Playboy sexuality, separated from any backdrop of cosmic lawfulness, is a negotiated matter, the body's essential inviolability may be more clearly apprehended than in the ascetic framework. In asceticism sexuality occurs within a basic conformity to law which establishes a certain "right" over the body within orders of creation. The right over the woman's body on the part of the male and the "duty" toward sexuality under the pressure of the bearing of offspring both result in objectifying the body by

making it the occasion of a cosmic *telos* toward the continued repro-
duction of the species. In the negotations of sexuality in the bachelor model, personal body is not available to another's right, thus is
intuited its connection with the self and its inviolability.

We are not trying in this example to assess the merits of these two
forms of social existence. That would obscure our basic point that
each one's co-intentionalities carry insights and appresentations about
the personal body which the other one misses. Furthermore, this
form of social mediation of reality differs from the creation of special
perceptivities in the following way. Perceptivities are simply capacities, ways of being disposed toward things, which must yet be
actualized before concrete apprehensions occur. Intersubjective
appresentation differs from this in that realities are pre-reflectively
grasped in conjunction with these co-intentionalities. Furthermore,
while our example of personal body is also an ontological stratum
of the human being, this itself appresents in these determinate social
settings many other matters involving sexuality, marriage, and play,
which insights may not be acknowledged in the actual institutions
of that social world. It is because of these appresentations which
transcend the empirical and institutional situation of a given society
that criticism, creativity, and constructive change can be generated
out of that social world, thus altering and reforming its framework.
Accordingly, both monasticism and the Playboy phenomenon may
carry appresentations which generate self-criticism and change within
their own communities.

Chapter 9

PRESENCE AND APPRESENCE

He always left the impression that there was more; that he knew
there was more; and that the more to come, might, for all one
knew, throw a very different light on the matters under discussion.
He respected the universe too much to believe that he could carry
it under his own hat.[1]

Ralph Barton Perry

We are conducting this exploration against the background of the
problem of faith and reality. In this background is the suspicion
that faith is not reality-directed nor is it a vehicle of reality-apprehensions. This suspicion dominates the present secular consensus in
two forms. First, faith is reality-less because of its apparent lack of
interest in verification and evidence. Faith listens to what supports
it and ignores what counts against it. Second, faith seems to be
inevitably locked in the prison of immanence; hence, even if it has
a content, that content is "solely and without remainder" anthropological. Insofar as this suspicion infiltrates theology, theology tends to
fall into a state of paralysis, unable to take even a first step. The overall theological response to this suspicion has been a fluctuation between a sheer repudiation of the problem by taking its stand within
justification, Christocentrism, or the Word of God which cannot permit any measurement by such autonomous formulations of knowledge
and a semi-acknowledgment of the suspicion in which one does

1. R. B. Perry, *The Thought and Character of William James* (Boston:
Little, Brown and Co., 1935), vol. II. p. 704.

206

theology by exploring its anthropological content or its "perspectives" on the world. Our proposal draws from both of these responses. The principle of positivity makes it impossible for us to formulate the issues of knowledge, evidence, meaning, and verification in merely universal terms. If faith has a cognitivity, that cognitivity will be actualized in the determinate situation of faith, a matrix which we characterized as faith-world and ecclesia. In this sense our proposal remains within the tradition of religious determinacy which goes from Schleiermacher to Barth. On the other hand, we are convinced, as the present chapter will show, that faith's cognitivity begins with apprehensions within its own immanent and anthropological realm. We do not mean this chronologically or biographically but structurally. We can elaborate this in the following distinction.

Not only are presence and appresence part of the very structure of all apprehensions; certain types of realities correspond with one or the other of these two modes. Some realities are able to be directly present such as a human being before our eyes; some are only indirectly indicated such as the center of the earth or the other's flow of consciousness. Most realities are present to us only in the indirect mode as are most of the things to which we give credence. When we turn our attention to faith and its "realities," we discover a similar distinction. The devotional literature of Christendom as well as its theological tradition contains the distinction between the experience of God and "belief," the conviction of things not seen. In the Old Testament a few individuals experience theophanies but most of the people of God simply participate in the cultus and remember the religious figure and his theophany. Throughout the history of the church believers experience the divine in their own biographical situation, but at the same time their "believing" is based on the indirect mediation of an authority. The Christian church does distinguish between direct and indirect mediation of reality, and it does so by distinguishing between "religious experience" and trust in an authority (Scripture, the tradition). Our formulation continues but also alters this distinction between immediate and mediate modes of the presence of reality to faith.

We want to propose that faith does have immediate apprehensions of realities which are "at hand." But we hesitate to identify these apprehensions with what usually count as "religious experience" which connotes both conscious and explicit affections and discrete units of experience.[2] We would argue instead that these apprehensions occur in conjunction with the shaping effect of determinate intersubjectivity rather than isolatable biographical "experiences." Faith also resembles the everyday world in that most of the realities to which it is directed are only mediately or indirectly present. At this point we depart from the traditional version because we do not regard the mode of indirect presence as the mode of authority. The reason for this is because the realities at hand appresent realities not at hand; hence, there is a structural relation between the two modes of presence which precedes and in fact founds the authorities. We are not, however, prepared to say whether appresentation simply replaces the whole way of authority or whether it is a clue to the peculiar sense in which authorities occur in ecclesia. It is not our intention to impose on ecclesia something alien or strange nor simply to offer a speculative possibility. We are persuaded that appresentational apprehending actually occurs in this historical faith.

A. Ecclesia and Realities at Hand

We must now explore the sense in which realities are directly present through the social mediations of that determinate intersubjectivity which we are calling ecclesia. Our thesis is that ecclesia mediates realities which are directly present, "realities at hand." What are realities at hand? Tautologically expressed, they are simply realities grasped in apprehension. Husserl used to speak of originary (primordial, immediate) presence. He had in mind an entity directly viewed; the surface of the desk before me, the gestures and sounds of a person talking to me, my own flow of consciousness. Our claim is that faith too is directed to certain realities at hand, and that these are corporately mediated.

1. *The interdependence of the three components of the faith-world and the priority of ecclesia*

We begin with the question of the interrelationship among the three

2. Cf. the phenomena treated in William James, *Varieties of Religious Experience* (New York: Longmans, Green and Co., 1904).

components or dimensions of the faith-world. These dimensions are individuality (existence), sociality, and linguisticality; or more specifically, the existing individual and the redemptive modification of his transcendental and disrupted existence, ecclesia and its inter-subjectivity, and story and image. First of all, it seems evident that these dimensions are not simply discrete entities which are inter-dependent in some way but are actually inter-permeating. The very *being* of the individual in transition toward redemption is social, bound up intersubjectively with the other in ecclesia and with the stranger. His being is also linguistic since the consciousness which is the background of all his specific acts and valuations is the re-ceptacle of images which help guide these acts and rank the evalua-tions. The determinate intersubjectivity of ecclesia is linguistic be-cause of the story and images which correlate to its collective inten-tion or *telos*. It is also comprised of existing individuals who are not mere parts of a collective but contributors to an open community.

Second, ecclesia has a certain precedence over individual redemp-tive existence and over language. This is not because we can con-ceive ecclesia without language or redemptive existence, but because the order of dependence is one in which the individual depends on ecclesia and not the other way around. Redemption involves the shaping of a consciousness toward freedom and obligation and the way the shaping is effected is through ecclesia. The individual does not transform himself, nor does God transform him by directly act-ing upon his consciousness. We note that theophanies and discrete experiences of God in both Testaments are not redemptive but usually initiate and legitimate the career of a religious leader. Al-though the individual does also affect ecclesia, his affecting does not account for its very existence. Ecclesia is the matrix of redemptive (individual) existence; the individual is not ecclesia's matrix. And while we might say that ecclesia is instrumental for redemption, we can as easily say that in its ideal form it *is* redemption. Or to put it differently, redemption itself is a social and intersubjective situation. To be redeemed means to participate in the co-intentionalities of freedom and obligation rather than idolatry and flight. Furthermore, ecclesia has priority in relation to faith's language. Since ecclesia is a determinate intersubjectivity, that corporate form of human ideality which requires freedom from and for the other, it is the *telos* of faith's language which is ordered toward it.

Third, images which constitute the "story" told in the community of faith and which are correlates of the acts and intentions of faith function indispensably in the other two components of ecclesia. In the intersubjective component it is by means of images that co-intentionalities can take place. In ecclesia human beings co-intend each other through ecclesia's story, the story of God founding through Jesus Christ a non-provincial redemptive corporate existence. In these co-intendings human beings "mean" or constitute each other through the images which express their essential being (creation), their disrupted existence (idolatry, flight), and their redemptive existence (freedom, obligation). We have already attempted to clarify that the concrete linguistic carriers of the story and its images are complex mixtures of the story and images with contemporaneous world-pictures, mythologies, and doctrinal and ethical formulations.

The language of faith permeates the other dimension, individual existence viewed in its transition toward redemption, primarily as the "means" by which redemptive existence retains continuity or permanence. We have described redemption as a modification of disrupted existence which itself had modified transcendental human structures. Disrupted historical existence is a persisting stage, something a human being *is,* because it involves persisting modes of intersubjectivity and a distorted consciousness which functions as the background for particular acts of evil. The same holds for redemptive existence. As a modification of disrupted existence, it is not to be thought of simply as occurring in units such as thoughts, feelings, acts, or behaviors. It too is an altered intersubjective structure which has a certain persistence or duration. One way of expressing this is that the transcendental refusal of chaos as one's ultimate context and the insistence that one's structural openness be honored by the other take on a determinate intentionality. The general refusal of external manipulation is translated into an intentionality about the self and the other in the light of which particular decisions are made. Without *images* these persisting intentionalities would have no endurance. Redemptive existence is a matrix of particular decisions, life-styles, valuations, and affections. What gives continuity to this matrix (shaped-consciousness) are interiorized images of the story of faith. Therefore, these interiorized images serve to guide the way in which one conducts his life against the background of that inclusive concern for the "meaning of life" and the questions of one's *telos* and destiny. Therefore, insofar as the images imbedded in the Adamic myth or the story of Jesus are interiorized and are determinative of the shape of one's ·consciousness, he will conduct the business of everyday life in a certain way. This does not mean necessarily a conscious referral to these images or to this shaped consciousness. They now stand for "what one is" insofar as he has a continuity at all. Out of that matrix he pursues activities of gratification, sacrifice, and competition, and out of that matrix he exists in determinate ways in a family (or out of it), as a citizen (or revolutionary) and in relation to a career (or rejection of one).

2. *Social and anthropological realities at hand*

In Chapter 8 we set forth two ways in which a social grouping mediates distinctive cognizings; the determinate social form exists as a content to be grasped, and special perceptivities are created. We find both of these mediations occurring in the community of faith. Ecclesia is itself a new form of historical existence involving a distinctive historical consciousness as well as depth or intersubjective structures and social relations. To this extent ecclesia resembles other concrete forms of human existence such as tribal religion, Buddhism, and East European Marxism. These forms of existence are "realities" which have emerged in human history and which have their own essential and empirical content. Like other historical religions the Christian religion can be grasped both from without (as in phenomenological and historical disciplines) and by way of ecclesial participation. The difference is not so much that some aspects of the Christian religion are accessible to the participant and hidden from the external observer. If anything, the reverse is true. The systematic student of a religion is typically aware of more "aspects" of a religious faith than the members of its cultus. Neither is the observer totally barred from intersubjective and subjective levels insofar as the psychological and sociological distinctiveness of a historical faith is available in its literature, cultic forms, and institutional expressions. The difference between the participant and the observer is their mode of apprehension. The modification of existence and co-intentional intersubjective consciousness are apprehended by the participant, the man of faith, in an originary or immediate manner. These "realities" are apprehended by him in and through his own modified consciousness and his own intersubjective relations. The believer, therefore, "testifies" while the systematic observer only describes, interprets, and explains. What then is immediately present in ecclesia? First, this distinctive social entity which we are calling ecclesia is present to me both as a dimension of my own social being and as a determinate historical reality.[3] Second, my own modified existence is a new reality, something which neither I nor anyone else has hitherto apprehended.[4]

In these two mediations realities at hand are restricted to the corporate and subjective content involved in faith. While we would not question the reality status of this content, its significance seems to be reducible to historical and psychological contingencies. We recall, however, that redemptive existence involves a threefold structure, a redemptive modification of a disrupted modification of an *essential human makeup*. Present in this immanent situation of faith and ecclesia is an *ontological* pattern, the pattern of what is distinctively and properly human. Because this pattern permeates redemptive existence and is in part restored in it, participation in ecclesia

3. In claiming that a social entity qualifies as a reality, we stand in the tradition of Tönnies, Mannheim, and Durkheim. Durkheim rejects the view that society is simply an epiphenomenon of individual life, and argues for the relative autonomy of collective representations and social facts. He describes collective representations as "realities which . . . are to a certain extent independent of the physiological sub-stratum." Even as human individuals represent a transcending of physical and chemical associations, so do social units represent a transcending of the level of individuality. See "Individual and Collective Representations," in *Sociology and Philosophy* (Glencoe, Ill.: The Free Press, 1953). Mannheim also describes human relations as realities. See his *Essays on the Sociology of Culture* (London: Routledge and Kegan Paul, 1967), p. 69.

4. This modification of my own existence available to me for *re*-presenting and reflection is the basis of the possibility of "story" in the more autobiographical sense. However, because it is only one among a number of realities both present and appresent in the situation of faith, it is impossible to restrict theological reflection to simply autobiographical storytelling, personal testimony, and the like. To do so involves an abstracting of most of the content and components in the situation of faith.

includes apprehensions of something about the human being which is universal and constitutive. We repeat that such apprehensions are largely pre-conscious, being concomitants of participation in ecclesia's intersubjectivity. The reason we suspect that these apprehensions or prehensions are in fact present is that they actually function as guiding "presuppositions" in the behaviors and evaluations of believers. When reflective thought attempts to justify such behaviors, it uncovers apprehensions which are not simply about the historical contingencies of a religious piety but pertain to the human being as such.

The second way social relationships mediate realities is their capacity to effect new powers of perceptiveness. Recent philosophies of perception have successfully established not only the variety of perceptive powers, but the immense role of interest, motivation, and even training in physical perception. Combinations of inherited traits, acculturation, and individual biographical exposure result in vast differences between human beings simply in visual and auditory perceptions. Some perceive in more detail than others. All perception involves bringing an object into the foreground, and this act depends in part on both the gradation of interests and the presence of skills. The biologist for example perceives a stratum of events occurring in his life-world which most people miss. What is true for physical perception carries over, it seems, into the more subtle realms of insight or perceptiveness into various regions of reality; the nuances of poetry, the complex interrelations of a bureaucracy, the shadings of human vocabulary.

In addition to these variations of perception and perceptiveness which are traceable to hereditary and cultural differences, disrupted historical existence affects the perceptive powers. In the imagery expressive of disrupted existence, this means that an attachment to an object in the hope that it can secure us against chaos sets up an unhistorical relationship between ourselves and that object blinding us to its historical and contingent aspects. Furthermore, when we view the contents of our world as mere ciphers of chaos, our response is one of fear, enmity, or flight, all of which obscure those contents in their order, function, and beauty. Something of the sort appears to operate in all racist, ethnic, and national conflict. When idolatrous inclinations are combined with our incipient vulnerability to ridicule and our insistence on our own survival, integrity, welfare, and freedom, more self-deceptions take place.

For these reasons the redemptive shaping of the consciousness affects the mind, or better, all our antennae through which we perceive and respond. Redemptive existence cannot alter disrupted historical existence without increasing and refining perceptivity. The most immediate region toward which that perceptivity operates is what we have just treated, the immanent situation of the self and the other person in ecclesia. However, because this perceptivity is a "power," a capacity, it has no regional restrictions except those which an object itself fosters upon it. And this pushes us beyond our "immanent" or provincial formulation of the realities at hand. Hitherto, we have simply considered realities which are immediate in the sense of the ecclesially altered social and individual existence. With this alteration comes a perceptivity directed toward the ever-changing situations of human life. The man of faith, the believer in the sense of a participant in ecclesia, is not simply one whose individual existence is altered and who resides in a strange intersubjectivity. We have already argued that one mark of that intersubjectivity was the incorporation of the stranger, mankind as such, into the imagery of redemptive existence. Now we are saying that the perceptive power of redemptive existence opens up the realities of whatever life-world surrounds that existence. The status of being as such is altered from mere chaos or a cipher of chaos to something at the disposal of a more ultimate power. A consciousness altered in this way should therefore be disposed toward any given situation · more in the mode of interest, delight, use, receptivity than fear or enmity. And such a disposition should carry with it a new capacity for insight into possibilities, beauties, and relationships of whatever is before us. This means nature, politics, interpersonal relations, animals, anything confronting us in the environment.

This interpretation is clearly incompatible with the view that religious knowledge is simply a different "perspective" on things. Neither of these apprehensions of realities at hand involves simply new "perspectives." In both cases we are talking about new "realities"; states of affairs which at one time had no existence and which now have emerged in the course of history and individual existence. Redemptive existence and ecclesia are new realities and

apprehension and reflection. Over and above
nd cultural realities are perpetually appearing.
es for self-deception or for insight. In other
:ness which arises with faith is directed at the
leveloping world. This is one reason why this
:o be ethically imperialistic and culture-dominat-
:nerates insights and then convictions about its
ice, about the state, war, slavery, exploration,
iort about the total contents of the life-world.
ts convictions final and official has been due to
ionary view of reality and its identification of
tive and authoritative institution. These con-
l obscure the intrinsic feature of faith, the
he perceptiveness which redemption effects.

PPRESENTED REALITIES

ew that faith is reality-less, we have contended
:cclesia involves the apprehension of realities
: view that these realities are simply universally
ilities, we have proposed that the situation of
ne and that the social reality of ecclesia and
of the human being (transcendental, disrupt-
e correlative with that determinacy. The
re not simply universal furnishings of the
focuses a "perspective." Even if these state-
ments represent some forward progress in our inquiry, they do not
confront that paralyzing problem of religious knowledge formulated
in Chapter 1, the violation on the part of faith of the axiom of
object-evidence correspondence. Faith has cognitive intentions toward matters of fact (historical events) and toward realities which
transcend the region of ecclesia and redemption (the cosmos), but
appears to be indifferent to evidence appropriate to the level of the
claim. Even when faith's interpreters make use of historical method,
as in the interpretation of Scripture, historical evidence so gathered
is not the original basis of faith's affirmation of its own historical
beginnings or its testimony to Jesus Christ as historical.

The realities which disclose this apparent logical peculiarity of faith's cognitivity are realities which are not present in a direct or originary way. Not since its actual occurrence in the first century has any believer directly grasped the event of Jesus' crucifixion. The creation of the world is never immediately present to any believer either in the semi-mythological sense of something pertaining to beginnings or in the more sophisticated sense of a persisting feature or structure about the world. As we have said before, the traditional way of justifying such affirmations is to defend the rationality of trusting the authorities to which the revelation of God is entrusted. We find this way of authority unacceptable on two counts. One, historical consciousness and method has relativized these authorities, rendering them ambiguous as norms or sources. Two, we find that the matters about which we have been talking (Jesus Christ *qua* historical, the cosmos) are not present to the believer simply and solely through a mediating authority. The way of authority only pushes the question back one step to those prophets and apostles whose testimonies and formulations comprise the cited authority. Even the way of authority presupposes that the authority itself contains a pre-authority mode of apprehending these indirectly present realities. Expressed in the language of the previous chapter, this pre-authority way of apprehending these realities is appresentation. In our view appresentation is inherent in all of faith's apprehensions, hence is something all believers share. It cannot therefore differentiate "prophets and apostles" from believers.

We shall explore appresence as a component of presence by way of examples of appresent realities in ecclesia. The three examples chosen, the historical, the cosmological, and the transcendent, represent current issues and disagreements, and they serve as dramatic indications of faith's seeming indifference to evidence. In the language of recent controversy, the three examples are the "historical Jesus," creation-providence, and God and the death of God. The paralysis caused by the suspicion that faith has no real foundation for its claims about these regions reaches beyond the dialectics of theological journals into piety itself. The secularized piety of the present-day church, especially as it appears among the young, is not at all persuaded that "there *is* a God," that the world depends on

216

God in any way, or that a historical figure in the past is decisive for redemption. The old reasons, metaphysical and authoritarian, make little sense, and the only alternative seems to be to turn Jesus over to the historians, creation over to the astrophysicists, and the transcendent over to the metaphysicians.

The following thesis states our attempt to reopen these matters. The realities-at-hand which faith apprehends present not only themselves but appresent other realities. Note our way of formulating the issue. We are not saying that the experience of redemption, the transition to redemptive existence, or even the intersubjective structure of ecclesia appresent realities, although this may also be the case and could be a significant subject for inquiry. Rather, the *realities* which are prehended in conjunction with the redemptive modification and the intersubjective ecclesial shaping of consciousness appresent other realities. Whether this means other aspects of themselves, as in a perceived space-time object, the field in which they are located, or something else, remains yet to be determined.

1. *The appresence of the historical redeemer*

We begin our exploration of the way in which faith grasps the historical redeemer by "questioning back" or uncovering the pre-reflective levels of faith. We must push beneath the strata of conscious piety, doctrine, and myth to the linguistic correlates of the modification of human existence toward redemption (to story and image), and to the pre-reflective co-intentions which utilize these images to constitute the other human being in ecclesia. We have already found that the transition toward redemption involves the actualization of freedom and obligation in the face of idolatry and flight. Furthermore, we argued that freedom and obligation rest on the constitutive structure of human being since they express the transcendental refusal of external determination. Obligation expresses, therefore, conditions necessary for the mutual honoring of the other's self-determination which range from the prevention of murder to more subtle protections against manipulation. If I am to be free to be, to grow, to change, to create, I need an honoring or acknowledgment of this by the other and I need to honor this in the other, thereby creating the residual intersubjective structure of obligation. In short redemptive existence involves *nomos*.

Insofar as our intersubjectivity is an obligatory intersubjectivity, there is intrinsic to our very being a point of reference for evaluations. Some events threaten our existence and others do not. Individuals around us (even as we ourselves) only partially acknowledge their obligation and direct themselves toward us in acts of murder, stealing, exploitation, manipulation, and propagandizing for their own purposes. These actions become embodied in the social order, in cultures, nations, and societies, times and places past and present, and in causes, trends, social tendencies. Obligation actualizes the normativeness latent in all self-determining being and creates a measure by which the human being lives his life in a continuing series of assessments. When obligation comes to the surface in human sociality, it effects a moralization of human relations, events, governments, nations. That is, they are intended in their relation to human welfare according to whether or not they embody the obligation which structures this intersubjectivity. Events, then, are measured according to their power and importance in disturbing or promoting this welfare. When this happens, *history* comes into being. But for there to be history in the sense of a continuity of human sociality carried by significant remembered events, events must be assessed and measured according to their moral status. Hence, history is only beginning to dawn in societies which are mythical in the sense of maintaining themselves by means of seasonal reenactments of the powers of the beginning. The appearance of history does not mean inevitable progress, but a continuing struggle occasioned by the perpetual assessment of leaders, policies, and institutions. What we are contending in this lengthy example is that obligation appresents history. It is not simply inferred in an intellectual act. It is appresent as the field *necessary* to the social manifestation of obligation. And with history we have the possibility of some events being more significant than others in the struggle between good and evil.

We take a second step by recalling ecclesia's central feature of dispelling provincialist requirements of God's presence and the intentional presence of any possible stranger in that community. We are confronted here with a community which is not permitted to make itself coincident with any natural or cultural human boundary or institutionalization. It can never *be* simply a white community, a black community, a national community, or a class community. The redemptive existence of this community demands the negation of all social boundaries as conditions of the redemptive presence of God. What replaces bounded conditions of redemption is simply a testimony to one whose death and resurrection was the occasion of this negation and the creation of ecclesia. According to the Christian story and its imagery, the breaking of the power of evil, the establishing of freedom, the universalization of the religious community are all connected with the redeemer, Jesus of Nazareth. If we grant that Jesus of Nazareth is, image-wise, intrinsic to the constellation of images of the Christian story, is it conceivable that the image of Jesus of Nazareth be the image of a mythical figure? Here we must return to obligation's appresenting of history.

Obligation and the appresentation of a realm of human action in which some events are decisive for human good combines with the communal matrix of redemptive existence, a specific (ecclesial) community which has a historical beginning, to appresent a historical redeemer. Empirically speaking, it can be argued that the processes of testimony, corporate memory, oral tradition, and written records all functioned to preserve the ministry and teachings of this man. We are saying that the historical figure who is the subject of this tradition is appresent to the reality of ecclesia. Because redemptive existence is a displacement of flight by obligation, the past presents itself historically, that is, as comprised of significant, even decisive events which establish the conditions of obligation. Because redemptive existence is existence in a community which negates provincialist conditions of divine presence, the beginning of that community presents itself as involving an event powerful enough to accomplish this negation. Such an appresentation is not in itself Jesus of Nazareth. But given the traditional witness to the ministry and teachings of this man as well as the connection between his death and resurrection and the emergence of ecclesia, the result is that Jesus of Nazareth of the tradition is appresented as a historical figure. His historicity is not "proved" by the tradition alone or by appresentation alone. The tradition's imagery, the participation in

219

ecclesia, and the appresenting of obligation in ecclesia work together to appresent a historical rather than mythical figure.

It should be clear that the content and significance of Jesus is not contained in this appresentation. Such an inclusive Christological interpretation would necessarily involve theological criteriology, hence the role of the literature and witness of the primitive church as well as a hermeneutic of the image of the redeemer set within the total story. Our only point is that the redeemer of that story, tradition, and imagery is appresented as a *historical* redeemer by the realities of ecclesia and obligation. To participate in ecclesia is to participate in a re-formed history and re-formed community. Although this appresentation does not carry us very far into the content of this ministry, it does suggest that faith's intention of Jesus as a historical figure is not simply an arbitrary, superstitious, or unfounded act. It also suggests why faith does not wait for the judgment of the professional historian before claiming that its redeemer is a historical figure. In the light of this appresentational aspect of faith, we find the recent terminology of a "paradigmatic event" somewhat misleading. Insofar as a paradigm is simply an example or model, the paradigmatic event serves as a model for the self-understanding of Christians or Christian existence. This language borders on an unhistorical understanding of the redeemer and seems to bypass the appresented historical dimension of the redeemer and the events surrounding him. The reason for this bypassing is a narrowly hermeneutical formulation of the problem which has largely ignored the ecclesial matrix of faith.

2. *The appresence of the cosmos as creation*

Cosmology like history has been the occasion of increasing embarrassment for the theologies of this post-metaphysical and post-historical-critical era. The relation between God and the world as it is expressed in the cultus and its piety seems to border on mythology, and the theological formulations of these matters have seemed ever more vulnerable to rational critique. The salvaging of such cosmological themes as creation and providence has, with the exception of the recent renascence of process theology, tended to fluctuate between tradition-oriented approaches (neo-Reformation theologies)

220

and an existential reduction in which creation symbolizes something about the relaton of the human being to his environment but has nothing to do with the cosmos itself.

In our view cosmological matters are present to faith as an appresent reference of freedom and not simply as something mediated through an authority nor as something which is the end product of an intellective act. Freedom is a "reality" which concerns the possibilities, transcendental structures, and actualized power in the being of man. This reality appresents the world in a twofold way or, we might say, in two aspects. We have argued that freedom involves a breaking of the power of idolatry, that perpetual attempt to secure onself against chaos by means of unqualified attachments. We are not thinking here of obvious or dramatic instances of conscious "worship" but the ever-present way human beings intend their environment through a mixture of fear and hope that somehow the total mix of nature, nation, and self will suffice. Freedom transforms this intention of the world as the region capable of dispelling the threat of chaos, and in that transformation the world is appresented as a power incapable of being the recipient of this search for security. Expressed in traditional language, freedom discloses the world's *finitude*. We submit that this is not simply an expression of a subjective experience but an appresentation of a feature of the cosmos itself.

Freedom, furthermore, creates a perceptiveness about the nature and origin of the rift in the human being of which idolatry and flight are expressions. Insofar as the transition to redemption involves a restoration of the essential transcendental structures of human consciousness, it is clear that the origin of evil is not simply in man's transcendental constitution. The rift does not break forth from man's own "nature" which in turn is the mere product of world processes. Furthermore, if the rift is rooted in the response the human being makes to his own insecure situation, this rift is not insecurity itself nor is worldly contingency the explanation or cause of the rift. Accordingly, the second feature of the world appresented by freedom is, to express it negatively, that the world itself is not evil nor is it the cause of evil. The events, processes, and strata of worldly being threaten man's refusal to settle for a final victory of chaos over him, but they also serve as the necessary conditions of his transition to redemptive existence. In the language of classical theology the world is not only finite but "good." It is not itself evil and it offers supportive conditions for obligation and Torah. The positive, supportive character of the cosmos is also appresented by redemptive existence and as such is co-present with the intersubjectively shaped consciousness of ecclesia.

In these appresentations the cosmos is disclosed in its intrinsic character of finitude or contingency, unfit to be the anti-chaos, and in its capacity to be a supportive environment for good. These features in themselves do not amount to "the doctrine of creation" in the sense of a certain relation between God and the world. But they anticipate it and provide ingredients for it. When such appresentations combine with the imagery and appresentation of the transcendent who is himself the anti-chaos and the origin of redemptive existence, it becomes apparent that he can be positively related to redemption only if he has the same relation to the cosmos. If redemption means a modification of disrupted existence which involves human sociality and if this in turn has worldly conditions and means a certain way of having a world, the redeemer cannot be adequate toward man and powerless toward the world. The "doctrine of creation," therefore, originates in the reflection of Israel on these appresentations.

We have stressed that appresentations are usually not consciously grasped and formulated. For example, in the everyday world human beings behave toward each other by way of appresentations of the selfhood and personal body of the other without personal body being conceptually formulated. Similarly, the cosmos was appresent to the Israelites as both finite (an unfitting anti-chaos) and good (a fitting context for Torah) long before this appresentation became a theme of cultic celebration or part of Israel's story. Our point is that what made the thematization of cosmos possible was Israel's redemption appresenting cosmos. Students of Israelite religion all tell us that Israel's faith is "non-speculative" and non-dogmatic, but they give us little help beyond this in accounting for Israel's story. They tend to leave us with antiquated myths and supernaturally given revelations, hence no way of grasping why Israelite faith has to do with realities, including realities in the cosmos itself.

3. *The appresence of the transcendent*

What follows is not a full theological account of the "knowledge of God." Such an account would necessarily involve the presence of God in ecclesia and in the world, and the issues and problems of the interrelation between providence and revelation and the contemporaneity of God's Word, all of which are bound up with the central theological issue concerning the relation between the world and God and his so-called personhood. We are restricted in this study to the very basic problem concerning the "reality" of God and his reducibility or non-reducibility. We should also say that these remarks do not add up to a "proof" of God's existence. Our aim is to see how faith apprehends God as a reality not coincident with human subjectivity. Negatively, our thesis is that God is apprehended neither at the transcendental levels of the religious a priori, nor in and through a trusted authority, nor by means of the intellective acts of which the "proofs" are examples. God being what he is, there appears to be no way of really "accounting" for how he is present, or why the reality of God is irreducible. Such accounts themselves invariably reduce him. Therefore, the appresence of God does not fall within any of the ordinary types of appresence, and in one sense it does not even qualify as appresence. On the other hand, appresence describes the mode in which faith grasps the transcendent better than any other available epistemological notion.[5]

The transcendent like history and cosmos is appresented by the realities grasped in the transition toward redemptive existence. To explicate this we recall the threefold scheme of that transition which

5. One phenomenological philosopher has used Husserl's notion of appresentation in a theory of how the transcendent is grasped. Maurice Natanson argues that the transcendent is appresented in the typification of everyday experiencing because such typifications always have an interior horizon of negation by which we limit what is before us in order to grasp it. Natanson's concern is more with a theory of religion and the universal reference to the transcendent than the positivity of a specific religious faith. Thus Natanson's approach pertains more to the religious a priori than to a determinate theology of redemption. See *The Journeying Self: a study in philosophy and social role* (Reading: Addison-Wesley, 1970), chap. 7.

includes the transcendental refusals, human evil in historical existence (idolatry and flight), and redemptive existence. The religious a priori does not enable the apprehension of "God" because its noema or intended reference is an indeterminate "whatever" which could support the refusal of chaos. The object of this refusal is not a reality or actuality. Furthermore, as the correlate of a transcendental structure, its noematic content is simply its capacity to disperse chaos as man's ultimate context, replacing a meaningless framework with meaning.

When we move to disrupted historical existence, we find the refusal of chaos still operative but its noema, the Something, is made determinate in the mode of mundanization. Refusing chaos, disrupted historical man secures himself against chaos and its emissaries by intentions, relations, expectations of unqualified loyalty toward *a* something in his environment, which can of course include the environment itself as well as an environmentally conceived deity. Disrupted historical existence lives in the deception that chaos is dispersed or is dispersable by this mundane Something. Furthermore, self-securing, self-deceptive existence sets up essentially fearful, protective, and manipulative relations with the other human being which disrupt the mutual acknowledgments appropriate to human sociality. Disrupted historical existence appresents the transcendent or the anti-chaos in the mundanized form of an *idolum*.

Since the refusal of chaos is an essential human feature, it persists through the transition to redemptive existence and the breaking of the power of self-securing. Freedom and obligation replace idolatry and flight. The world is appresented in its incapacity to disperse chaos (its finitude and contingency) and as an environment supportive of obligation in harmony with man's constitutive normativeness. What effects this transition and the breaking of deceptive and self-securing powers? Three possibilities present themselves. One, man's transcendental constitution is modified so that he is no longer self-transcending; hence, he does not refuse but accepts chaos as his proper context and destiny. We find no evidence for such a modification, and all the evidence points the other way. Two, man affirms his refusal of death, chaos, and meaninglessness in the knowledge that there is no evidence that chaos is dispersible. Here self-securing and its disruption is overcome by the sheer *assertion* of meaning in the face of absurdity. This Unamuno-like alternative is logically possible but psychologically and historically unconvincing. In addition it is not consistent with the actual experience of the transition to redemption found in ecclesia.

Third, the power of self-securing is broken because the fundamental *problem* which served as its occasion is addressed, namely, the threat of chaos and the actual need for an anti-chaos which is not a mere subterfuge. In redemption the power of self-securing is really broken. The threat of chaos is really dispersed, and therefore what disperses it is not a mundanized deity which is itself a cipher of chaos and exists under its threat. In other words the transcendent itself is appresented in genuine redemption, and only a mundanized transcendent or *idolum* is appresented in the self-deception of disrupted existence.

It should be apparent that we are speaking of the *essence* of the matter, the level of the *Wesen des Christentums*. The actual Christian community, reflecting as it does the continuation of disrupted historical existence, is not incapable of transforming the transcendent into an *idolum*. But this very act helps illustrate the essential structure of appresentation of the transcendent. There simply is a correlation between self-securing and an idol (even if that idol is called God) and between the breaking of self-securing and the transcendent.[6] At this point we observe the circular nature of the faith-world. The transition to redemptive existence is made possible by

6. Although I am sympathetic to the criticisms of the classical doctrine of God's impassibility and unchangeability on the part of Whiteheadian theism (panentheism), these criticisms are so preoccupied with the *doctrinal* level of language with its metaphysical formulations that it fails to do justice to the rootage of impassibility in the pre-doctrinal story and image of ecclesia. If my interpretation is correct, ecclesia resists ascribing motion, suffering, and change to the transcendent because the transcendent is appresented by redemption as the only true anti-chaos. In the background of the *via negationis,* therefore, is not the metaphysics of hellenistic Platonism but the problem of self-securing and disrupted historical existence. The Platonic tradition offered patristic theology a way of formalizing this concern, a way which may have been misleading and unfortunate, but it is not the sole origin of the impetus to place the transcendent beyond "change." Needless to say, the problem of self-securing and disrupted existence is not very prominent in the writings of Whitehead and Hartshorne.

a relation to the transcendent, which itself is accounted for as an appresence of redemptive existence. In our view both themes do justice to what occurs in ecclesia. In the concrete process of the corporate shaping of consciousness, ecclesial man does not first experience redemptive existence and then the transcendent. We are not dealing here with chronology or the psychology of conversion but with modes of presence of the realities which ecclesial man confronts. The transcendent is not grasped in originary presence but is appresented by redemptive existence. On the other hand, this appresented transcendent is that which accounts for the breaking of self-securing.

So far it seems that what is appresented is still an indeterminate transcendent and not "God." In ecclesia the transcendent is not simply an "absolute" which founds the world and to which chaos is subordinated. The appresenting reality is redemptive existence, and this means that the transcendent is appresented both as able and willing to disperse the threat of chaos and its ciphers, and as one whose relation to the world can produce the conditions for actualizing obligation. Noematically speaking, these two aspects (ultimacy and goodness, freedom and love) constitute the very meaning of "God" and differentiate God from the transcendent, the sacred, and the absolute. "God" in meaning and content is in correlation with ecclesia and cannot be translated into the synthesizing, transcendental, or descriptive programs of history of religions or philosophy of religion.

We hope that our typology of three possibilities of how self-securing might be broken will not be taken as an argument, an attempted demonstration of the rationality of the third option. The purpose of the typology is to show that the first two options are not possibilities within the redemptive experience of ecclesia. Our overall purpose is to illustrate the appresence of God to redemptive existence.[7] It should be clear that most of the issues in this matter remain unclari-

7. Formally speaking, this approach may resemble Kant's description of the indirect reference to God out of the moral structure of things. Kant's view seems to be a version of what we are calling appresentation. It is the principle of positivity which marks the difference between this approach and that of Kant. In our view it is determinate sociality (ecclesia and redemptive existence) which appresents God, not the more general phenomenon of the moral structure of man and the world.

fied. One region of possible exploration is the temporal dimension of the appresence of the transcendent. In the language of recent theology, the transcendent is present primarily in the mode of hope. Such an emphasis accords with both the experience and the imagery of primitive Christianity where the dimension of futurity is expressed in the "reign of God" theme of Jesus' teaching as well as the continuing apocalyptic element in hellenistic Christianity.

If we are in some way on the right track in arguing that immediately prehended realities of faith *appresent* other realities, what have we in fact established? In one sense very little has been claimed. Viewed from the perspective of someone who would decide what can and cannot be confessed about Jesus, about creation, and about God, our portrait of these things as appresented is exceedingly minimal. This calls for some clarification. That which is appresented is not, in content, the complete or full reality intended in the religious cultus. Much more can legitimately be confessed about Jesus than simply a bare, almost empty historical event. "God" for religious faith refers to more than a mere transcendent. At this point we recall that our problem is the pre-methodological problem of reality reference, not the problem of theological method itself. The question of Jesus Christ, methodologically considered, is a question of Scripture, of hermeneutics, of tradition, of the interrelation between symbols. Appresentation does not, therefore, in itself provide an object in its fullness. At least it does not do so when it is abstracted from the function of tradition in redemption and revelation. This is why we have established very little in our case for appresentation. On the other hand, if faith is in fact appresentative, we are faced here with a staggeringly immodest claim. We are actually claiming that Feuerbach is overcome. And we do so not by appealing to the overpowering otherness of revelation, but by exposing the inadequacy of his formulation. For if faith's immediate realities are appresentative of the transcendent, the historical, anthropological immanence is broken and transcended.

4. *Two clarifications: originary presence and "religious experience"*

We are persuaded that in ecclesia historical, cosmological, and transcendent realities are appresented by immediately grasped realities, and that this appresentation occurs in the pre-reflective mode and is mediated through ecclesia's determinate intersubjectivity. Nevertheless, our case amounts to little more than limits and suggestions, starting points for further explorations. In anticipation of more specific inquiries, we shall now pose in some detail two specific issues: originary presence and "religious experience."

Most of the puzzles which attend this appropriation of appresentation arise in connection with the sense in which appresentation in ecclesia retains or departs from ordinary perceptual appresentation. In Chapter 8 we argued that appresentation in Husserl's thought was not simply an *association* of two entities, the validity of which depends on some past experience of their conjunction. Appresentation involves an intuiting of an indirectly present reality which is bound up with the originarily present reality in an a priori way. We also noticed that in perception some appresented aspects can be transformed into originary presence, while in other cases (other minds, the field beyond the horizon) the appresented entity is in principle untransformable. All three examples of faith's appresentation appear to retain the first feature. The historical redeemer, the finitude and goodness of the world, and the transcendent as God are bound up a priori with redemptive existence, and are grasped in intentions which accompany the intersubjectively shaped consciousness of ecclesial man. With regard to the second issue of the transformability of the appresented entity into originary presence, the situation differs in each of the three appresentations. None of the three entities are subject to transformation into originary presence. In this respect they resemble the appresented self of the other more than the appresented back-side of a space-time object. A past historical object, a feature of the world as such, the transcendent, cannot by a change of stance be brought into originary presence. A past historical object, however, resembles the other mind in a way that the cosmos and the transcendent do not. We do grasp in the mode of originary presence "present" historical entities, the stuff of history, so to speak, even as we grasp in an originary way our own conscious-processes and personal body. Hence, in the case of the appresented historical redeemer, we know on the basis of immediate apprehension what a historical object is. Furthermore, historical method resembles common-sense confirmations which occur in interpersonal relations to the degree that it offers a way of filling out and confirming the detail of the appresented object. For this reason, commitment to historical method is not inconsistent with the knowledge of historical entities in redemptive existence by way of appresentation. Contradictions arise when appresentation is coupled with authority commitments and historical details are affirmed prior to historical evidence. In our view redemption appresents a historical redeemer but does not appresent phases of his ministry or the specific relation he had with his disciples.

With the cosmos and its features, we are in a different situation. Like history the cosmos is something with which we have some immediate familiarity. Like history we never grasp the cosmos in its totality. Here the similarity seems to stop. For while historical entities are present before us as quantities of our everyday world, the "features" of the cosmos are not. Even if we prehend features of the world such as the asymmetrical structure of events in process, this comes to awareness only in rather sophisticated acts of reflection. The possibility of this reflective repetition of our apprehensions of the world suggests that the appresented features of the cosmos are not mere contentless projections. As with history our pre-reflective familiarity with the cosmos founds a reflective discipline which can fill in, confirm, or disconfirm interpretive details of the appresented world. Here philosophy and faith need not necessarily contradict each other except when faith fixes the details of its appresentations from its authorities.

The appresence of the transcendent, as we have said, is the farthest removed from the general structure and types of appresentation. The transcendent is neither transformable into originary presence, nor is there any direct human experience of anything like the transcendent. The appresence of the transcendent, therefore, is different in structure from the situation of other minds and also from a historical entity and the cosmos. The transcendent is appresented neither in an association of two known quantities nor by a reality of its ontological type. What prevents the transcendent from being a sheer projection is that it is the intuited "field" which redemptive existence requires.

But since there is no originary acquaintance at all, the transcendent is not appresented in its own mode of reality. This in fact comprises the negative aspect of the *noema,* transcendent.

A second region of perplexities centers around the traditional motif of "religious experience." Our assigning of priority to the social dimension may find further clarification in relation to this theme. One way in which the theme of religious experience appears is that of the inner testimony of the Holy Spirit. The main value it has is negative. It serves as a warning to those who so cast the question of religious knowledge that it can account for itself exhaustively and without remainder. However, the traditional formulation of the positive role of the Spirit in religious knowledge has been within an intellectualist and individualist framework. The result is a crypto-gnosticism. Presupposing the priority of revelation and redemption, these formulations make redemption the result of receptive acts of the intellect. The attempt to correct this in pietism and in recent existentialist theology with its stress on encounter, I and Thou, pre-understanding, and *fiducia* does not escape this crypto-gnosticism. For it is still the individual person in focus, and the case for religious belief depends on formulating the condition of his voluntary and conscious response. In our interpretation the transition to redemption occurs by means of participation in a form of corporate historical existence (ecclesia). The realities of faith are founded here and are concomitant with this participation. Proceeding in this way, we must bluntly say that there is no such thing as an "inner testimony of the Holy Spirit" in the sense of an individualized supernatural action of God which enables belief in God, adherence to Scripture, or which grants cognitions. There is a work of the Spirit in ecclesia which modifies the human being. In connection with this modification and its co-intentionalities, perceptive powers are created and insights and apprehensions occur. To say that the Spirit directly "causes" them or enables them simply loses sight of the very phenomenon of Christian faith. Such formulations resemble the mind-invading stories of science fiction more than the redemptive transformation of Jesus Christ in ecclesia.

Does this social formulation of religious knowledge exclude what is sometimes called "religious experience," that watchword of liberal theology and taboo-word for dialectical theology? No one can deny that there are religious experiences of a dramatic nature nor that faith itself occurs more through affections and emotions than intellection. Are such experiences reality-mediating? The question is not a clear one. Are we asking whether cataclysmic emotional experiences can be vehicles by which God communicates cognitive content to an individual? In our view religious experience is not cognitive, partly because Hepburn's arguments about the matter seem to us valid, and partly for reasons stated above.[8] On the other hand, a vivid emotional experience representing a crisis in a human life can serve as the occasion of perceptivity or insight. In these situations, the structure of presence and apprecence and the social mediation of reality in ecclesia are presupposed. The religious experience represents a conjunction of the cumulative shaping effect of ecclesia with a critical juncture of individual biography, aided perhaps by institutionalized patterns of emotional expression in given churches. Only in this sense would we acknowledge that "religious experience" has a cognitive dimension.

C. CONCLUSION

It is time to summarize. We have struggled with the question of faith and reality-orientation partly guided by suspicions of recent philosophy that faith is indifferent to reality but mostly concerned about the paralyzing effect this suspicion has on theological work from criteriology to confession. Working from a commitment to the positivity and determinacy of faith's situation, we focused upon that form of corporate historical existence which serves as the matrix of faith; ecclesia and ecclesial man. Our exploration was conducted at two levels. First, drawing largely from Husserlian phenomenology and especially the life-world analyses of Husserl's final period, we set forth several operative principles which include the principle of positivity, the notion of concrete apprehension or intuition, the life-world, intersubjectivity, and appresentation. We do not see these as mere empty methodological instruments but as expressions of something about reality itself, that is, something about world,

8. Ronald Hepburn, *Christianity and Paradox* (London: C. A. Watts and Co., 1958), chaps. III and IV.

knowledge, human consciousness, and social man. Second, we discovered that in its own distinctive way ecclesia reflects these realities. In ecclesia the life-world is a faith-world. It retains a unique set of co-intentionalities. Apprehensions occur in its "collective unconscious" of matters both present and appresent. Generally, our argument has been that little progress can be made in the question of faith's reality-orientation apart from a morphology of faith's situation. The reason this is the case is that faith's apprehensions do not occur as products of theological ratiocination but as concomitants of a largely unconscious shaping of the consciousness. The problem then is to isolate the components of faith's situation such as language, existence, and sociality to discover their interrelationship and how that interrelationship functions in cognition, and to gain access to the depth strata of this situation; the images and story beneath the doctrines and myths, the transcendental structure beneath redemptive existence, the intersubjectivity beneath the conscious social interactions. After a brief attempt to indicate general ways in which reality is socially mediated, we argued that the realities of faith appear in the depth strata of ecclesia in the two modes of presence and appresence.

It may be clearer now why we insist that phenomenological theology in the sense of this inquiry must precede criteriology and in fact provide the clues to the vexing questions about theological norms and authorities. First, if reality-apprehensions occur in the mode of presence and appresence at the depth levels of ecclesia, this means that authorities (Scripture, tradition) are not *principia* in the Aristotelian sense of Protestant scholasticism, the first and immediate starting point from which everything else is constructed. Historically speaking, the authorities did not produce but grew out of a social and redemptive existence which preceded them. Systematically speaking, the authorities are authorities only if their usage conforms to what ecclesia is, which includes the constitutive structure of redemptive existence. To reverse the procedure makes ecclesia vulnerable to arbitrary and idolatrous uses of authorities, uses so habitual in both Catholic and Protestant Christendom that to question them is to question faith itself. Our proposal is that the transition to redemptive existence, the story and imagery correlative to this, and the co-intentionalities involving mankind as such provide ways of assessing what kind of authority is appropriate in ecclesia and how the writings of prophets and apostles are to be used in the community of ecclesial man.

The reader may or may not sense in this essay a peculiar way of relating philosophy and theology. The question of phliosophy and theology is hopelessly ambiguous insofar as philosophy offers two unresolved pictures of itself: the one, technical and analytical in service to reality-oriented sciences; the other substantial, directed to being or regions of being. It is also ambiguous given a similar division in theology itself. In my view philosophy's proper business is ontology, both fundamental and otherwise, and theology's proper business is the transposing of the basal apprehensions which occur in ecclesia into the modes of understanding. The question of their relationship is at an impasse because the merely technical use of philosophy in theology does little to criticize the persistent obscurantist element which attends a religious community nor does it relate whatever is involved in faith to the larger questions of reality. On the other hand, a theory of religion advanced within the framework of a metaphysical commitment resides above the level of positive religion and does little to illuminate it or relate it to being or its regions. Furthermore, "interpretations" of determinate religious faiths within that metaphysical framework tend to transform that faith and its realities into something else. The impasse, therefore, is produced by the two undesirable alternatives of irrelevant clarification and the subjugation of faith by philosophy.

It is obvious that our proposal is not a systematic portrayal of the relationship between philosophy and theology. Presiding over our whole enterprise is the Husserlian view of world which locates "reality" in determinate processes, entities, and configurations rather than in the general structure in common to such. Although these general structures can be described (as in a science of life-world), they cannot serve as criteria for determinate realities since they undergo modification at determinate levels. The contribution of philosophy to theology is the discovery of these general structures (transcendental, cosmological, historical, epistemological) which reappear in modified form in the religious community. Using such discoveries, the theologian is helped to uncover what is in fact there in the religious community, but the reality principle itself prevents him from using the general structures as criteria or from bending the realities of faith to fit the general scheme. Faith like all determinate regions of human experience confronts the philosopher with a many-sided reality to be taken seriously rather than simply engulfed into a system. Philosophy confronts faith with descriptions of reality at inclusive levels, to be taken seriously and utilized in the attempt to uncover transcendental, ontological, and epistemological dimensions in the situation of faith. The relationship between philosophy and theology is neither merely technical nor one of subjugation because "reality" resides in both.

Appendix

PHENOMENOLOGY IN CATHOLIC AND PROTESTANT THOUGHT

A. THE TWO MAJOR PERIODS

The effect of Husserlian phenomenology on types of twentieth-century religious inquiry (history of religions, philosophy of religion, theology) presents something of an enigma. In history of religions phenomenology effected a virtual methodological revolution. In theology with a few exceptions and until very recently, Husserlian phenomenology has been all but ignored. Philosophy of religion has seen sporadic and usually unrelated attempts to appropriate phenomenological method. The situation can be summarized in the following generalization. The more universal and "phenomenal" is the discipline the more explicit is the appropriation of the Husserlian method and conceptual apparatus. The more normative and determinate is the discipline, such as theology, the more phenomenology is present indirectly and without the Husserlian categories. Phenomenology's presence in twentieth-century theology is mostly in the altered form of philosophies of existence or existential phenomenology. We should not be surprised about this. The theological community has always participated in the general consensus that Husserlian phenomenology is a neo-Kantianism, a reality-bracketing methodology which continued Kant's transcendental philosophy. Accordingly, it was not drawn to Husserl but to Heidegger, the ontological and anthropological turn of the Husserlian program. Even as we are not surprised that a theology which expresses a religious faith oriented toward human bondage and redemption would gravitate toward ontological analyses of human temporality and its concomitant existentials, neither are we surprised that history of religions would be interested in a method which would illuminate the intentional aspect of religion.

Except perhaps for history of religions, the appropriation of phenomenology in religious studies has never had the character of a school or unified movement. There has never been a "phenomenological theology" in the sense of a self-conscious group of scholars. On the other hand, a number of monographs in philosophy of religion and theology do explicitly utilize Husserlian methods and categories. They are few in number, limited in influence, and for the most part remain in the background of the movements which have carried the day since the turn of the century. In this Appendix we shall turn our attention to phenomenology in philosophy of religion and theology rather than history of religions. In twentieth-century religious thought the appropriation of phenomenology falls into two distinct periods. The first covers the 1920's and early 1930's and is dominated by Max Scheler. The second ranges from the 1950's to the present and reflects post-Husserlian "existential" phenomenologies.

1. *From Scheler to Reiner: 1921–1934 (phenomenology and religious philosophy)*

The first period includes the 1920's and 1930's and goes from Scheler's *Vom Ewigen im Menschen* (1921) to Hans Reiner's *Das Phänomen des Glaubens* (1934).[1] The immediate background of this cluster of writings is the "older phenomenological movement."[2] Besides Husserl himself the key figures in the older movement were Alexander Pfänder, the central figure at the University of Munich,

1. Scheler, *Vom Ewigen im Menschen* (Leipzig: Neuer Geist, 1921). See the English translation, *On the Eternal in Man,* trans. Bernard Noble (New York: Harper & Row, 1960). Hans Reiner, *Das Phänomen des Glaubens* (Halle: Niemayer, 1934).
2. For a summary of the older movement and its main participants see Spiegelberg, *The Phenomenological Movement,* I (The Hague: Nijhoff, 1965), parts IV and V. A picture of this period is also provided by the essays of Hocking, Löwith, Conrad-Martius, and others in *Edmund Husserl 1859–1959* (The Hague: Nijhoff, 1959).

Adolf Reinach, who taught with Husserl at Göttingen, and Max Scheler. None of them slavishly continued Husserl's life-time programmatic, but each developed his own philosophy by applying phenomenological analyses to such themes as the will, oughtness, social acts, and religion. From the very beginning of the movement we have phenomenologists who did not continue Husserl's transcendental program but who did apply his method(s) to problems and themes beyond the founding transcendental region. The result was that a number of students of phenomenology wrote monographs applying Husserlian methods to religion. The first phenomenologist to be concerned about the relation between phenomenology and the religous sphere was probably Reinach, a Göttingen *Privatdozent* who was killed in the First World War. However, he left only brief hints in sections of his collected writings on the subject of religion.[3] The first major works on religion produced by the phenomenological movement appear in 1921, and this brings us to Max Scheler. Scheler, unsystematic but with powerful and original insight, clearly dominated the period. His *Vom Ewigen im Menschen* (1921) was the most ambitious and mature piece of writing among a number of monographs on phenomenology and religion, many of which were doctoral dissertations or were based on such.

Most of the thinkers who applied Husserlian methods to philosophy of religion in this period are not heard from, at least in the role of phenomenologists, after the early 1930's. The one clear exception is Dietrich von Hildebrand, a Roman Catholic moral philosopher associated with Scheler who submitted significant publications in the early 1930's on community and on moral attitudes, and who continued on the same lines when he immigrated to America.[4] Some of those writing in this early period who were Roman Catholics saw in Husserlian methods a way of modernizing the perennial philosophy. Edith Stein's *Endliches und ewiges Sein* (see p. 241, n. 11), written in this period but published posthumously in 1950, was

---

3. For instance, Adolf Reinach, *Gesammelte Schriften* (Halle: 1921), pp. xxviii ff.
4. See his *Metaphysik der Gemeinschaft* (Augsburg: Haas und Grabher, 1930) and *Sittliche Grundhaltungen* (Mainz: Matthias Grünewald Verlag, 1933).

one of the more industrious attempts along this line. Arnold Metzger's *Phänomenologie und Metaphysik* (1933) addressed the problem of the relativity of knowledge using Husserlian concepts and methods but moving to a Christologically grounded understanding of man to solve the problem.[5]

Most of these works of this early period display a theologically neutral tone with the sectarian tradition played down. Their area of focus tends to be "philosophy of religion," the nature of religion, or "religious experience."[6] Winkler's *Phänomenologie und Religion* (1921) is a Heidelberg dissertation whose proposals are mostly formal and methodological. He uses Husserl's "insight into essence" to obtain a grasp of the "primordial phenomenon" of religion which founds and unifies all other religious phenomena. He thinks this to be a more scientific approach than the usual empirical psychologies and compares his proposal to Wobbermin's religious-psychological method.

Otto Gründler's *Elemente zu einer Religionsphilosophie auf phänomenologischer Gründlage* (1922) is not only stimulated by Scheler, who wrote the Foreword, but draws on phenomenologically oriented thinkers in the history of religions; Otto, Heiler, and Söderblom. Structurally, this little work anticipates Van der Leeuw since it poses the question of the nature of religion by focusing on the religious act as it is determined by its object, the Holy. He locates a correspondence between the inclinations of religious subjectivity like world-denial and world-affirmation with noematic qualities in God such as eternal rest and eternal work. When one obtains to these *Urphänomenen* of religion, he has taken only the first step of

5. *Phänomenologie und Metaphysik: Das Problem des Relativismus und seiner Uberwindung* (Stuttgart: Neake, 1933).

6. Robert Winkler, *Phänomenologie und Religion: ein Beitrag zu den Prinzipienfragen der Religionsphilosophie* (Tübingen: J. C. B. Mohr, 1921); Otto Gründler, *Elemente zu einer Religionsphilosophie auf Phänomenologischer Gründlage* (Munich: Kösel und Pustet, 1922); Kurt Stavenhagen, *Absolute Stellungnahme: eine ontologische Untersuchung über das Wesen der Religion* (Erlangen: Verlag d. philos. Akademie, 1925); Jean Hering, *Phénoménologie et Philosophie religieuse* (Strasbourg: 1925); Charles Hauter, *Essai sur l'objet religieux* (Paris: Alcan, 1928); Hans Reiner, *Das Phänomen des Glaubens.*

philosophy of religion, beyond which arise questions of reality and existence.[7]

Jean Hering's dissertation, *Phénoménologie et Philosophie Religieuse* (1925), begins a tradition of using phenomenology in philosophy of religion at Strasbourg, France, which persists to the present day in Roger Mehl and Georges Gusdorf. The focus of the work is on methodological issues raised by the crisis of post-Feuerbach religious thought and the possibility that religious content can be exhaustively derived from an anthropology. Hering's grasp and interpretation of Husserl's philosophy is much more rigorous than Winkler's, but his constructive proposals concerning the use of eidetic analysis to procure the essence of religion are very close to Winkler. However, he goes beyond Winkler in his desire to incorporate the efforts of empirical religious psychology, empirical religious sociology, and eidetic religious psychology. Similar to Hering's monograph is Charles Hauter's *Essai sur l'objet religieux* (1928), which is also written in the Strasbourg milieu, and which applies phenomenological methods to the sphere of religious philosophy in a Christian context. In 1925 appeared one of the most cited contributions of the decade, Kurt Stavenhagen's *Absolute Stellungnahmen.* He was intrigued by Reinach's brief programmatic hints about the possibilities of using phenomenology to uncover the essence of religion, and he cites Otto Pfänder and Scheler as his primary sources of inspiration. His work is in one way the most impressive of these monographs of the 1920's since it contains what amounts to a natural theology. He argues that there are consciousness acts or *noeses* which are incapable of further enhancement. They are absolute noeses, and they involve "absolute personal attitudes." Examples of personal attitudes are hate, love, and honoring, and he argues that a certain type of personal attitude is incapable of gradation; for instance, honoring another simply for himself. These attitudes serve

7. Resembling Gründler's work but less explicitly phenomenological is Paul Hofmann's *Das religiöse Erlebnis: seine Strukture, seine Typen und seine Wahrheitsanspruch* (Charlottenburg: Rolf Heise, 1925). Hofmann continues the Ritschlian motif of value-judgments but uses Heiler, Otto, and Wobbermin for a more explicit grasp of the unity of various religious acts, a unity which he finds in a salvation pertaining to one's total life.

as the condition of man's power to grasp the Holy, and function as the bridge between the worlds of sacred and profane. In these absolute noeses we have the clue to the very essence of religion.

In 1929 two rather significant articles were written by Johannes Heber on the methodology of phenomenological philosophy of religion. They occur against the background of the early Husserl and the German literature of phenomenological philosophy of religion (Reinach, Scheler, Gründler, and Stavenhagen).[8] Johannes Heber's thesis is little more than a direct repetition of Stavenhagen's work. He too thinks that phenomenological philosophy of religion offers an indispensable moment for both history of religions and philosophy of religion by isolating and describing the "essence of religion." To elaborate this he expounds Husserl's distinction (in the *Ideas*) between fact and essence and the corresponding distinction between sciences of fact and sciences of essence. Phenomenological philosophy of religion is the science of the "essence" of religion, and through essence-insight (*Wesenschau*), it discovers the irreducible and distinctive content of the religious act and its object. Hans Reiner's *Phänomen des Glaubens* (1934) is the last monograph of the period and draws on the work of both Husserl and Heidegger. Reiner attempts an eidetics of faith but in the light of Heidegger's ontology of *Dasein*. This work therefore is a transitional work from the "eidetic" and methodological monographs of the early period to the existential and anthropological focus of the later period.

We would miss an important feature of the first period if we failed to observe that several theologians who later achieved visibility without association with phenomenology were concerned with Husserl in the 1920's. None of these theologians are "phenomenological theologians," yet phenomenology played some role in the formative period of their thought. On the Catholic side are Erich Przywara and Joseph Maréchal. Phenomenology seems to have little effect on Przywara's constructive work, yet in 1923 he wrote an appre-

8. Johannes Heber, "Problemstellung und Eigenart der religionsphänomeno-logischen Methode," and "Die phänomenologische Methode in ihrer Bedeutung für die Religionsphilosophie," in Karl Girgensohn, ed., *Christentum und Wissenschaft,* Fünfter Jahrgang (Dresden: Ungelenk, 1929).

ciative book on Scheler and Newman and the renascence of an Augustinian school of intuition. He thinks there are affinities between Newman and this school, and he finds that the new method is made possible by phenomenology.[9] In a key article published in 1930 Maréchal urges a correction of Blondel's philosophy of action by means of the analytic rigor of Husserl.[10] Phenomenology played some role in the thought of three young Protestant theologians of the 1920's; Karl Löwith, Dietrich Bonhoeffer, and Paul Tillich. Both Bonhoeffer and Löwith saw in phenomenology a possible method for a new understanding of human community.[11] We shall postpone the complex problem of Tillich's use of phenomenology until later in the chapter. Suffice it to say that his writings in the 1920's give evidence of an exposure to Husserl's *Investigations* and to the *Ideas,* and reflect both criticism of Husserlian phenomenology and a partial incorporation of it.

In summary the early period is almost exclusively dominated by single monographs on phenomenology and "religious philosophy." These are exploratory in character and do not engender a life-time programmatic. Theology in the period is concerned with the critique of the Ritschlian heritage, and those writings which do make use of Husserlian phenomenology attract little attention among the resounding battle cries raised by the dialectical and confessional theologies which were carrying the day.

9. Erich Przywara, *Religionsbegründung: Max Scheler und J. H. Newman* (Freiburg: Herder, 1923).
10. "Phénoménologie pure ou philosophie de l'action?" in *Mélanges Joseph Maréchal* (Paris: Bruxelles, 1950), vol. I, pp. 181–206.
11. The philosophical problem of the knowledge of other minds and the broader problem of intersubjectivity (the relation between selves) were present in the older phenomenological movement almost from the beginning. Edith Stein had written a dissertation on the subject in 1917 *(Zum Problem der Einfühlung).* It was Scheler, however, who gave most attention to the pre-reflective and corporate structures which founded human community. He published his very intriguing theory of "sympathetic" knowledge of the other in the same year as Husserl's *Ideas,* entitled, *Zur Phänomenologie und Theorie der Sympathiegefühle und von Liebe und Hass* (Halle: Niemayer, 1913). Bonhoeffer's work was his Berlin dissertation, written in 1927, *Sanctorum Communio: eine dogmatische Untersuchung zur Soziologie der Kirche* (Munich: Chr. Kaiser, 1954). Löwith's study was *Das Individuum in der Rolle des Mitmenschen* (Darmstadt: Wissenschaftliche Buchgesellschaft, 1928).

2. "Existential phenomenology": 1950 to the present

The early application of phenomenology to philosophy of religion came to a halt in the middle 1930's and was not resumed until the 1950's. There are some exceptions. The works of Otto, Heiler, and Van der Leeuw established a method which continued unabated in northern Europe in the history of religions field. Furthermore, some individual efforts (von Hildebrand) persisted beyond the 1930's while others (Thévenaz) began their work in the interim period. Otherwise, we can say that the philosophies of religion written against the background of the older phenomenological movement had no continuing successors. The use of phenomenology in philosophy of religion lapsed in the middle 1930's and recommenced with a new generation of thinkers in the 1950's.

This demise and renascence more or less follows the course of Husserlian phenomenology itself. After 1933 Husserl's own publications as well as attention and response to his thought more or less went underground.[12] From the publication of Heidegger's *Being and Time* (1927), the ontology of *Dasein* more and more dominated the interest of European philosophers. The publications of Jaspers, Sartre, and Marcel supplemented the Heideggerian influence so as to turn the phenomenological movement into the philosophies of existence of the late 1930's and 1940's. Interest in Husserlian phenomenology as a philosophical option seems to have been reborn first in France. Sartre had been a close student of Husserl's early writings, and both Merleau-Ponty and Ricoeur studied the Archives materials, and especially the *Crisis*. Although their philosophies have an existential and hermeneutical dimension, they also retain a

12. The political situation in Germany made it difficult for Husserl with his Jewish background to lecture or publish in Germany. Most of his research and writings of this later period were not brought to publication. When he died in 1938, his papers and unpublished manuscripts were smuggled from Freiburg to the University of Louvain with the help of the Belgian Embassy in Berlin. See Van Breda's "Die Rettung von Husserls Nachlass und die Gründung des Husserl-Archives" in *Husserl und das Denken der Neuzeit* (The Hague: Nijhoff, 1959). Van Breda and others worked over these papers during and after the war, first translating Husserl's private code into German, and then preparing publishable portions for *Husserliana,* the multivolume edition of Husserl's works. Accordingly, in the period of the 1940's, most of Husserl's materials were available only to the few who consulted the Louvain Archives. The volumes of *Husserliana* did not begin until the 1950's.

clear eidetic or essence-oriented step. Further, both worked from an exposure to the later Husserl and from a perspective on his total development, not simply on the basis of the *Investigations* and the *Ideas,* the only works which the 1930's reflect. In short Husserlian phenomenology begins to return to the philosophical community in the 1950's, and with the publications of Husserl's later works as well as the postwar accessibility of the Archives, a massive amount of research began to see publication.

With the broadened access to Husserl and the broadened picture made possible by it came a renewed interest in phenomenology in the theological community. This 1950's rebirth of interest in phenomenology occurred almost exclusively in Roman Catholic circles. If we do not count Ricoeur and Thévenaz who are primarily philosophers, the only exception to this is the Lutheran theologian, Theobald Süss, who attempted to apply Husserlian concepts (horizon, intentionality) to theological themes. Beyond this, phenomenology was present in Protestant theology only in the ontological developments of existentialist philosophy, especially in the concern with hermeneutic. Toward the end of the 1960's phenomenology in its Husserlian sense begins to appear again in a few Protestant theologians who develop a fundamental theology.

A number of influences were at work to stimulate the rebirth of phenomenology in Roman Catholic circles in the second period. Scheler had been the most prominent thinker in phenomenology and religious philosophy in the early period. Blondel's philosophy of action had used a "phenomenological" method in opening up a priori structures of the human will. Maréchal had pioneered a major attempt to appropriate the critical philosophy into Thomism. Furthermore, the seeds of Maréchal's work fell on receptive soil and a continuing effort to use transcendental method persisted after him. The centuries-long apologetic tradition of Roman Catholic theology combined with transcendental method to create attempts to correlate transcendental structures in the religious subject with the religious object; hence, interest increased in rigorous (Husserlian) methods in dealing with such matters. It is no surprise then that the renascence of Husserlian studies in philosophy plus the heritage of Scheler, Blondel, and Maréchal created new appropriations of phenomenology in the 1950's. These appropriations are of many kinds, ranging from Catholic personalism to the transcendental method.

If Scheler dominated phenomenological religious philosophy in the early period, Henri Duméry dominates the later one. His has been the most thoroughgoing methodological exploration and the most inclusive application of Husserlian methods to the whole range of theological questions. In addition to Duméry, Albert Dondeyne, August Brunner, Raymond Vancourt, and Carlos Cirne-Lima published phenomenological investigations in the 1950's with others entering the picture in the following decades.

Phenomenology in the second period is present in both Roman Catholic and Protestant circles in such different ways that it is difficult to characterize the period as a whole. We can confidently say that no "school" of phenomenology and theology has formed. It is also clear that most of those who utilize phenomenological methods and categories work not simply with Husserl but with Husserl by way of Merleau-Ponty, Heidegger, or Marcel; in other words the "existential turn" of the phenomenological movement. Yet these efforts vary significantly from the existential theologies of Bultmann, Buri, or Ebeling. Duméry and his Protestant counterparts are more committed to the Husserlian method of illuminating a consciousness-act by focusing on its meant or noematic object. To this degree the efforts of the second period recall those of the first although with more explicit theological interest. We find it, therefore, somewhat strange that while the second period is born from the renascence of Husserl studies which opened up the late Husserl and the life-world theme, the theological uses of phenomenology in the 1950's and 1960's almost uniformly bypass this theme, restricting themselves to the eidetic reduction of the early Husserl.

B. HUSSERLIAN PHENOMENOLOGY IN CATHOLIC AND PROTESTANT THEOLOGY

The present Appendix is little more than an outline of the presence of phenomenological philosophy in twentieth-century theology and philosophy of religion. We are, therefore, omitting that part of religious studies in which phenomenology has had its most extensive and fruitful influence, the history of religions.[13] Neither the study

13. For brief accounts of this influence see the introduction to Van der

of religious "phenomena" nor even "phenomenological" investigations are necessarily dependent on Husserlian phenomenology.[14] Yet
those studies which are dependent share certain common characteristics. They organize their data on the basis of a view of the
"essence" of religion, and they portray this "essence" through an
eidetics of the religious act or the religious consciousness. Further,
the typologies in which the data are arranged reflect a noetic-noematic, that is, the intentional structure is threefold: the divine object,
the act or acts in which such is experienced, and the mediating rites,
authorities of communities through which the divine "power" is
present.[15] In Husserlian language the "phenomenology" of history
of religions is an eidetics of the religious consciousness. Major
works of phenomenology of religion occur throughout the two
periods of our typology. Anticipated by Otto's classic work on the
Holy in 1917, they go from Heiler's work on prayer in 1923 to the
present.[16] The appropriation of phenomenology outside of history

Leeuw's *Einführung in die Phänomenologie der Religion* (Darmstadt:
Wissenschaftliche Buchgesellschaft, 1961). See also *Religion in Essence
and Manifestation* (London: Allen & Unwin, Ltd. 1938), chap. 110, and
R. F. Merkel, "Zur Geschichte der Religionsphänomenologie," in the *Fest-
schrift* for Heiler, C. M. Schroder, ed., *In Deo Omnia Unum. Eine Samm-
lung v. Aufsätzen Friedrich Heiler zum 50. Geburtstage* (Munich:
Reinhardt, 1942). One of the fullest summaries published to that time
was Eva Hirschman's Groningen dissertation, *Phänomenologie der Religion*
(Würzburg-Aumuhle: Konrad Triltsch, 1940). Written under the influence
of both Van der Leeuw and Wach, the book incorporates almost all of
the significant literature into an elaborate typology of approaches. See
especially Part I for a history of the use of phenomenology in the history
of religions.

14. For instance note the "Phänomenologische Teil" in P. D. Chantepie de
la Saussaye's *Lehrbuch der Religionsgeschichte* (Freiburg: J. C. Mohr,
1887), I, pp. 103–35. The author sees the "outer appearances" of religion
as reflecting "inner processes" (acts, presentations, and feelings), and
characterizes the study of this "important group of religious appearances"
as phenomenology, a discipline closely allied to psychology. In this section
he takes up such phenomena as holy stones, trees, and animals, the venera-
tion of nature and man, sacrifice and prayer, holy places, times, and
persons, the religious community, mythology, etc.

15. For descriptions of the phenomenological method employed in history
of religions see Van der Leeuw, *Religion,* "Epilegomena," and also Friedrich Heiler, *Erscheinungsformen und Wesen der Religion* (Stuttgart: W.
Kohlhammer, 1961), pp. 18 ff.

16. Rudolf Otto, *The Idea of the Holy* (New York: Oxford University
Press, 1958); Friedrich Heiler, *Prayer: A Study in the History and Psychology of Religion* (New York: Oxford University Press, 1958); (the

of religions occurs along the sectarian lines of Protestant and Catholic thought. In the second period phenomenology in the original Husserlian sense is more a story of Catholic than Protestant thought and that is where we shall begin.

1. *Phenomenology in Roman Catholic circles*

So close has been the relation between modern Catholic thought and the phenomenological movement that some critics have described phenomenology as a "Catholic philosophy."[17] We have already mentioned several factors which created a receptive climate toward phenomenology in Roman Catholic circles; namely, the influence of Scheler, the "phenomenology" of Blondel, and the transcendental program of the Maréchal school. In addition Catholic-related universities played a significant role in the revival of Husserlian studies. The University of Freiburg, where Huserl taught and resided from

German original was published in 1923); Van der Leeuw, *Einfuhrung* (1925) and *Religion* (1933); Widengren, *Religionsphänomenologie* (Berlin: de Gruyter, 1969); the original edition appeared in 1945; W. B. Kristensen, *T,ie Meaning of Religion: Lectures in the Phenomenology of Religion* (The Hague: Nijhoff, 1968), a posthumous publication of lectures given in Leyden prior to 1953; W. King, *Introduction to Religion: A Phenomenological Approach* (New York: Harper & Row, 1968); Heiler, *Erscheinungsformen* (1961). See also various works by Mircea Eliade.

17. Karl Manheim notes the dependence of Husserl himself on Bolzano and Brentano whose philosophies to some extent reflect scholastic philosophy. He also argues that certain features of phenomenology lend themselves to Catholic thought such as the sharp distinction between fact and essence which can reappear in the Catholic framework as the time-eternity distinction and which "prepares the terrain for the construction of a non-formal, intuitionist metaphysics." *Essays in the Sociology of Knowledge* (New York: Oxford University Press, 1952), p. 155. Further, Scheler was suspected of turning phenomenology into a "common whore" by making it serve the purposes of Catholic apologetics. See the "Preface to the Second German Edition," *On the Eternal in Man*, p. 18. Scheler replied to this criticism by pointing out that pheonomenology is not *productive* but *reproductive*, proceeding from given ideas which it merely rediscovers. In this passage Scheler stressed the evaluative and metaphysical neutrality of "reproductive" phenomenology. On the other hand he did think that phenomenology has a deeper relationship with "the fundamental propositions of traditional Christian philosophy than any other modern philosophical school since Descartes" (from Scheler's "Foreword" to Gründler, *Elemente*). Van Breda, the salvager of Husserl's literary estate for the University of Louvain and the general editor of *Husserliana,* stresses phenomenology's philosophical autonomy and denies that it offers presuppositions favorable to Catholic thought (*Edmund Husserl 1859–1959,* pp. 119–20).

1916 until his death, retained a Roman Catholic theological faculty. Husserl's papers were salvaged and stored at the Roman Catholic University of Louvain, which then became one of the earliest post-World War II centers of Husserlian studies, and from which phenomenology spread to other Roman Catholic schools such as Fordham and Duquesne. Because of this Catholic receptivity to phenomenology, the most extensive and ambitious attempts to utilize phenomenology in religious philosophy in both early and late periods are found in Roman Catholic thinkers.

The widest context in which to understand the Roman Catholic appropriation of phenomenology is the response of Catholic philosophers to post-Cartesian or modern philosophy. Contentwise this means the question of whether simply to reject or to work with that set of epistemological and ontological problems generated by the unveiling of the *cogito,* or, more broadly expressed, the unreducible region of the human subject.[18] As Scheler saw it, the issue was not simply between Thomism and Kantianism, but rather between rationalistic Thomism which was shaped by the Enlightenment and which had lost sight of the *cogito* and transcendental or phenomenological philosophies which could serve as a corrective. For Przywara, post-Cartesian philosophy and especially phenomenology aid Roman Catholic thought to return to the Augustinian strand of its own tradition and he finds such "Augustinianism" a common element in both Newman and Scheler.[19]

Although Scheler is the central and dominant figure in initiating a rapprochement between Catholic thought and Husserlian phenomenology, he does not typify the way this rapprochement took place thereafter. Excluding the dissertation-like monographs on phenom-

18. According to Charles Courtney, Eduard LeRoy's lectures on the cogito (published in his *Le Problème de Dieu,* 1930) were important in creating a receptivity toward phenomenology in Roman Catholic circles in France. "Phenomenology and Theism, Henry Duméry's Proposal," unpublished Ph.D. dissertation, Northwestern University, 1965, p. 2.

19. This association of Newman and Scheler may not be so farfetched as it sounds. Newman like Jonathan Edwards and Friedrich Schleiermacher read and profited by the philosophy of John Locke. And Locke and Hume were important sources of Husserl's thought. He offered seminars in the British empiricists, and Diemer suggests that this tradition is as crucial for Husserl as neo-Kantianism.

enology and religious philosophy written in the 1920's, we find two clearly distinguishable ways in which phenomenology was taken up in Catholic thought. The first is represented by those whose primary concern is fundamental theology, and who, reflecting the Maréchal school, employ Husserlian phenomenology to perform transcendental analyses of faith. The second is represented by those who work out a synthesis of Husserlian and existentialist philosophies and utilize this "existential phenomenology" to reformulate theological or dogmatic materials in the church tradition. Max Scheler, profound and unclassifiable, falls into neither camp. His first major effort was an attempt to find an objective basis for philosophical ethics by tracing formal and imperative levels of ethics back to the concrete and interpersonal structures of human life.[20] In his *The Nature of Sympathy* Scheler argued for an immediate "sympathetic" knowledge between the ego and the other.[21] His insistence on the primacy of emotions anticipates later existentialist philosophies but also indicates the complex way in which Scheler amalgamated the personal, religious, and moral dimensions of Catholic faith with the universal concerns of the philosopher. He was careful to distinguish in a formal way various kinds and levels of phenomenology as applied to religion.[22] Such distinctions are more difficult to locate in Scheler's actual analyses which at one point appear to set forth the religious act in the universal sense of history of religions and at the same time is an act directed toward an object, the divine, which

20. This massive and incomparable work, *Der Formalismus in der Ethik und die materiale Wertethik: neuer Versuch der Gründlegung eines ethischen Personalismus,* was published originally in the series edited by Husserl, the *Jahrbuch für Philosophie und Phänomenologische Forschung* (1916), no. 2.

21. *Zur Phänomenologie und Theorie der Sympathiegefühle und von Liebe und Hass* (Halle: Niemeyer) was originally published in 1913. *The Nature of Sympathy,* trans. Peter Heath (London: Routledge and Kegan Paul, 1954), translates the second German edition published under the title, *Wesen und Formen der Sympathie* (1923).

22. *On the Eternal in Man,* pp. 18–20. This work includes Scheler's most extensive writings on religion and philosophy, the heart of the work being "Problems of Religion" (pp. 105–353), which is Scheler's "phenomenology" of religion and of the religious act. The threefold structure of the "essential phenomenology of religion" (the divine or religious object, the forms of revelation, and the religious subject) very closely resembles that of Van der Leeuw's *Religion.*

appears in the determinate form of classical Catholic thought. Hence, Scheler's influence was exercised in such divergent directions as Catholic moral philosophy (von Hildebrand), personalist and interpersonalist theology (Przywara), and phenomenologies of faith and the religious act.

a. Phenomenology at the edge of transcendental Catholic thought

The most impressive strand of recent Catholic religious philosophy is, from a technical point of view, the Maréchal school following what is called transcendental method.[23] Transcendental Catholic philosophy is the attempt to construct a sound epistemology which retains a basically Thomist framework but expands and revises it with the help of Kant and the disclosure of the transcendental conditions of knowledge. Transcendental method lends itself to Catholic fundamental theology in which the foundations of theology itself are revealed by analysis of the human conditions of the act of faith and the predisposition of man toward revelation.[24] Transcendental Catholic thought does have an indirect relation to Husserlian phenomenology. Maréchal himself had read and reacted to Husserl. Both Rahner and Lotz absorb Husserlian motifs insofar as they persist in Heidegger's thought. On the other hand, it is clear that Kant rather than Husserl himself is the central figure in transcendental philosophy. Furthermore, the interpretation of Husserl in Catholic transcendentalism does not go beyond the portraits of Husserl which were in vogue in the 1920's and 1930's. These accounts are restricted to Husserl's *Logical Investigations* and the *Ideas,* and they interpret

23. Maréchal's *Le Point de Départ de la Metaphysique* (Louvain: 1927) is the founding work of the movement, and Emerich Coreth's *Metaphysique: eine methodisch-systematisch Gründlegung* (Innsbruck: 1961), Karl Rahner's *Geist im Welt* (Munich: Kösel-Verlag, 1957), and Lonergan's *Insight: A Study of Human Understanding* (New York: Philosophical Library, 1957) are all landmarks in the development of Catholic transcendental philosophy. For two excellent accounts of the movement see Otto Muck, *The Transcendental Method* (New York: Herder & Herder, 1968), and Hansjürgen Verweyen, *Ontologische Voraussetzungen des Glaubensaktes* (Düsseldorf: Patmos, 1969).
24. Karl Rahner's *Hearers of the Word* (New York: Herder & Herder, 1969) is the most definitive expression of a fundamental theology within transcendental Catholic thought.

Husserlian phenomenology as simply a reality-bracketing eidetics.[25]

However, it is within or "at the edge of" transcendental Catholic thought, especially to the degree that it is also a fundamental theology, that Catholic thinkers of this second period reflect Husserlian phenomenology. The key figures are Raymond Vancourt, Auguste Brunner, and Carlos Cirne-Lima. All three attempt "phenomenologies of faith"; hence, they represent the reappearance of the early Scheler-inspired investigations of the religious act. All three make the category of the personal central, and in the thought of of Brunner and Vancourt, Husserl is clearly the main philosophical resource. We describe them as at the edge of transcendental Catholic thought not so much because they are disciples of Maréchal but because they attempt to understand faith in relation to personal and social structures of the human being.

Of the three Cirne-Lima has least relation to Husserl. His work, *Der personale Glaube* (1959), is a philosophical study of belief and certitude, emphasizing belief as a personal act in an interpersonal situation.[26] Vancourt began his publishing in the 1940's with studies on Maine de Biran, Husserl, and Kierkegaard, including a translation of Hartmann's *Principles of a Metaphysics of Knowledge*. He

25. Coreth, for example, describes Husserl's philosophy as an eidetic science which turns away from the "real and actual" self-operations of the ego (*Metaphysik*, pp. 76–77). Lonergan sees Husserlian phenomenology as following a formal and descriptive method which shrinks the subject to intentional acts and therefore is restricted to the realm of immanence (*Insight*, p. 415). According to F. P. Fiorenza, Rahner assimilated Heidegger's critique of Husserl and reacted to Husserl by way of that critique ("Karl Rahner and the Kantian Problematic," in Rahner's *Spirit in the World* [New York: Herder & Herder, 1968]). These portraits of Husserlian phenomenology as a "subjective idealism" are fairly standard outside the circles which drew on the unpublished materials which contained the late philosophy of Husserl. In transcendental Catholic thought this view goes back to Maréchal himself who saw the Husserlian ego as indeterminate and phenomenal and an insufficient ground for any enterprise which concerns itself with reality and validity. Verweyen, commenting on this interpretation, regrets that Maréchal had no continuing exposure to Husserl's philosophy after his essay of 1930, and calls for a correction of this Cartesian interpretation on the basis of Husserl's total work (*Ontologische Voraussetzungen*, pp. 105–107).

26. The English translation by G. Richard Dimler is *Personal Faith: A Metaphysical Inquiry* (New York: Herder & Herder, 1965).

250

lays the foundation of his constructive thought in *La Philosophie et sa structure.*[27] Like Cirne-Lima he has written a "phenomenology of faith."[28] And like most of the Catholic phenomenologists of the second period, Vancourt's phenomenology makes an existential turn, influenced, as he says, by Merleau-Ponty and DeWaelhens. This existential turn guides his view that Husserl's transcendental consciousness is a real, effective existence. This determines his version of phenomenological analysis as "the analysis of the presence of man in the world."[29] With other phenomenologists, he opposes the reduction of the act of faith to subjective states and insists that faith is constituted by its content. The analysis of faith is therefore not an analysis of interior man but of man in the world.

Auguste Brunner like Vancourt and Duméry began his philosophical labors with a work on knowledge which draws heavily on Husserl.[30] Reminiscent of Husserl he distinguishes between the kinds of understanding which pre-reflectively grasp various sorts of entities (personal, vital, cultural, etc.) and more reflective and formal modes of knowledge carried by concepts and judgments. And like Cirne-Lima and Vancourt he followed his methodological work with a phenomenology of faith.[31] Of the three phenomenologies of faith Brunner's *Glaube und Erkenntnis* is the one closest to a fundamental theology because it distinguishes natural faith and Christian faith and attempts to show a common structure between the two. This work offers little that is explicitly Husserlian but is written within the phenomenological attitude and on the basis of procedures defended in his *Erkenntnistheorie.* Brunner's framework is clearly classical Catholic theology, and he uses phenomenology to illumine or reformulate that framework but never decisively to change it. He

27. (Paris: Bloud & Gay, 1953). Part I of this work is "Philosophie et phénoménologie."
28. *La Phénoménologie de la Foi* (Belgium: Desclee and Co., 1953).
29. Ibid., p. 45.
30. *Erkenntnistheorie* (Cologne: J. P. Bachem, 1943).
31. *Glaube und Erkenntnis: philosophisch-theologische Darlegung* (Munich: Kösel, 1957).

argues that the philosophical tradition from Kant through Husserl can be used by Catholic thinkers because of the essentially religious character of idealist philosophy.[32]

b. *Phenomenology and the personalization of Catholic theology*

The second way Husserlian phenomenology appears in Roman Catholic thought parallels its presence in Protestant thought. From the time of the 1920's, both Protestant and Catholic thought were receptive to philosophical anthropologies in which subject-to-subject relations were paramount.[33] "Personalism" as I am using it designates a broad stratum in twentieth-century Roman Catholic thought which attempts to reformulate the Catholic tradition with the aid of philosophies of the cogito, the human spirit, or personal reciprocity. The personalist movement of Emmanuel Mounier and the periodical *Esprit* are only one strand of a more general phenomenon that ranges from Guardini to Dewart. Most Catholic personalism occurs without conscious dependence on Husserlian phenomenology. The founding figure was Ferdinand Ebner whose "dialogical personalism" was taken up later by Theodore Steinbüchel, who wrote a book on Ebner, and by Romano Guardini.[34]

The chief contemporary inheritor of early dialogical personalism is Edward A. Schillebeeckx. Like other Catholic philosophers

32. *La Personne Incarnée: étude sur* la phénoménologie et la philosophie *existentialiste* (Paris: Beauchesne, 1947), p. 120.

33. We cannot elaborate the extremely complex problem of the sources of philosophical personalism. We can only indicate that Kierkegaard and Nietzsche are key figures, that the combination of Husserlian analyses with the primacy of existence occurs in Heidegger and Sartre, that Dilthey played a key role in sensitizing a whole generation to the problem of the sciences of the human spirit, that Max Weber had attempted to do justice to the dimension of subjective meaning in the social sciences, and that in France a long post-Cartesian philosophical tradition had kept open the philosophy of the *cogito* in such thinkers as Bergson and Maine de Biran.

34. For an account of "dialogical personalism" in Catholic thought which summarizes Ebner and Steinbüchel, see Bernard Langemeyer, *Der dialogische Personalismus in der evangelischen und katholischen Theologie der Gegenwart* (Paderborn: Bonifacius, 1963). Steinbüchel's work on Ebner is *Der Umbruch der Denkens* (Darmstadt: Wissenschaftliche Buchgesellschaft, 1966). Typical expressions of this personalism are Ebner's *Das Wort und die geistigen Realitäten* (1921) and Guardini's *Welt und Person* (Würzburg: Werkbund-Verlag, 1939) which argues for an I-and-Thou or dialogical structure of personal existence. See especially pp. 103–35.

Schillebeeckx is materially committed to Thomism; hence, he registers strong criticism of contemporary phenomenological philosophies (e.g., Merleau-Ponty) which portray man as simply self-directed without reference to transcendence or to a separate soul. However, he tries to overcome the scholastic stress on the conceptual nature of human knowledge. In doing this he has studied and appropriated much from Merleau-Ponty, Binswanger, and Buytendiik.[35] He develops a phenomenology of encounter which opens up new perspectives on providence and the sacraments. He decries extremes and sees himself correlating the valid element of phenomenological thought with perennial philosophy.[36] Hence, he associates himself with Rahner and is suspicious of the work of Duméry.[37]

The strand of Catholic personalism which explicitly claims to be an "existential phenomenology" has been especially associated with the University of Louvain in Belgium and Duquesne University of Pittsburgh. Although Husserl is not unimportant here, the key figures are Merleau-Ponty and Alphonse DeWaelhens who has made brilliant contributions on the subject of the relation of phenomenology and existentialism and the philosophy of self and body in natural experience.[38] Albert Dondeyne's lectures at the University of Louvain in 1951 resemble Schillebeeckx with their Thomist framework and their strong critique of existentialist philosophy.[39] But they go beyond Schillebeeckx, however, in utilizing Husserlian concepts to explore the "noematic aspect of faith." Furthermore, this work is not simply a fundamental theology since it applies these concepts to dogmatic themes such as God, the Church, and Mariology. William

35. Edward A. Schillebeeckx, *Christ, the Sacrament of the Encounter with God* (New York: Sheed and Ward, 1963), p. xiv.
36. Schillebeeckx, *The Concept of Truth and Theological Renewal* (London: Sheed and Ward, 1968), p. 6.
37. Ibid., pp. 18–20, pp. 120–121.
38. See Alphonse DeWaelhens, "Les constant de l'existentialisme," *Revue Internationale de Philosophie*, 9 (1949), and "L' Idée de l'intentionalité" in *Husserl in den Denken der Neuzeit*. See also his work on natural experience, *La Philosophie et les expériences naturelles* (The Hague: Nijhoff, 1961).
39. Albert Dondeyne, *Contemporary Thought and Christian Faith* (Pittsburgh: Duquesne University Press, 1958). Cf. Dondeyne's "Foi, Théologie de la Foi, et Phénoménologie," in *Foi Théologale et Phénoménologie*, a supplement to *Recherches et Debats* (Paris: C.C.I.F., 1951).

A. Luijpen has written introductory works on "existential phenomenology" (Heidegger, Sartre, Merleau-Ponty) and has applied this phenomenology to certain areas in Catholic thought such as atheism, humanism, and natural law, most of which publications appear in the Philosophy Series of Duquesne Studies.[40] Although Maurice Nédoncelle may not subscribe to "existential phenomenology" in the sense of Dondeyne and Luijpen, nevertheless, he too applies an "existential" phenomenology to such matters as prayer, fidelity, and love.[41] His *Réciprocité des consciences* (Paris: Aubier, 1942) and *Vers une philosophie de l'amour et de la personne* (Paris: Aubier, 1957) are his most indicative and significant works. Like Przywara he has made his own contribution to Newman studies. More than any other figure in Catholic personalism, Nédoncelle has used phenomenological analyses to clarify theological or dogmatic themes. The Catholic thinker who is closest to Heidegger is probably Bernhard Welte, who has attempted a rapprochement between Thomism and Heidegger. Welte's thought resembles therefore Protestant Heideggerian theology and includes such matters as pre-understanding, the hermeneutic task of theology, and the analysis of *Dasein,* especially as bearer of death and guilt.[42]

Among twentieth-century Catholic phenomenological programs, Henri Duméry's appropriation of phenomenology for theological purposes is the most ambitious, extensive, and original. The framework of his efforts is clearly not transcendental Thomism of the Maréchal school. His program is carried out primarily under the tutelage of Husserl but with an existential turn guided by Sartre and Merleau-Ponty. Beginning in the late 1940's, Duméry has been a productive scholar, although few English translations or interpretations of his thought are yet available.[43] His first writings are on

40. William A. Luijpen, *Phenomenology of Natural Law* (Pittsburgh: Duquesne University Press, 1967), *Phenomenology and Atheism* (Pittsburgh: Duquesne University Press, 1964); *Phenomenology and Humanism: A Primer in Existential Phenomenology* (Pittsburgh: Duquesne University Press, 1966).

41. *De la fidélité* (Paris: Aubier, 1953), and *Prier humain, prière divine. Notes phénoménologiques* (Paris: Desclee de Brouwer et Cie, 1962).

42. Bernhard Welte, *Heilsverständnis: philosophische Untersuchung einiger Vorraussetzungen zum Verständnis des Christentums* (Freiburg: Herder, 1966).

43. The most extensive treatment of Duméry's thought in English is the previously cited dissertation by Charles Courtney, "Phenomenology and

Blondel and also include two extensive methodological works.[44] Sounding a bit like Pascal, Duméry rejects a philosophy of religion whose datum is simply the speculatively obtained God of the philosophers. All philosophy depends for its subject matter on "lived experience," and the same holds for philosophy of religion. Accordingly, philosophy of religion exists between philosophy and theology, making every attempt to be philosophically rigorous, and required to do justice to the concrete ways in which the object (God) is given to reflection. The God reflected on by the philosopher must be the God of the religious man. Hence, Duméry is committed to philosophy but is fearful lest the philosopher's assessments simply pass by the religious object or reduce it to something other than itself. Although the existence and nature of God has been Duméry's main concern, he plans to extend his work to other major theological themes. He goes far beyond the merely terminological level of phenomenological theology (Dondeyne) and uses phenomenological method to delve into the institution distinctive to Christian faith, tracing the relationship between a realized messianism and the kind of institution it generates.[45]

2. Phenomenology in Protestant circles

Husserlian phenomenology has dominated Catholic more than Protestant thought, while existentialist philosophy has more deeply influenced Protestant than Catholic thought. In the period of the early phenomenological movement, there were a few rather temporary flirtations with phenomenology on the part of Protestants. If there was any one school associated with phenomenology, it was the

Theism." Two of Duméry's own works are available in English translation: *The Problem of God in Philosophy of Religion* (Evanston: Northwestern University Press, 1964), and *Faith and Reflection,* ed. by L. Dupré (New York: Herder & Herder, 1968), which is a book of selections from Duméry's works. See Courtney's "Introduction" to *The Problem of God* for a brief account of Duméry's thought, and also Jean Daniélou's essay on Duméry, "Phenomenology of Religions and Philosophy of Religion," in M. Eliade and J. Kitagawa,, eds., *The History of Religions: Essays in Methodology* (Chicago: University of Chicago Press, 1959).

44. *Critique et Religion: Problèmes de Méthode en Philosophie de la Religion* (Paris: SEDES, 1957), and *Philosophie de la Religion,* 2 vols. (Paris: P.U.F., 1957).

45. *Phénoménologie et Religion: structures de l'institution chrétienne* (1962).

Protestant faculty of the University of Strasbourg. We have already mentioned the dissertation-like monographs of Reiner, Hering, and Winkler. Several other Protestant theologians were concerned, even if indirectly, with phenomenology in this early period. Karl Heim's first book-length publication was an exploration of the "psychologistic" and metaphysical grounding of logic, in which he expounds and defends Husserl's critique of psychologism in the *Logical Investigations* and the new alternative offered there.[46] Although Heim's subsequent works contained themes shared with the phenomenological movement, especially the intentional interpretation of world (the relation of world to the consciousness-acts of the individual) and the theme of the plurality of egos (intersubjectivity), his work on these motifs does not seem to depend directly on Husserl or any other phenomenological philosopher.[47]

A second "young" theologian who drew indirectly from the early phenomenological movement was Dietrich Bonhoeffer. Bonhoeffer's attempt to construct a sociology of the church in his Berlin dissertation draws on phenomenology as it appears in the sociologists Simmel, Tönnies, and Vierkandt.[48] In this period the Protestant theologian who had the fullest grasp of phenomenological literature including Husserl's writings was Karl Löwith. In addition to making his own constructive contribution to the problem of the self and the other, he was one of the few Protestants to address systematically the relation between phenomenology and Protestant theology.[49] Work-

46. Karl Heim, *Psychologismus oder Antipsychologismus* (Berlin: C. A. Schwetschke, 1902).

47. Later Heim tended to dismiss Husserl as a philosopher of the Kantian a priori, working in the line of Descartes. *Glaube und Denken: Philosophische Gründlegung einer christlichen Lebensanschauung* (Berlin: Furch, 1931), pp. 23 ff., p. 439. He saw Husserl therefore as concerned only with insight into the essences of the region of logic, thus disinterested in being and value.

48. Bonhoeffer says that phenomenological method, by which he means the attempt to grasp the essential constitutive acts in empirical acts, is "the only one which can overcome the genetic approach which turns sociology into a mere branch of history." *The Communion of Saints* (New York: Harper & Row, 1960), p. 20. See also p. 209, n. 31.

49. The following two articles by Löwith show a rare mastery of the phenomenological literature of the day. "Grundzüge der Entwicklung der Phänomenologie zur Philosophie und ihr Verhaltnis zur protestantischen Theologie," *Theologische Rundschau; Neue Folge,* II (1930), pp. 25–64

ing primarily with Husserl's *Investigations* and the *Ideas,* he saw the Husserlian contribution occurring at the level of description. This he calls "phenomenology" and it develops into genuine philosophy only when ontological questions emerge, as for instance in Heidegger. Löwith's 1930 article was a sign of what was to come, for in his view the importance of phenomenology for Protestantism was its Heideggerian culmination. All of these early efforts reflect only temporary flirtations with phenomenology which eventually develop into some other programmatic. Protestantism had no major representative in the early phenomenological movement itself such as Scheler. Its reactions to Husserl were either indifferent or polemical, and interest picked up only after the Heideggerian shift to the analysis of *Dasein* or existential ontology.

When we consider the presence of phenomenology in Protestant thought in the last twenty-five years, we find two fairly clear groupings. One is comprised of philosophers who maintain some relation to the Protestant faith. All of these philosophers with the exception of Pierre Thévenaz participate in the post-Husserl shift to existential philosophy represented by Heidegger. The second group is made up of theologians, who, with the exception of Theobald Süss, are "phenomenologists" only in the sense of existential phenomenology.

a. *The existential phenomenology of "Protestant philosophers"*

"Protestant philosophy" sounds like a misnomer. It does not mean a view of knowledge and being based in some way on Protestant dogma. We are using it to describe a group of French-speaking philosophers who are at the same time committed Protestants. The group includes Pierre Thévenaz, Paul Ricoeur, Georges Gusdorf, and Roger Mehl.[50] We have contended that the use of

and 333–61; and "Phänomenologische Ontologie und protestantische Theologie," *Zeitschrift für Theologie und Kirche,* 11th year, pp. 365–399.
50. We are tempted to include Jean Nabert among phenomenological Protestant philosophers. Nabert is a philosopher of religion and of ethics in the French tradition of reflective philosophy. He clearly represents what we have called the phenomenological attitude, and Ricoeur finds a similarity (though not influence) between Nabert and Husserl in the way Nabert understands the relation between the act and the significations in which the act objectifies itself. See Ricoeur's "Preface" to Jean Nabert *Elements for an Ethic* (Evanston: Northwestern University Press, 1969),

phenomenology in religious analyses falls into two periods; 1921–1934 and 1950 to the present. The writings of the Protestant philosophers fall within the second period, roughly from the late 1940's to the present. Exceptions are an occasional early work and Thévenaz, most of whose writings occur in the 1940's. He is one of the few thinkers whose work bridges the two periods. Unlike the others Thévenaz's thought depends directly on Husserl himself rather than on the existentialist refraction of Husserl in Sartre or Merleau-Ponty. On the other hand, Pascal plays a strong role in Thévenaz, and his criticism of Husserl's transcendental consciousness resembles that of Sartre. Although Thévenaz died at the age of forty-two when he was just beginning his life-time project of a Protestant philosophy, he set the tone of the relation between philosophy and theology for those who followed. He laid strong stress on the inability of the philosopher simply to produce from his reflections a God other than the God of faith. At best the Protestant philosopher could philosophize "before God" rather than "about God." Thus Protestant philosophy is a philosophy without the Absolute, a philosophy this side of the Absolute, clarifying in radical ways man's finitude and limit.[51]

While Thévenaz was a Swiss who taught at the University of Lausanne, Mehl and Gusdorf (now retired) continue the tradition of phenomenology in the Protestant faculty of the University of Strasbourg which goes back to the early period and to Jean Hering and Charles Hauter. Georges Gusdorf is a contemporary of Ricoeur and Merleau-Ponty, and his many publications range from the late 1940's to the present. His writings indicate a special interest as

p. xxii. However, Nabert's three published works, *L'Expérience intérieure de la liberté* (1923), *Eléments pour une Ethique* (1943), *l'Essai sur le mal* (1955), and his *Le Désire de Dieu,* published posthumously in 1966, do not indicate significant participation in the phenomenological movement. The prominent figures in Nabert's background are Kant and Maine de Biran.

51. For brief expositions of Thévanaz, see the Preface (by John Wild) and Introduction (by James Edie) to Thévenaz, *What Is Phenomenology and Other Essays,* trans. Charles Courteney, et al (Evanston: Northwestern University Press, 1962), and Paul Ricoeur's "Pierre Thévenaz, un Philosophe Protestant," the Preface to the two-volume collection of Thévenaz's essays, *L'homme et sa raison: raison et conscience de soi* (Neuchâtel: Editions de la Baconnière, 1956).

well as an important contribution to the field of ethics, and they reflect a set of issues which had occupied Scheler. He has offered profound phenomenological descriptions pertinent to philosophical anthropology, taking up themes of time and memory, human freedom, self-affirmation, and the motif of self-sacrifice. Gusdorf has his own version of the shift to existence; hence, it is never simply transcendental consciousness but lived-existence which he specifies through phenomenological method. His most ambitious and important work is *Traité de Metaphysique* (1956) in which he investigates many of the main themes of Husserl and Scheler and the phenomenological tradition. He struggles with the hermeneutical problem of myth in the constructive way which we associate with Ricoeur. He also offers original analyses of Marcel's motif of embodiment or incarnation, as well as that of intersubjectivity and the problem of the other. He also offers analyses (what Husserl would call regional ontology) of natural and cultural "worlds" and takes up the problem of God in the personalist manner of Pascal and Thévenaz.[52]

Roger Mehl teaches both philosophy and theology on the Protestant faculty of the University of Strasbourg. Like Gusdorf his shift is to lived-experience with a special focus on the problems of ethics and society.[53] Mehl's first significant work, *La condition du philosophe chrétien* (1947), indicates strong dependence on Husserl and Scheler and on Gaston Berger's Husserl research.[54] Although he

52. The only work of Gusdorf available in English is his ingenious and suggestive *Speaking* (Evanston: Northwestern University Press, 1965) in which P. T. Brockelman, the translator, has written a brief introduction to Gusdorf's thought. In addition to *Traité de Metaphysique* (Paris: Colin, 1956), the reader should consult *Mémoire et Personne* (Paris: P.U.F., 1951); *La Découverte de soi* (Paris: P.U.F., 1948); *Traité de l'existence morale* (Paris: A. Colin, 1949); and *L'Expérience humaine du sacrifice* (Paris: P.U.F., 1948).

53. Mehl's works on ethics and society are the following. *Images of Man* (Richmond: John Knox, 1965); *Society and Love: Ethical Problems of Family Life* (Philadelphia: Westminister Press, 1964); *The Sociology of Protestantism* (Philadelphia: Westminster Press, 1970); *De l'autorité des valeurs; essai d'éthique Chrétienne* (Paris: P.U.F., 1957); and *La recontre d'autrui* (Paris: Délachaux & Niestle, 1955).

54. Gaston Berger, *La Cogito dans la philosophie de Husserl* (Paris: Aubier, 1941).

follows Berger in a criticism of Husserl's notion of the transcendental ego, he also corrects the frequent caricatures of phenomenology as a subjective idealism, a philosophy trapped in the subjective consciousness. He sees the intentional nature of consciousness as phenomenology's central discovery, a concept which he uses as an instrument to detect the meaning of a datum.[55] More important, perhaps, he shares with the other French-speaking Protestant philosophers the conviction that metaphysics should divest itself of constructive pretensions in relation to religion and the religious object. Metaphysics can only take seriously the unreducibility and integrity of faith. The relation between philosophy and religion is, therefore, a dialogue rather than a competitive struggle between a God of philosophers and a God of faith. Mehl employs phenomenology in subsequent works in the sense of descriptive analysis of a reality given in the mode of generality. These works include a phenomenology of community and a phenomenology of authority.[56]

Paul Ricoeur's thought is so complex and original and ranges over such a massive programmatic that it negates attempts to summarize it. Ricoeur is a careful Husserl scholar, attentive to Husserl's total work, and sensitive to its spiral development. In his own use of phenomenology he himself reflects various levels of phenomenological analysis which range from eidetic analysis applied to the realm of the cogito seen as the will to hermeneutics of symbols and myths. He too reflects in his own very original way the focus on lived-experience, although he thinks this does not mean abandoning Husserl for existential philosophy because Husserl himself made this move in the life-world philosophy of his last years.[57] As he works his way through a philosophical anthropology, he displays the "particularism" or positivity found in all of the French-speaking Protestant philosophers, a particularism which refuses to lose sight of the concrete situation of man in history and in a specific historical faith.

55. *The Condition of the Christian Philosopher* (Philadelphia: Fortress Press, 1963), pp. 62–63 and p. 102.
56. See *La recontre d'autrui* for Mehl's phenomenology of community and *De l'autorité des valeurs* for his phenomenology of authority.
57. Most of Ricoeur's Husserl studies appeared in the 1950's and are translated into English in *Husserl*. See especially "Existential Phenomenology" which he wrote originally for the *Encyclopédie Française* (1957).

For this reason, Ricoeur cannot be in his view a true philosopher and ignore human evil and its transcendental conditions or the hermeneutical problem of penetration and assessing myths of bondage and salvation. In these approaches Ricoeur is working as a "Christian philosopher" in Mehl's sense of a certain spiritual orientation but not in the sense of constructions grounded in "Christian" data.[58]

The French-speaking Protestant philosophers are self-consciously Protestant, and they philosophize out of a formulated relation between philosophy and religious faith and from a focus on the particularity of revelation. In addition to them there are also philosophers who work in the framework of an existentially oriented phenomenology who are Protestant and who are not unconcerned about theological questions, but who are not self-conscious "Protestant philosophers" in the sense of Thévenaz or Gusdorf. John Wild, William A. Earle, and James Edie, all of Northwestern University, have explored the relation of existential thought to "Christian philosophy."[59] Wild, lately concerned with the *Lebenswelt* philosophy of the late Husserl, has contributed several works pertinent to religious thought, the most important being his book on Christian ethics and social philosophy (1959).[60]

58. Many of Ricoeur's most important essays are available in English in a volume dedicated to Roger Mehl entitled, *History and Truth* (Evanston: Northwestern University Press, 1965). Ricoeur's programmatic philosophy of the will is also available in English in the following works: *Freedom and Nature: The Voluntary and the Involuntary*, trans. Erazim Koháčk (Evanston: Northwestern University Press, 1966); *Fallible Man*, trans. Charles Kelbley (Chicago: Regnery, 1965); and *The Symbolism of Evil*, trans. Emerson Buchanan (New York: Harper & Row, 1967). Ricoeur's hermeneutics are formulated in his book on Freud, *Freud and Philosophy: An Essay on Interpretation* (New Haven: Yale University Press, 1970), and in the collection of essays, *Le conflit des interprétations: essais d'herméneutique* (Paris: Editions du Seuil, 1969). Don Ihde's *Hermeneutic Phenomenology: The Philosophy of Paul Ricoeur* (Evanston: Northwestern University Press, 1971) is a helpful and accurate interpretation. See also David M. Rasmussen, *Mythic-Symbol Language and Philosophical Anthropology: A Constructive Interpretation of the Thought of Paul Ricoeur* (The Hague: Nijhoff, 1971).

59. William A. Earle, et al., *Christianity and Existentialism* (Evanston: Northwestern University Press, 1963).

60. *Human Freedom and Social Order: An Essay in Christian Philosophy* (Durham: Duke University Press, 1959). Wild's writings range impressively over many literatures and themes which include Plato, existentialism, "Christian philosophy," and ethics. Early in his career he studied and drew

b. *Existential phenomenology in Protestant "fundamental theology"*

"Fundamental theology" is now the new jargon.[61] The term, originating in Catholic circles of the nineteenth century, is a useful one, since it formulates as a task and as a conscious problematic what was little more than a structural aspect of certain nineteenth- and twentieth-century theologies. As a task it means the attempt to overcome heteronomous formulations of the relation between revelation (or reconciliation) and essential humanity. What is it about the human being which makes the salvific imagery of the Christian faith (freedom, justification, community, Word of God) restorative and creative rather than destructive? Fundamental theology in this sense is the unifying feature of recent Protestant existentialist theologies. The phenomenological movement is present in these theologies primarily through Martin Heidegger.

From the 1940's Rudolf Bultmann and the Bultmann school has been the most prominent Protestant existentialist theology, and this includes both the early stress on the analysis of *Dasein* and the new hermeneutic. The two most prominent English-speaking representatives of this school have been Carl Michalson and John Macquarrie. Michalson used Heideggerian categories to formulate a "critique of theological reason" by displaying the fundamental historical situation of faith. He is conscious of the importance of Husserl's ground-

on existentialist philosophy but within a "realist" critique. See *The Challenge of Existentialism* (Bloomington: Indiana University Press, 1955). For his religious philosophy see his essay in Earle, *Christianity,* and "An Existential Argument for Transcendence" in *Existence and the World of Freedom* (Englewood Cliffs, N.J.: Prentice-Hall, 1963). Although *Lebenswelt* occupies a central place in Wild's formulation of Christian philosophy, he argues that the *Lebenswelt* as such is marked by the experience of transcendence, and he does not, under the principle of positivity, reflect out of the ecclesial determination of *Lebenswelt.*

61. The following articles are adequate introductions to fundamental theology. See H. Vorgrimler, "Fundamental Theologie," in Hofer and Rahner, eds., *Lexicon für Theologie und Kirche* (Freiburg: Herder, 1960); H. Fries, "Fundamental Theology," in Rahner, et al., eds. *Sacramentum Mundi* (New York: Herder & Herder, 1968), vol. II; and the essay on fundamental theology and apologetics by Gössman in E. Neuhausler and E. Gössmann, *Was ist Theologie?* (Munich: Hueber, 1966). The fullest historical and systematic study of the term in Protestant theology is by Gerhard Ebeling, "Erwägungen zu einer evangelischen Fundamentaltheologie," in *Zeitschrift für Theologie und Kirche,* vol. 67 (December, 1970), pp. 479–524.

breaking work behind Heidegger, and has an appreciation for Husserl's late writings. Further, he attempts to go beyond Heidegger himself to a more dynamic or historical (and less ontological) portrait of man.[62] Macquarrie, for whom Heidegger is the dominant figure, sees phenomenology in the framework of the old caricatures, as merely a methodology without metaphysical significance.[63] Nevertheless, the methodology plays a positive role in three avenues of approach to theology's content, serving as the first "descriptive" step. This enables theology to begin on the secure ground of viewing what there is to be viewed, the phenomenon indicated by words like "sin," "man," and 'history." In the second step, which is interpretation, hermeneutical principles are applied to the symbolic language of faith thereby revealing the existential-ontological referents of this language. For Macquarrie, therefore, Husserl's phenomenology enables an initial description of the phenomenon, but it is with Heidegger's help that fundamental theology really occurs.

The most inclusive twentieth-century attempt at a Protestant fundamental theology is the theology of Paul Tillich. Fundamental theology, the constitutive structure whereby the human being is predisposed toward revelation, God, and new being as proper to his being, serves as one side of the correlational structure of Tillich's theology. Phenomenology plays an important but elusive role in Tillich's fundamental theology. We must initially distinguish between the way Tillich interprets phenomenology and the role it actually plays in his thought. In the 1920's Tillich was one of the few Protestant theologians to recognize the importance of and call attention to Husserl's *Logical Investigations.*[64] Unlike many of his day, he saw Husserlian phenomenology as distinguishable from neo-Kantianism and an important alternative to the critical method.[65]

---

62. Carl Michalson, *The Rationality of Faith: An Historical Critique of Theological Reason* (New York: Charles Scribner's Sons, 1963), p. 17, p. 41, and p. 128. Cf. also *Worldly Theology: The Hermeneutical Focus of an Historical Faith* (New York: Charles Scribner's Sons, 1967).

63. John Macquarrie, *Principles of Christian Theology* (New York: Charles Scribner's Sons, 1966), p. 20.

64. *The Religious Situation* (New York: Meridian Books, 1956), p. 69, pp. 74–75.

65. The basis of this difference is phenomenology's rootage in immediately grasped essences. This means that a phenomenological philosophy of

He does not write off Husserl as a subjective idealist, and he can agree with and appropriate the eidetic analyses of the *Investigations* which enable one to obtain the unreducible realm of structural presuppositions. On the other hand, Tillich always saw phenomenology as an essentialism, a philosophy in the Platonic tradition indifferent to existence and unable to be normatively systematic. Phenomenological method describes simply "meanings" and thus disregards the realities to which the meanings refer.[66] Therefore, Tillich was instrumental in mediating to a whole theological generation in America that interpretation of existential philosophy which so played down the ground-breaking work of Husserl as to lose sight of it.[67] Hence, what Tillich says about Husserlian phenomenology is based

religion focuses on the essence and qualities of religion, thus going much farther than critical method which is limited to the transcendental conditions of religious meanings and their synthesis. *Religionsphilosophie* in *Gesammelte Werke,* Band I (Stuttgart: Evangelische Verlagswerk, 1959), pp. 308–309.

66.. *Das System der Wissenschaften nach Gegenstanden und Methoden* (Göttingen: Van den Hoeck and Ruprecht, 1923), pp. 236–237; *Systematic Theology* (Chicago: University of Chicago Press, 1951), vol. I, pp. 106–107. "Trennung und Einung im Erkenntnisakt," *Ges. Werke,* IV, p. 110.

67. The issue is the following: Is the matrix of existential philosophy primarily the phenomenological movement or is Husserlian phenomenology a minor moment in existential philosophy? In Tillich's account of existential philosophy Husserl's place is described in one sentence, "The third and contemporary form of Existentialist philosophy has resulted from a combination of this 'Philosophy of Life' with Husserl's shift of emphasis from existent objects to the mind that makes them its objects, and with the rediscovery of Kierkegaard and of the early developments of Marx" ("Existential Philosophy," *The Journal of the History of Ideas,* V [January, 1944], p. 46.) In Tillich's view existential philosophy insists that "Reality or Being is existence, Reality as immediately experienced" (p. 44). This permits him to find anticipations of the philosophy in Böhme, to locate its decisive beginning in anti-Hegelian polemics of the 1850's, and to interpret Heidegger and Jaspers as contemporary forms of that anti-Hegelianism and the priority of "Reality immediately experienced." This sort of historical work reminds us of the attempts on the part of some personalists (Boston) to discover "personalism" in every period of the history of philosophy. There is a certain cogency about Tillich's approach insofar as these thinkers do share some general features. The portrait is drawn at the cost of abstracting away most of the historical elements and philosophical issues. To obtain this portrait of existentialist philosophy, Tillich isolates certain common characteristics of such thinkers as Trendelenberg, Kierkegaard, Bergson, Marx, Freud, Dilthey, and even William James, on the basis of which he posits his three forms of existential philosophy. He isolates these figures from the actual religious and philosophical movements

mostly on the *Investigations* and the *Ideas* and falls within those views of phenomenology as a mere eidetics. Tillich seems unaware of Husserl's transcendental program as it groped and spiraled its way into the life-world theme of the last period.

When we take up the question of Tillich's actual incorporation of phenomenology into his thought, we begin by noting that Tillich himself tells us in what sense his theology is phenomenological. Acknowledging his debt to Rudolf Otto and Max Scheler, he appropriates "phenomenological theology" as that stage of analysis which focuses on *meanings* essential to religious experience.[68] Hence, each of the five sections of his system begins with an eidetics (an essence-analysis) of the motif of that section as that motif is carried in the symbolism of the Christian religion: revelation, "God," the Christ, Spirit, and the Kingdom of God. However, Tillich's thought is phenomenological in a far more pervasive sense than his term *phenomenological theology* indicates. In the first place Tillich uses Husserl-Heideggerian methods to pursue a "fundamental ontology," an ontology of the human being in the sense of both essential features and the alteration of such under the conditions of existence. Second, these features (human reason, finitude, existence, life, history) carry a double intentionality. First, they "intend" in the pre-reflective or transcendental sense the *meaning*-dimension of the symbols of the Christian faith. For example, the symbol *the Christ*

which were their matrix; hence, the problems which formed the actual schools and debates are mostly omitted: the attempt to found a science of human *Geist,* the issues generated by the British empiricists to which Kant responded, the problem of the foundation of the a priori sciences (Frege, Husserl), the problem of historicism, and the issues addressed by the new psychologies (Meinong, James, Stumpf). Furthermore, to obtain this view of contemporary existential philosophy as a third wave of an anti-Hegelian stress on existence, whose main representatives are Heidegger, Jaspers, and "religious socialism" (p. 46), Tillich must ignore most of the actual writings of French and German phenomenology, the "existential" elements in Husserl himself (intentionality, world, time-consciousness) which are methodically though not terminologically present in Heidegger, Sartre, and Marcel, and the issues of the exact relation between Heidegger and others to Husserl. In our view Heidegger and Sartre, while rejecting Husserlian terminology and the egology of the *Ideas,* take their basic problematic and method from Husserl, and it is more misleading than illuminating to describe them as a later phase of nineteenth-century anti-Hegelianism.

68. *Systematic Theology,* I, p. 43.

is the noematic object of an intending which is constitutive of fallen existence. Second, these features intend the "realities" in which the symbols participate. For example, the question of God in human finitude is related intentionally both to "God" (the symbol) and to being-itself of which "God" is a symbol. In this complex structure Tillich has ingeniously combined several levels of phenomenological analysis; the "experiential" dimension of human individuality, the universality of the human situation, the particularity and concreteness of the cultus, and the cosmic and/or "worldly" dimension. Although the Husserlian conceptual apparatus is almost totally absent, overshadowed by Schelling, Heidegger, and Kierkegaard, the structure of Tillich's system is more Husserlian than Heideggerian because it attempts to do justice to the intentional or noetic-noematic structure of both universal and cultic aspects of a historical faith, and to the complex interweaving of the many facets of a life-world modified in a religious way. The Husserlian element tends to be obscured, not only because of the absence of Husserlian terms, but because the theologies influenced by Tillich simplified his program to a single intentionality, a correlation of existential states with relevant symbols.

Two recent Protestant theologians whose work is heavily influenced by Tillich, and who are pursuing a fundamental theology within a phenomenological framework, are Ray L. Hart and Langdon Gilkey. Hart, working explicitly with Husserlian concepts, but after the so-called shift to ontology of Merleau-Ponty and Heidegger, has written the most probing and original attempt at a Protestant fundamental theology in the post-Tillich era. His thesis is that the *imagination* (the pre-reflective capacity to apprehend an aesthetic object) is that which predisposes unfinished man toward revelation and is that which grasps the salvific imagery of the religious tradition.[69] Gilkey's fundamental theology rises from his attempt to show in the face of the challenge of secularism and secular theology that religious language does have a transcendent referent. Tillich-like, he argues that secular existence or secular man hides within himself questions, needs, and intentional structures which go beyond

69. Ray L. Hart, *Unfinished Man and the Imagination* (New York: Herder & Herder, 1968).

secularity itself to an ultimate dimension. Gilkey finds little help in what he calls original or pure phenomenology because it simply dealt with "essences within the stream of experience" and bracketed transcendent reality.[70] He dismisses such phenomenology as inadequate because its concern is with "experience," and religious experience is problematic.[71] However, Gilkey wants to make his case about secular existence by recovering "the character and structure of immediate experience," and he finds aid in doing this in those phenomenologists (Heidegger, Sartre, Merleau-Ponty) who deal with "concrete experience as lived." Method for Gilkey is a way to lived-experience, the tones of our living, thereby unveiling a dimension which is lost sight of in the preoccupation of secular consciousness with the everyday world. Gilkey's use of the phenomenological tradition is that of existentialist phenomenology for the purposes of fundamental theology. In this he seems to be a Protestant counterpart to Auguste Brunner or Vancourt, without, however, their technical control of the Husserlian literature and without their constructive epistemological prolegomena.[72]

70. *Naming the Whirlwind: The Renewal of God-Language* (Indianapolis: Bobbs-Merrill, 1969), p. 244. Since Gilkey is speaking about Husserl in this passage, it should be stated that Husserl's *essences* are not in the *Erlebnisstrom* which for him is a matter of psychological introspection not phenomenology, and that the purpose of Husserl's reality-bracketing even in the *Ideas* was to expose the intentional structures present in all reality appearance.

71. Ibid, p. 246.

72. Gilkey is one of the few Protestant theologians to deal explicitly with Husserl in a methodological work. Yet I must confess almost utter perplexity about his interpretation. In one passage he describes the philosophy of the *Ideas* as a complete subjective idealism, which repudiates ontological systems and is concerned only with immanent objects (Ibid., p. 244). In another passage he cites Merleau-Ponty's very careful essay on Husserl which makes the opposite point, namely, that "Husserl's essences are destined to bring back all the living relationships of experience" (p. 278, n. 18). Merleau-Ponty had carefully studied Husserl's late philosophy and this essay is one of the many in the renascence of Husserl studies to correct the caricature of "subjective idealism."

More strange still, Gilkey uses Husserl's own term, *Lebenswelt,* to characterize a hermeneutical phenomenology which "has not so much uncovered, as Husserl did, the eternal, timeless, and necessary forms apparent to consciousness and the Absolute Ego, as it seeks to bring to expression the characteristic structures of man's immediate awareness of himself as a concrete, contingent being in interaction with the world" (p. 280). Although Gilkey has already acknowledged that *Lebenswelt* is a Husserlian notion, this passage gives the impression that Husserl's *Lebens-*

Our portrait of phenomenology in contemporary Protestant thought would be incomplete without reference to two thinkers who fall outside of the Bultmann and Tillich spheres of influence, Theobald Süss and Gibson Winter. We should add that their resistance to being classified within our twofold typology is about the only thing they have in common. Süss is a Lutheran theologian who applies Husserlian categories to the actual content of classical Protestant theology. In this effort he has written articles on the inspiration of Scripture, on the certainty of salvation, on baptism, and on the resurrection of Christ.[73] Süss characterizes his own approach as "phenomenological theology," which he sets forth programmatically in an article by that title.[74] The article investigates the relation between theology and Husserlian phenomenology which finds its solution in Süss's own program. Süss is aware of the

welt, the theme of the *Crisis,* is an invention of Heidegger's! Furthermore, has Gilkey forgotten that "essential structures" connote a transcendental not empirical program? Gilkey praises phenomenology "after Husserl" for its turn away from ideal, essential experience to concrete, actual experience (p. 278). The anomaly of "ideal experience" aside, it is clear Husserl's life-world and the structures pertaining to perception, the body, the will, the other, and temporality even in Heidegger and Sartre are not "concrete, actual experiences" but essential structures of the human being as such.

Further, all three ways in which "hermeneutic phenomenology" supposedly differs from Husserl are clearly applicable to Husserl himself (p. 280, n. 21). Perhaps much of this is explained by excessive dependence on the *Ideas,* the only work Gilkey quotes at length. There is little concern in this rare Protestant passage on phenomenology to struggle with the place of the *Ideas* in the total program, to work with Husserl's late philosophy and the sense in which it is the key to the early philosophy, or to formulate the relation between the *Lebenswelt* program of Husserl as a transcendental philosophy and the being-in-the-world philosophy of Heidegger or Sartre. Gilkey does take over the phenomenological reduction, but without differentiating the several reductions in Husserl's thought. The result is that, while it is clear Gilkey would bracket "secular assumptions," that to which the reduction obtains eludes us. He says it has nothing to do with ontology, that it is "experience," and "appearances and their appropriate language" (p. 283). Such talk confuses us all the more since it seems to return to the "original phenomenology" which Gilkey has criticized and rejected as irrelevant because it was restricted to "essences within the stream of experience" and repudiated "ontological systems" (p. 244).

73. Theobald Süss, "L'inspiration de l'Ecriture," *Pos. luth.,* no. 1 (Novembre, 1953); "Menschenwort und Gotteswort: zur Frage der Schriftinspiration," *E.L.K.Z.* no. 20 (1955); "Heilsgewissheit. Eine dogmatische Meditation in phänomenologischem Stil," in *Die Leibhaftigkeit des Wortes* (Hamburg: 1958).

74. "Phänomenologische Theologie," 1963. See Chapter 2, n. 12.

explorations of the 1920's, most of which were philosophies of religion, but his own concern is systematic theology. Like other phenomenologists of religion he is attracted by the Husserlian approach to the given which permits a determinate appearance to remain determinate. Furthermore, it is Husserlian not existential phenomenology which dominates Süss's approach. Süss uses certain categories from Husserl's philosophy of consciousness to illuminate classical theological motifs. Thus he argues that in Heidegger's view of human consciousness Christ's resurrection is simply not conceivable because the particular horizon through which human beings are predisposed toward death restricts them to their own death. Süss would correct this with a Husserlian view of consciousness in the sense of an unrestricted horizon of possibilities for human subjectivity, one of which is the possibility of resurrection. In fact resurrection seems to be the central motif in Süss, establishing as it does the new man or new being. Süss's use of Husserl within the classical Lutheran framework resembles those Roman Catholic thinkers who use phenomenology within the classical Thomist framework. He is distinctive in his primary usage of Husserl over against existentialist thought, his concern to apply phenomenology to *theological* problems, and his attempt to work on the basis of a Husserlian view of consciousness. However, his efforts amount more to suggestions and proposals than to an elaborated position, and his failure to take up the radical challenges to religious knowledge with which twentieth-century theologians are struggling reduces the significance of his liaison with phenomenology.

Gibson Winter is a social ethicist whose work has opened up to Christian ethics and social thought the fascinating researches of social phenomenology. He draws on Scheler and Schutz (as well as G. H. Mead) in a critique of traditional sociologism, a reformulation of the problem and method of the social sciences, and a beginning at founding a social ethic in the structures of the social world. Unlike Süss whose work is isolated and uninfluential, Winter may mark the beginning of a new epoch in social ethics.[75]

75. Although Winter has written a number of other works, his appropriation of social phenomenology occurs in *Elements for a Social Ethic* (New York: Macmillan, 1966).

C. CONCLUSION

Our survey of the literature of phenomenology in Protestant and Catholic thought suggests the following generalizations. The early phenomenological school stimulated some explorations in the 1920's and 1930's, most of which were discontinued, which stressed eidetic analysis, and which were either concerned with the essence of religion or philosophy of religion. When phenomenology reappeared after World War II, it was largely as a hidden if not forgotten strand of the philosophies of existence, and this remained its dominant form in the second period. The exceptions to this were certain Protestant (Thévenaz) and Catholic (Duméry) philosophers who participated in the renascence of Husserl studies and for whom Husserl was as important as his successors. But for most Protestant and Catholic theologians, "phenomenology" meant primarily an eidetics, an analysis of meanings, which could play a legitimate role in theological prolegomenon but which required existential, ontological, or "reality" supplementation.

The specific way in which postwar existential phenomenology occurred in Protestant and Catholic thought was that it founded a new philosophical anthropology centered around the theme of human self-transcendence or the *for-itself*. This new anthropology along with the new method (*Dasein*-analysis) of investigation emerged in Protestant and Catholic thought in different forms. First, we find it in fundamental theology, that is, in Catholic phenomenologies of faith and in the Protestant return to a religious a priori (Hart, Gilkey). Second, this anthropology so pervaded theology that various classical themes underwent "personalistic" reformulation.

Third, the problem and motif of intersubjectivity, which had been so prominent in phenomenological philosophy from the beginning, has continually appeared in theological writings in fascinating but usually ignored ways. Husserl had struggled with the problem from the time of *Ideen* II, but it did not appear in his published writings until the *Cartesian Meditations*. In the early period of the 1920's and 1930's Scheler, Stein, Schutz, von Hildebrand, Löwith, and Gerda Walther all explored the problem of the other, with Schutz's work attempting a phenomenology of the social world. Inheriting

270

this problematic of community and social world were phenomenologists such as Maurice Natanson, R. C. Kwant, John Wild, Georges Gurvitch, and F. J. J. Buytendiik, as well as Sartre, Marcel, and Merleau-Ponty.

What is not so well known is the importance of this theme of community and social world in the Protestant and Catholic appropriation of phenomenological philosophy. Stein and von Hildebrand as Roman Catholics and Löwith and Bonhoeffer as Protestants offered studies in the early period, although of these four only Bonhoeffer's was for an exclusively theological purpose. In the second period most of the attempts to import the phenomenology of interpersonal relation into theology occur in Catholic thought. The work of Scheler, Stein, and von Hildebrand did not fall on barren soil. Such philosophers as Stephan Strasser and Nédoncelle wrote significant pieces on the philosophy of encounter.[76] Furthermore, most of the Catholic phenomenologists of the second period have not only done philosophical explorations of the problem of human community but have gone on to apply their insights to the community of faith.[77] In Protestant thought Löwith's early investigations of interpersonal structures are not taken up except in Protestant philosophers John Wild and Roger Mehl. Their investigations of life-world and of the "other" remain mostly philosophical. Hence, Bonhoeffer's early attempt in *Sanctorum Communio* to formulate the constitutive corporate structures of a community of faith has not been pursued.

When we ask about the interpretation of phenomenology which dominates Catholic and Protestant thought, we find a consensus running through the literature. Most theologians seems to retain the 1920's picture of Husserlian phenomenology as an extractable

---

76. Stephan Strasser, *The Idea of Dialogal Phenomenology* (Pittsburgh: Duquesne University Press, 1969), and Maurice Nédoncelle, *La réciprocité des consciences* (1942).

77. See Nédoncelle's "Personne et Communauté dans l'Eglise" in his *Le Chrétien appartient à deux mondes* (Paris: Centurion, 1970). Duméry's *Phénoménologie et Religion* (1962) is a brief but significant investigation of Christian institutionality. Auguste Brunner's phenomenology of faith culminates in an investigation of the religious community, although the results are disappointingly traditional (*Glaube und Erkenntnis,* chap. 10). Cirne-Lima's phenomenology of faith also stresses interpersonal faith. And the role of interpersonal structures in the thought of Schillebeeckx is well known.

method of obtaining essences or meanings. They see this corrected and supplemented by the existential philosophies. Therefore, some simply reject "phenomenology" because it dispenses with reality, while others (Tillich, Macquarrie) incorporate it as an eidetic moment of a theological program. Such a response has resulted in a certain impoverishment in contemporary theology. Insofar as the appropriation of phenomenology has been reduced to existential anthropology with the intersubjective or social world strand of phenomenology ignored, the result has been a religious individualism which correlates the religious message with existential states or needs. The strong but latent individualist piety of American Protestant theologians has been exceptionally apparent in this regard, permeating the new hermeneutic, radical theology, and Wittgensteinian fideism. The intersubjective matrix of faith is thereby totally passed over. A by-product of this impoverishment is the almost complete inattention to that strand of phenomenological philosophy which had its beginnings in Husserlian phenomenology and which worked in aesthetics (Dufrenne, Ingarden), language (Gusdorf, Kwant), psychology (Aron Gurwitsch, Strasser), and especially sociology and the social world (Schutz). The influx of translations of this literature, the new accessibility of Husserl, and the increased receptivity to the general problem of human community seem to promise a near-term correction of this impoverishment.

INDEX

INDEX

Manipulation, 136–139
Mannheim, Karl, 212 n, 246 n
Marcel, Gabriel, 26, 61, 91, 242
Maréchal, Joseph, 240–241, 243, 249 n, 250 n
Mehl, Roger, 239, 258–259, 271
Merleau-Ponty, Maurice, xiii n, 26, 35 n, 46 n, 61, 77 n, 91, 114 n, 201 n, 242, 251, 267 n
Metzger, Arnold, 238
Michalson, Carl, 262–263
Mounier, Emmanuel, 252
Muck, Otto, 249 n
Myth, 120–124

Nabert, Jean, 257 n
Natanson, Maurice, xiii n, 223
Nédoncelle, Maurice, 254, 271
Newman, J. H., 247
Niebuhr, H. Richard, 176 n, 183 n
Nielson, Kai, 52 n
Nietzsche, Friedrich, 132, 252 n
Noematic analysis, 112–114
Noesis-Noema, xv, 26, 44, 68–69, 79, 81, 112–115, 133, 196, 239, 265–266

Obligation, 147–149, 159–161, 218–219
Ontology, 45, 212
Operative principles, 51–57
Originary presence (*Urpräsenz*), 197–198, 208, 227–229
Otto, Rudolf, 239 n, 245 n, 265

Ownness sphere (*Eigenheitssphäre*), 40, 46, 69, 94–95, 200

Pannenberg, Wolfhart, 5, 15 n
Pascal, Blaise, 57, 258
Perception, 87–88, 194–196
Perceptivities, 191–192, 213–214. *See also* Apprehensions
Personalism, 252–255
Pfänder, Alexander, 28, 236
Phenomenal content, 13 ff.
Phenomenological reduction, 22, 38–42, 62
  eidetic reduction, 27, 47, 49, 244
  transcendental reduction, 41–42
Phenomenological theology, 18–23, 24, 51–54, 70–82, 127, 151 n
Phenomenology, 24–29, 32
  descriptive (eidetic) phenomenology, 27 n, 28
  phenomenological attitude, 26, 28 n, 51
  phenomenological method, 25–26, 33
  transcendental phenomenology, 27, 38
Phillips, D. Z., 52 n
Plato, 60, 103
Plessner, Helmuth, 30 n
Pluralistic social world. *See* Social world

principle
formula
program
paradigm
structure
  universal
  general
  abstraction
  idea
  apriori
  guarantees
  mode
stereotypes
inclusive
morphological
reality
deeper
higher
unity

typifications
stereotypes
way
existence
being
dimensions
depth